Malay

Phrasebook & Dictionary

T0384506

Acknowledgments

Product Editor Amy Lynch
Book Designers Mazzy Prinsep, Wibowo Rusli
Language Writer Susan Keeney
Cover Image Researcher Naomi Parker

Thanks

William Allen, James Hardy, Campbell McKenzie, Catherine
Naghten, Rachel Rawling, Angela Tinson, Juan Winata

Published by Lonely Planet Global Limited

CRN 554153

5th Edition – Jun 2020
ISBN 978 1 78657 588 3
Text © Lonely Planet 2020
Cover Image Tua Pek Kong Chinese Temple, Miri, Sarawak, Malaysia/
Chris Howes/Alamy Stock Photo ©

Printed in Malaysia   10 9 8 7 6 5 4 3 2 1

Contact lonelyplanet.com/contact

MIX
Paper from
responsible sources
FSC™ C021741

acknowledgments

about the author

Having lived in Malaysia on and off for 16 years, Susan Keeney first started to learn Malay in the kitchens and back rooms of obscure places like Kajang and Serdang. She wound up teaching communication courses (in both Malay and English) at various universities and colleges in Malaysia. She is now teaching elementary school students (in English) in California.

from the author

Many thanks to my three children, Johan (without whom this book would never have been finished on time), Sarah and Sabrina, for their help, advice and patience while I worked on this project. I would also like to thank my one and only *guru tatabahasa*, Awang Sariyan, who was a wonderful teacher and who certainly shared my love of grammar; and most of all, my father, Bob Keeney, for all his love and support.

from the publisher

Special thanks to Sofie Jussof for the creation of the Sustainable Travel chapter.

make the most of this phrasebook ...

Anyone can speak another language! It's all about confidence. Don't worry if you can't remember your school language lessons or if you've never learnt a language before. Even if you learn the very basics (on the inside covers of this book), your travel experience will be the better for it. You have nothing to lose and everything to gain when the locals hear you making an effort.

finding things in this book

For easy navigation, this book is in sections. The Tools chapters are the ones you'll thumb through time and again. The Practical section covers basic travel situations like catching transport and finding a bed. The Social section gives you conversational phrases, pick-up lines, the ability to express opinions – so you can get to know people. Food has a section all of its own: gourmets and vegetarians are covered and local dishes feature. Safe Travel equips you with health and police phrases, just in case. Remember the colours of each section and you'll find everything easily; or use the comprehensive Index. Otherwise, check the two-way traveller's Dictionary for the word you need.

being understood

Throughout this book you'll see coloured phrases on the right-hand side of each page. They're phonetic guides to help you pronounce the language. You don't even need to look at the language itself, but you'll get used to the way we've represented particular sounds. The pronunciation chapter in Tools will explain more, but you can feel confident that if you read the coloured phrase slowly, you'll be understood.

communication tips

Body language, ways of doing things, sense of humour – all have a role to play in every culture. 'Local talk' boxes show you common ways of saying things, or everyday language to drop into conversation. 'Listen for ...' boxes supply the phrases you may hear. They start with the phonetic guide (because you'll hear it before you know what's being said) and then lead in to the language and the English translation.

CONTENTS

5

CONTENTS

7

malay

Standard Bahasa Malaysia

Malay with dialect variations

Cambodia

Vietnam

Thailand

Phillipines

Papua New Guinea

PACIFIC OCEAN

Palau

Australia

South China Sea

Sulu Sea

Sulawesi Sea

Banda Sea

Arafura Sea

Timor Sea

Medan

Ipoh

PENINSULA MALAYSIA

KUALA LUMPUR

SINGAPORE

SINGAPORE

Palembang

JAKARTA

Bandung

Bandar Lampung

Surabaya

Pontianak

SARAWAK

BRUNEI

BANDAR SERI BEGAWAN

Niah

SABAH

Kota Kinabulu

Banjarmasin

INDONESIA

MALAYSIA

Java Sea

Denpasar

Ujung Pandang

East Timor

Joyapura

0   500 km
0   300 mil

The national language of Malaysia is Malay. Malaysians refer to it as *Bahasa Malaysia* (Language of Malaysia) or *Bahasa Melayu* (Language of the Malays). It's been the language in government and schools since the early '70s, so nearly every Malaysian speaks it, either as their first or second language.

Don't be confused by the terminology. 'Malays' are those who are racially considered Malay, usually Muslim, who also speak the language Malay. Malaysians are, of course, anyone who is a Malaysian citizen.

Malay is a member of the Western Austronesian language family and is spoken with slight variations throughout Malaysia and some parts of southern Thailand, Singapore and Brunei. In Malaysia, it's by no means the only language. Multiracial Malaysia is of course multilingual. Chinese Malaysians, who form approximately one third of the population, belong to many different dialect groups, including Cantonese, Hakka, Hokkien, Teochew and Hainanese, and many also speak Mandarin. Indian Malaysians have linguistic backgrounds in Tamil and Malayalee; other groups speak Punjabi, Gujerati and Bengali. They account for about 10% of the population.

Wherever you go in Malaysia you will see shop signs in a rainbow of languages and scripts. Malay uses the Roman alphabet, but was originally written in *jawi*, an adaptation of Arabic script created during the introduction of Islam in the 14th century. You might notice the *halal* sign in *jawi* script, which shows food is kosher for Muslims. At the crossroads of many trade routes, Malaysia's language has a potpourri of influences. In addition to Arabic (*mahkamah*, 'court'), there's Portuguese (*garfu*, 'fork'), Sanskrit (*istana*, 'palace'), Chinese (*mee*, 'noodles'), and English, (*elektrik*, 'electric').

Classical Malay was almost lost during British colonisation. It was the traders and merchants who kept the language alive

introduction

9

during these times. 'Bazaar Malay' became a lingua franca and was the basis for the Bahasa Melayu we know today.

Bahasa Melayu also forms the basis for *Bahasa Indonesia*, but while Indonesian has been influenced by Dutch, Malaysian has adopted more English words, making it a dream of a language to learn for English speakers. English is Malaysia's second tongue, and is a compulsory subject in schools from the age of seven. Words such as 'clinic' and 'antibiotic' are incorporated into Malay through a change of spelling (*klinik* and *antibiotik*) and educated Malays often tend to mix languages in their daily conversations. English is commonly spoken in urban areas and it's not difficult to find someone who speaks some, even in rural areas.

While standard Malay is spoken in Kuala Lumpur, other regions of Malaysia have their own dialects that vary in pronunciation and accent. Regional accents can be strong, with variations in vocabulary. In Kelantan, *Apa khabar?*, 'How are you?' becomes *Guano demo?*. But never fear, your attempts at standard Malay will definitely be understood!

bahasa malaysia or bahasa melayu?

In this country where racial tensions still bubble under the surface of every decision, the difference between these two terms is loaded with meaning.

After the race riots of 1969 the government made many moves to address economic inequities, including a declaration that Malay should become the national language and the medium of instruction in all schools. But what to call the language?

Bahasa Malaysia, 'the language of Malaysia', was considered a unifying name, implicitly for Malaysians of all origins. In 1989 however, the members of the *Dewan Bahasa dan Pustaka* (The Hall of Language and Publishing), who are predominantly Malay, decided to change it back to *Bahasa Melayu*, 'the language of the Malays'. This move was seen by some to be a racially possessive, 'our language, not yours' move. It remains the official name.

Bahasa Melayu is an easy language to learn to speak. The spelling is largely phonetic; tenses are simple to use and you don't have to worry about gender in grammar. This makes for fast progress and plenty of communication. You'll get a kick out of learning Malay, and remember that, even a simple *terima kasih*, te-*ree*-muh *kah*-si(h), 'thank you', will please the people you meet. *Selamat belajar*, se-*lah*-maht be-*lah*-jar, 'happy learning' and now *jumlah!* , *joom*-lah(h)! – 'let's get to it!'

Bahasa Melayu and *Bahasa Indonesia* have only a few differences in vocabulary and pronunciation. The structure and other aspects of grammar remain the same in both languages. This means that this book could stay in your bag for travels further south, and the same goes for our *Indonesian phrasebook* – a great read – in Malaysia. The differences in vocabulary include some of the most common words:

ENGLISH	MALAY	INDONESIAN
after	*selepas*	*sesudah*
afternoon	*petang*	*sore*
beef	*daging lembu*	*daging sapi*
brother	*abang/adik*	*kakak/laki-laki*
can (as in 'I can')	*boleh*	*bisa*
car	*kereta*	*mobil*
city	*bandar*	*kota*
cold (adj)	*sejuk*	*dingin*
cute (eg, baby)	*manis/cun*	*lucu*
invite	*menjemput*	*mengundang*
Mr	*Tuan/Encik*	*Bapak*
Mrs	*Puan*	*Ibu*
office	*pejabat*	*kantor*
room	*bilik*	*kamar*
shoes	*kasut*	*sepatu*
shop	*kedai*	*toko*
toilet	*tandas/toilet*	*WC; kamar kecil*

introduction

11

how to use this phrasebook

you *can* speak another language

It's true – anyone can speak another language. Don't worry if you haven't studied languages before, or that you studied a language at school for years and can't remember any of it. You just need to start speaking. Once you start, you'll be amazed how many prompts you'll get to help you build on those first words. You'll hear people speaking, pick up sounds from TV, catch a word or two from the local radio, see something on a billboard – all these things help to build your understanding.

plunge in

There are a few everyday words you could learn right away. The general greeting is *Selamat pagi*, se-lah-maht pah-gee. For other hellos and goodbyes, see page 40. If you are moving though a crowd or trying to get past people it is polite to say *Maafkan saya*, mah-ahf-kahn sai-yuh, which means 'Excuse me'. For tips on civilities and body language, see page 53. Two easy words to remember are *Tidak*, tee-dah(k), 'No' and *Ya*, ya, 'Yes'. If you're having trouble understanding someone, just say *Saya tidak faham*, sai-yuh tee-dah(k) fah-hahm, 'I don't understand'. 'How much is it?' is *Berapa harganya ini?*, be-rah-puh hahr-guh-nyuh ee-nee?. If you find yourself in an emergency situation, turn to page 203 for some handy phrases.

abbreviations used in this book

adj	adjective	lit	literal translation
col	colloquial	n	noun
excl	exclusive	pl	plural
incl	inclusive	pol	polite
inf	informal	v	verb

legend

The following notation is used throughout this phrasebook:

( ) parentheses
indicate words can be replaced with words of your choice:

Let's meet at (6 o'clock) at …

kee-tuh ber-*te*-moo *pah*-duh   *Kita bertemu*
(poo-kool e-*nahm*) dee …   *(pukul enam) di …*

indicate the words are optional:

Can you show me (on the map)?

to-long *toon*-joo(k)-kahn   *Tolong tunjukkan*
(dee *pe*-tah)?   *(di peta)?*

indicate one of the following:
- meaning, eg, demonstration (protest)
- usage, eg, date (time)
- aspect of grammar, eg, masculine (m) and feminine (f)
- literal translation, eg, (lit: I already eat)

/ forward slash
indicates when single words on either side of the slash are interchangeable:

To the left/right.   ke *ki*-ree/*kah*-nahn   *Ke kiri/kanan.*

denotes:

    To the left.   ke *ki*-ree   *Ke kiri.*
and **To the right.**   ke *kah*-nahn   *Ke kanan.*

indicates when single words are synonyms – or different forms of the same word (typically masculine, or feminine, singular or plural, informal or polite):

I'm a student.   *sai*-yuh *moo*-rid/   *Saya murid/*
                    pe-*lah*-jahr   *pelajar.*

| I'm not a Muslim. | *sai*-yuh boo-*kahn* moos-*lee*-meen/ moos-*lee*-mah(h) **(m/f)** | *Saya bukan Muslimin/ Muslimah.* |

This denotes:

| I'm not a (male) Muslim. | *sai*-yuh boo-*kahn* moos-lee-meen **(m)** | *Saya bukan Muslimin.* |

and

| I'm not a (female) Muslim. | *sai*-yuh boo-*kahn* moos-*lee*-mah(h) **(f)** | *Saya bukan Muslimah.* |

; semicolon
separates two (or more) alternative words where one (or more) consists of more than one word:

| chilli sauce | sam-bahl; sos chi-lee | *sambal; sos cili* |

denotes:

| chilli sauce | sam-bahl | *sambal* |

and

| chilli sauce | sos chi-lee | *sos cili* |

• bullet points
are used in the dictionary only to separate alternative words (synonyms):

| painter | pe-loo-kis • ahr-tis • se-nee-mahn | *pelukis • artis • seniman* |

If it is necessary to clarify the difference between alternatives, this is indicated in parentheses after each word.

Pronunciation

Malay is a breeze to pronounce. Unlike English, Malay is spoken as it's written, in Roman script, so getting your tongue around the correct way to say things isn't difficult. The Malay alphabet is the same as the English alphabet. You can hear little seven-year-olds reciting the 'ABC' song in schools, when they are beginning their English lessons.

There are some regional differences regarding how the language is spoken in the north-east and north-west of Malaysia, but standard Malay, *Bahasa Baku,* bah-*hah*-suh bah-*koo*, is what's taught in schools and understood everywhere.

Malays will be thrilled to assist you with correct pronunciation, so be sure to ask. The following pronunciation tips will help you to speak Malay and be understood.

stress

Most syllables have reasonably equal stress in Malay, but a good rule of thumb is to put more emphasis on the second-last syllable.

transliteration system

To help you understand the relationship between the letters and their corresponding sounds, a simple phonetic transliteration has been used throughout this book. All transliterations are in purple. We use a hyphen to indicate when a new syllable begins. The syllable to be stressed is written in italics, eg, tranz-li-te-*ray*-shuhn.

vowels

Malaysian vowel sounds are much more standard than in English. The following should help you to pronounce things correctly.

a	ah	as the 'a' in 'father'
	uh	as the 'u' in 'cup'
	ai	as the 'i' in 'aisle'

Sometimes, in the words borrowed from other languages, the 'a' sounds like 'ay' in day or the 'a' in cat – these will be transliterated as ay and a.

e	e	as the 'e' in 'water'
	eh	as the first 'e' in 'enter'
i	ee	as the 'ee' in 'teen'
	i	as the 'i' in 'bit'
o	o	as the 'o' in 'no'
u	oo	as the 'oo' in 'zoo'
	u	as the 'u' in 'put'

diphthongs (vowel combinations)

Malay has four vowel combinations.

ai	ai	as the 'ai' in 'aisle'
au	ow	as the 'ow' in 'cow'
oi	oy	as the 'oy' in 'toy'
ua	wah	as the 'wa' in 'swan'

---

get to the point

Adding -lah to a word gives it emphasis. Put a forceful -lah on the end of any phrase to really get your point across. You can liven up the dinner table when all you savour is *sedaplah!*, se-*dahp*-lah(h)!, (totally delicious!), or prevent near death when you tell your taxi driver to *Berhenti di sinilah!*, ber-*hen*-tee dee see-nee-lah(h)!, 'Stop here!'.

consonants

Some consonants that fall at the end of a word in Malay are not pronounced as clearly as they would be in English. It's as though the speaker starts to say the letter and then swallows it. This is shown in the transliteration system by brackets, eg, *boo-soo(k)*, 'smelly'. You will see it applied in particular to h and k.

Words ending in h have some rules all of their own. An (h) indicates a breathy h sound at the end of a syllable, and a slight lengthening of the vowel sound, which can indicate a different meaning. Don't get caught out! *Dadah*, *dah*-dah(h), means 'illegal drugs' and *dada*, *dah*-duh, means 'breast'. It's not unusual for tourists ordering a nice bit of chicken in a restaurant to accidentally ask for narcotics! Ask a Malay to pronounce some of these sounds for you and see if you can hear (and repeat) the difference. Most consonants are pronounced as they are in English, and the few exceptions are listed below.

c	ch	as the 'ch' in 'chair'
g	g	as the 'g' in 'garlic'
gh	gh	a throaty 'g' sound, as if you are clearing your throat
h	h	always pronounced. Stressed a little more strongly than in English, as if you were sighing sighing. This heavy pronunciation is especially evident for words of Arabic origin, when the 'h' appears between two vowels that are the same;
	(h)	at the end of a word, in brackets, a breathier, slightly prolonged version of the preceding vowel sound
k	k	as the 'k' in 'king';
	(k)	at the end of a syllable, in brackets, as a glottal stop – the sound made between the words 'uh-oh'
kh	kh	as the 'ch' in the Scottish loch
ny	ny	as the 'ny' in 'canyon'
ng	ng	as the 'ng' in 'singer'
r	r	always trilled clearly and distinctly
sy	sh	as the 'sh' in 'ship'

abbreviated talk

Many common words are abbreviated when you're speaking in a casual or intimate way. Sometimes the second syllable is used alone; sometimes a middle portion is dropped.

I (inf)	*aku/ku*	*ah-*koo/koo
you (inf)	*kamu/mu*	*kah-*moo/moo
you (inf)	*engkau/kau*	*eng-*kow/kow
near/at	*dekat/kat*	de-*kaht*/kaht
already/finished	*sudah/dah*	*soo-*dah/dah(h)
not/isn't it?	*bukan/kan*	*boo-*kahn/kahn
no/not	*tidak/tak*	*tee-*dah(k)/tah(k)
want	*hendak/nak*	*hen-*dah(k)/nah(k)
this/these	*ini/ni*	*ee-*nee/nee
that/those	*itu/tu*	*ee-*too/too
a little bit	*sedikit/sikit*	se-*dee-*kit/*see-*kit
a little while	*sekejap/jap*	se-ke-*jahp*/jahp
only	*sahaja/saja*	sah-*hah-*juh/*sah-*juh

So, the question:

How long have you been in Malaysia?

> *soo-*dah(h) be-*rah-*puh
> *lah-*muh *eng-*kow
> de-*kaht* mah-*lay-*see-ah?

> *Sudah berapa*
> *lama engkau*
> *dekat Malaysia?*

would become:

> dah(h) be-*rah-*puh *lah-*muh
> kow kaht mah-*lay-*see-ah?

> *Dah berapa lama*
> *kau kat Malaysia?*

Grammar

Many aspects of Malay grammar make it an easy language to learn. Verbs don't change according to subject or tense, nouns don't have to have plural forms, and there are no gender-related rules to remember. Like any other language, there are nuances to be learned, but for the purpose of basic communication, the grammar is quite straightforward.

word order

The structure of a Malay sentence is the same as in English: subject-verb-object.

I'm climbing the tree.
sai-yuh me-*mahn*-jaht *po*-ko(k)   *Saya memanjat pokok.*
(lit: I to-climb tree)

It's not unusual in Malay for the object to be mentioned first if it's being stressed. This causes some changes in verbs, so the beginner will find it easier to simply use the subject-verb-object construction.

articles

There's no word corresponding to 'the' or 'a/an'. Instead, they're understood from the context of a sentence. Alternatively, demonstrative adjectives *ini*, 'this/these', and *itu*, 'that/those' are placed after the noun.

this book	*boo*-koo *ee*-nee	*buku ini* (lit: book this)
that table	*meh*-juh *ee*-too	*meja itu* (lit: table that)

nouns

plurals

Plural forms of nouns can be indicated by doubling the noun or by the use of quantity words such as *ramai*, 'many/numerous'.

those books	*boo-koo-boo-koo ee-too*	*buku-buku itu* (lit: books those)
many visitors	*rah-mai pe-lah-waht*	*ramai pelawat* (lit: visitors many)

pronouns

personal pronouns

Saya, *sai-yuh*, is the Malay equivalent of 'I' in English. Referring to yourself as *saya* is considered polite. A more informal word for 'I' is *aku*, *ah-koo*, which is often abbreviated to *ku*. However, aku should only be used if you know the person you're speaking to very well, and if they're of roughly the same age and status. See the next page for polite ways of addressing people.

Malay pronouns can be a bit confusing, as Malaysians will often use a person's name, family status or title instead of the pronoun 'I' or 'you'. Malaysians also sometimes use their own names or titles when referring to themselves, rather than using 'I'. It might take a while to get used to an older Malay woman referring to herself as 'Auntie'.

Makcik boleh buat.
mah(k)-chi(k) bo-leh(h) boo-aht

Auntie can do it.
(lit: Auntie can do)

when the sense is:

Saya boleh buat.
sai-yuh bo-leh(h) boo-aht

I can do it.
(lit: I can do)

Other common age-related terms which Malaysians may use instead of 'I', even if there is no real familial relationship, include:

abang	ah-*bahng*	older brother; someone slightly older than the speaker
kakak	kah-kah(k)	older sister; someone slightly older
adik	ah-*di(k)*	younger brother or sister; slightly younger, or any child
pakcik	pah(k)-chi(k)	uncle; old enough to be the speaker's uncle or father
nenek	neh-*neh(k)*	grandmother; old enough to be the speaker's grandmother
datuk	dah-tu(k)	grandfather; old enough to be the speaker's grandfather

The pronoun 'you' causes problems for learners of Malay, because like 'I' there are hierarchical differentiations between various forms. The safest forms of 'you' to use when you want to make sure you are being polite are:

encik	en-*chi(k)*	**mister**
tuan	twahn	**sir**
puan	pwahn	**ma'am** or **missus**
cik	chi(k)	**miss**

singular pronouns		
I/me	*sai*-yuh, *ah*-koo	*saya, aku*
you (inf)	*kah*-moo, *eng*-kow, *ah*-wah(k)	*kamu, engkau, awak*
you (pol)	*ahn*-duh, *sow-dah*-ruh	*anda, saudara*
he/she/her/him	*dee*-uh	*dia*
it	*ee*-uh	*ia*

grammar

21

plural pronouns		
we/us/our (excludes person spoken to)	*kah*-mee	*kami*
we/us/our (includes person spoken to)	*kee*-tuh	*kita*
you	*ahn*-duh, *ah*-wah(k) se-*moo*-uh	*anda, awak semua*
they/them/their	me-*reh*-kuh	*mereka*
they (inf)	*dee*-uh o-rahng	*dia orang*

possessive pronouns

Malay uses possessive pronouns *after* the noun. The first and second person, 'my' and 'your', as well as the third person plural, 'their', are separate words placed after the noun they modify:

my money	*doo*-it *sai*-yuh	*duit saya* (lit: money my)
your umbrella	*pai*-yung *ahn*-duh	*payung anda* (lit: umbrella your)
their car	ke-*reh*-tuh me-*reh*-kuh	*kereta mereka* (lit: car their)

In the third person singular, 'he' and 'she', the suffix *-nya* (lit: of him/her) is added to the thing that's possessed, or the word *dia*, 'his/her' is used after the noun; *-nya* can also be used in place of the plural possessive pronoun *mereka*, 'their'.

her watch	jahm-*nyuh*; jahm *dee*-uh	*jamnya; jam dia* (lit: watch-of-her; watch her)
his keys	koon-chee-*nyuh*	*kuncinya* (lit: keys-of-him)

| their house | roo-mah(h)-nyuh | *rumahnya* |
| | | (lit: house-of-their) |

relative pronouns

The relative pronoun *yang* is used to mean 'who/which/that/
the one which/that which'.

This is the book that I want to buy.

ee-nee *boo*-koo yahng	*Ini buku yang*
sai-yuh *mah*-hoo be-*lee*	*saya mahu beli.*
	(lit: this book that I want
	to-buy)

The man who's big is crying.

lah-kee-*lah*-kee yahng	*Laki-laki yang*
be-*sahr ee*-too me-*nah*-ngees	*besar itu menangis.*
	(lit: man who big that to-cry)

adjectives

Adjectives always follow the noun they're describing.

big	be-*sahr*	*besar*
big car	ke-*reh*-tuh be-*sahr*	*kereta besar*
		(lit: car big)
clean	ber-*si*(h)	*bersih*
clean room	*bee*-li(k) ber-*si*(h)	*bilik bersih*
		(lit: room clean)

As there's no commonly used verb which means 'is/are', the
above constructions can also translate as 'The car is big' and
'The room is clean'. In writing or formal speech, the verb *ialah*,
ee-*ah*-lah(h), is used here.

The relative pronoun *yang*, 'which/who', is often used with
an adjective, especially when you want to describe more than
one thing about the noun.

the blue car with yellow tyres

| ke-*reh*-tuh *bi*-roo yahng | *kereta biru yang* |

ber-*tai*-yahr *koo*-ning   *bertayar kuning*
(lit: car blue which tyre yellow)

the big, white house
roo-mah(h) *poo*-ti(h)   *rumah putih yang besar*
yahng be-*sahr*   (lit: house white which big)

comparatives

The words *lebih*, 'more', and *kurang*, 'less', are used to indicate comparisons. They're placed before adjectives. The word *daripada*, 'than', appears after adjectives to form the following constructions.

lebih/kurang + adj (+ *daripada)*
(lit: more/less ... (than))

bigger   le-*bi(h)* be-*sahr*   *lebih besar*
(lit: more big)

slower than   *koo*-rang *che*-paht   *kurang cepat*
dah-ree-*pah*-duh   *daripada*
(lit: less fast than)

Daripada is also used if both objects being compared are mentioned.

**Mangoes are more expensive
than bananas.**
mahng-guh le-*bi(h)* mah-*hahl*   *Mangga lebih mahal*
dah-ree-*pah*-duh *pee*-sahng   *daripada pisang*
(lit: mango more
expensive than banana)

The way you compare quality in English, eg, 'as ... as', is indicated in Malay by the prefix *se-*.

as beautiful as   se-*chahn*-ti(k)   *secantik*
(lit: *se*-beautiful)

superlatives

To form the adjectives that correspond to 'most ... ' or '-est' in English, the word *paling,* 'the most', is used.

noun + *paling* + adj

cheap	*moo*-rah(h)	*murah*
the cheapest	*pah*-ling moo-*rah(h)*	*paling murah*
		(lit: most cheap)
good	bah-*gus*	*bagus*
the best	*pah*-ling bah-*gus*	*paling bagus*
		(lit: most good)

adverbs

As in English, adverbs can appear at the beginning, at the end or within a sentence.

also	*joo*-guh/pun	*juga/pun*
always	se-*lah*-loo/	*selalu/*
	sen-tee-*ah*-suh	*sentiasa*
here	dee *see*-nee	*di sini*
immediately	se-ge-ruh;	*segera;*
	de-*ngahn* se-ge-ruh	*dengan segera*
in this way	be-*gee*-nee	*begini*
in that way	be-*gee*-too	*begitu*
just now	*tah*-dee	*tadi*
maybe	*moong*-kin	*mungkin*
never	*tee*-dah(k) *per*-nah(h)	*tidak pernah*
not yet	be-*lum*;	*belum;*
	be-*lum lah*-gee	*belum lagi*
often	ke-*rahp*/se-*ring*	*kerap/sering*
perhaps	*moong*-kin	*mungkin*
possibly	*moong*-kin/bo-*leh(h)*	*mungkin/boleh*
rarely	jah-*rahng*	*jarang*
really	*soong*-gu(h)/be-*gee*-too	*sungguh/begitu*
sometimes	*kah*-dahng-*kah*-dahng/	*kadang-kadang/*
	kah-dahng-*kah*-luh	*kadang-kala*
so that	soo-*pai*-yuh/*ah*-gahr	*supaya/agar*
there	dee *sah*-nuh	*di sana*
very	sah-*ngaht*	*sangat*

verbs

Malay verbs are divided into a number of different classes, and are formed from a root word plus a suffix and/or prefix. The root word conveys the meaning, while adding suffixes and/or prefixes indicates that it's a useable verb – one you can use in a sentence. However, the bare root-word form can always be used in everyday speech and you'll still be understood.

1. The simplest type of verb stands alone and never requires a prefix. Fortunately, many of the most commonly used verbs fit into this category:

to bathe	*mahn*-dee	mandi
to eat	*mah*-kahn	makan
to go	*per*-gee	pergi
to laugh	ke-*tah*-wuh	ketawa
to sit	*doo*-du(k)	duduk
to sleep	*tee*-dur	tidur

2. The second type of verb requires the *me-* prefixes which include *meng-*, *mem-*, *men-* and *meny-* and *me-*. These are added to the root word.

me- is used with root words beginning with *l, m, n, ng, ny, r, w* or *y*. For example, the root word 'look' becomes useable: 'to look'.

| look; to look | *lee*-haht/me-*lee*-haht | lihat/melihat |
| record; to record | *rah*-kahm/me-*rah*-kahm | rakam/merakam |

meng- is used with words beginning with *g, h, k, q, a, e, i, o, u*. The *k* is dropped to make the verb.

change; to change	*gahn*-tee/	ganti/
	meng-*gahn*-tee	mengganti
pardon; to pardon	*ahm*-poon/	ampun/
	me-*ngahm*-poon	mengampun

mem- is used with words beginning with *b, v, p* or *f*. The *p* and *f* are dropped to make the verb and an *m* used instead.

buy; to buy	be-*lee*/mem-be-*lee*	*beli/membeli*
cut; to cut	po-tong/me-*mo*-tong	*potong/memotong*

men- is used with words beginning with *c*, *j*, *d*, *t*, or *z*.

search; to search	*chah*-ree/men-*chah*-ree	*cari/mencari*
climb; to climb	*dah*-kee/men-*dah*-kee	*daki/mendaki*

meny- is used with words beginning with *s*. The *s* is replaced by a *y*:

touch; to touch	*sen*-tu(h)/me-*nyen*-tu(h)	*sentuh/menyentuh*
rent; to rent	*seh*-wuh/me-*nyeh*-wuh	*sewa/menyewa*

3. The third type of verb requires the prefix *ber-* followed by the root word. For example, the root word *tanya*, 'ask', becomes *bertanya*, 'to ask'. If the root word starts with *r*, such as *renang*, 'swim', the prefix drops the *r* and the verb becomes *berenang*, 'to swim'.

walk; to walk	*jah*-lahn/ber-*jah*-lahn	*jalan/berjalan*
get ready; to get ready	se-dee-*uh*/ber-se-dee-*uh*	*sedia/bersedia*
speak; to speak	bee-*chah*-ruh/ ber-bee-*chah*-ruh	*bicara/ berbicara*

4. The fourth type of verb requires the prefix *me-* and the suffix *-kan*. With the addition of *-kan*, the verb must have an object.

witness; to witness	*sahk*-see/ me-*nyahk*-see-kahn	*saksi/ menyaksikan*
clean; to clean	ber-*si(h)*/ mem-ber-*si(h)*-kahn	*bersih/ membersihkan*

5. The fifth type of verb requires the prefix *me-* and the suffix *-i*. If the root word starts with *k*, it is replaced with a *g*.

enjoy; to enjoy	*nik*-maht/ me-*nik*-mah-tee	*nikmat/ menikmati*
love; to love	*kah*-si(h)/me-*ngah*-si-hee	*kasih/mengasihi*

to be able (can)	bo-*leh(h)*	*boleh*
to agree	ber-se-*too*-joo	*bersetuju*
to become	men-*jah*-dee	*menjadi*
to bring	mem-*bah*-wuh	*membawa*
to come	*dah*-tahng	*datang*
to cost	ber-*hahr*-guh	*berharga*
to depart (leave)	ber-*to*-lah(k)	*bertolak*
to do	mem-*boo*-aht	*membuat*
to give	mem-*be*-ree	*memberi*
to go	*per*-gee	*pergi*
to know (someone)	ke-*nahl*	*kenal*
to know (how to)	*pahn*-dai/*tah*-hoo	*pandai/tahu*
to like	*soo*-kuh	*suka*
to live	*hee*-dup	*hidup*
to make	mem-*boo*-aht	*membuat*
to meet	ber-*joom*-puh	*berjumpa*
to need	per-*loo*	*perlu*
to prefer	le-*bi(h)* soo-kuh	*lebih suka*
to return	*bah*-li(k)/	*balik/*
	poo-lahng	*pulang*
to say	ber-*kah*-tuh	*berkata*
to stay	*ting*-gahl	*tinggal*
to take	me-*ngahm*-bil	*mengambil*
to understand	*fah*-hahm	*faham*
to want	*mah*-hoo/	*mahu/*
	hehn-dah(k)/	*hendak/*
	nah(k)	*nak*

Don't be too concerned about these prefixes – you'll still be understood if you use the root word in a sentence. They mainly need to be used in formal settings or when writing.

tense

Luckily for the learner of Malay, verbs don't change their form acccording to tense. The tense of a verb can be easily worked out by context or by the inclusion of a time word such as *se-*

malam, 'yesterday', and *nanti* or *kemudian*, 'later'.

I went swimming yesterday.

se-*mah*-lahm *sai*-yuh   *Semalam saya*
per-gee be-re-*nahng*   *pergi berenang.*
                   (lit: yesterday I to-go to-swim)

I will eat later.

sai-yuh *mah*-kahn   *Saya makan*
ke-*moo*-dee-ahn/*nahn*-tee   *kemudian/nanti.*
                   (lit: I to-eat later)

Another way to indicate tense is by placing certain adverbs immediately before the verb. The most common are:

already	*soo*-dah(h)	*sudah*
currently	se-*dahng*	*sedang*
have just	bah-*roo*	*baru*
not yet	be-*lum*	*belum*
still	*mah*-si(h)	*masih*
will	*ah*-kahn	*akan*

I have already eaten

sai-yuh *soo*-dah(h)   *Saya sudah*
mah-kahn   *makan.*
                   (lit: I already eat)

to be

There's no direct equivalent of 'to be' in conversational Malay. The words 'is' and 'are' are implied in a sentence. In writing or formal speech, the verb *ialah*, ee-*ah*-lah(h), is used.

My name is Abu.

nah-muh *sai*-yuh   *Nama saya*
ee-*ah*-lah(h) *ah*-boo **(pol)**   *ialah Abu.*
                   (lit: name I is Abu)

I am here.

sai-yuh dee *see*-nee   *Saya di sini.*
                   (lit: I in here)

grammar

That baby is hungry.
   bai-yee *ee*-too *lah*-pahr   *Bayi itu lapar.*
                                  (lit: baby that hungry)

To say that something does or doesn't exist, the word *ada* 'there is/are' (lit: to-exist) can be used in a sentence with no definite subject.

Is there a night bus?
   ah-duh bahs *mah*-lahm?   *Ada bas malam?*
                                  (lit: to-exist bus night?)

to have

Ada can also be used to mean 'has/have'.

I have a younger brother.
   sai-yuh ah-duh   *Saya ada adik lelaki.*
   ah-di(k) le-*lah*-kee   (lit: I have younger-sibling
                                       male)

modals

There are other auxiliary words that can be used with a verb to indicate modality. These include *boleh*, 'can', *suka*, 'like to', *hendak/nak*, 'want to' and *tahu*, 'know how to', and they always come before the other verb.

can; be able to	bo-*leh*(h)	*boleh*

I can climb trees.
   sai-yuh bo-*leh*(h) *pahn*-jaht   *Saya boleh panjat pokok.*
   po-ko(k)   (lit: I can to-climb tree)

Where can I buy ...?
   dee *mah*-nuh sai-yuh   *Di mana saya boleh beli ...?*
   bo-*leh*(h) be-*lee* ...?   (lit: in where I can buy ...?)

like to	soo-kuh	*suka*

I like to eat curry.
  sai-yuh soo-kuh mah-kahn
  kah-ree

Saya suka makan kari.
(lit: I like-to to-eat curry)

I like to play soccer.
  sai-yuh soo-kuh main
  bo-luh seh-pah(k)

Saya suka main bola sepak.
(lit: I like-to to-play
  ball kick)

want to	*hehn*-dah(k)/nah(k)	hendak/nak

I want to dance.
  sai-yuh nah(k) me-nah-ree

Saya nak menari.
(lit: I want-to to-dance)

I don't want that one.
  sai-yuh tee-dah(k)
  hehn-dah(k) yahng ee-too

Saya tidak hendak yang itu.
(lit: I no want-to which/
  that that)

must; have to	hah-roos/mes-tee	harus/mesti

**What time do I have to be at
the airport?**
  poo-kool be-rah-puh sai-yuh
  hah-roos ah-duh dee
  lah-pahng-ahn ter-bahng?

Pukul berapa saya harus ada
di lapangan terbang?
(lit: hour how-much I
  have-to to-exist in
  field-fly?)

may/might/can	bo-*leh(h)*	boleh

May I speak to ...?
  bo-leh(h) sai-yuh
  ber-chah-kahp de-ngahn ...?

Boleh saya
bercakap dengan ...?
(lit: can I to-speak with ...?)

May I take photos?
  bo-leh(h) sai-yuh ahm-bil
  gahm-bahr?

Boleh saya ambil gambar?
(lit: can I to-take photo?)

| know how to | *tah*-hoo | *tahu* |

I know how to swim.
sai-yuh *tah*-hoo be-re-*nahng* *Saya tahu berenang.*
(lit: I know-how-to to-swim)

imperatives

If you're asking, insisting or demanding that someone does something, don't use the prefix on the verb.

Look! te-ngo(k)! *Tengok!*

To make a more polite command, add *silakan*, 'please', before the verb, in the context of offering someone something. *Tolong*, 'please' or 'help', is used when you're asking for something you need.

Please sit down.
see-*lah*-kahn *doo*-du(k) *Silakan duduk.*
(lit: please sit)

Please be quiet.
to-long *sen*-yahp *Tolong senyap.*
(lit: please/help quiet)

questions

As in English, a question can be indicated simply by raising the intonation of your voice at the end of a sentence. Other ways to form questions include ending a sentence or a word with *-kah*.

Where did he go?
dee *mah*-nuh-kah(h) *Di manakah*
dee-uh *per*-gee? *dia pergi?*
(lit: in where-*kah* he to-go?)

Do you like spicy food?
ah-wah(k) *soo*-kuh *Awak suka*
mah-kah-nan *makanan*

pe-*dahs*-kah(h)?   *pedaskah?*
                                           (lit: you like-to food hot-*kah?*)

Another option is starting a sentence with *adakah* (lit: is it that
...?).

Is the soup hot?
ah-duh-kah(h) soop *ee*-nee   *Adakah sup ini panas?*
pah-nahs?   (lit: is-it-that soup this hot?)

Or you can try adding *tak*, 'no', to the end of a question:

Is it spicy or not?
pe-*dahs* tah(k)?   *Pedas, tak?*
                                        (lit: spicy, no?)

Finally, with nouns and adverbs, add *kan* (short for *bukan*,
meaning 'not') to the end of the sentence.

We're going tomorrow, right?
kee-tuh *per*-gee *eh*-so(k)   *Kita pergi esok, kan?*
kahn?   (lit: we-(incl) to-go
                                            tomorrow, not?)

grammar

33

You can add a question word at the beginning or end of a sentence:

What?	*Apa?*

What's your name?
Apa nama kamu?
ah-puh nah-muh kah-moo?   (lit: what name you?)

Who?	*Siapakah?*

Who are they?
Siapakah mereka?
see-ah-puh-kah(h) me-reh-kuh?   (lit: who they?)

Where?	*Di mana?*

Where's the post office?
Di mana pejabat pos?
dee mah-nuh pe-jah-baht pos?   (lit: in where post office?)

When?	*Bilakah?*

When does the bus depart for Ipoh?
Bilakah bas akan berangkat ke Ipoh?
bee-luh-kah(h) bahs ah-kahn be-rang-kaht ke ee-po(h)?
(lit: when bus will depart to Ipoh?)

Why?	*Kenapa?*

Why is the food so oily?
Kenapa makanan ini terlalu berminyak?
ke-nah-puh mah-kah-nahn ee-nee ter-lah-loo ber-min-yah(k)?
(lit: why food this too-much oily?)

Which?	*Yang mana?*

Which is your book?
Yang mana buku anda?
yahng mah-nuh boo-koo ahn-duh?   (lit: which book you?)

How?	*Berapa?*

How much does a bus ticket to Melaka cost?
Berapa harga tiket bas ke Melaka?
be-rah-puh hahr-guh tee-keht bas ke me-lah-kuh?
(lit: how-much price ticket bus to Melaka?)

answers

Malaysians commonly answer questions concerning availability or possession with *ada*, 'have'/'to exist', or *tidak ada*, 'don't have'/ 'no to-exist'.

Do you have Western food?	*ah*-duh *mah*-kah-nahn *bah*-raht tah(k)?	*Ada makanan Barat, tak?* (lit: have food west, no?)
Yes.	*ah*-duh	*Ada.* (lit: have)
No.	*tee*-dah(k) *ah*-duh	*Tidak ada.* (lit: no have)

negatives

Three words are used to express the negative: *tidak*, 'no', *bukan*, 'not', and *jangan*, 'don't'. *Bukan* is used with nouns.

Not me.	boo-*kahn* sai-yuh	*Bukan saya.* (lit: not me)
Not that shirt.	boo-*kahn* bah-joo ee-too	*Bukan baju itu.* (lit: not shirt that)

Both *tidak* and *jangan* are used in relation to verbs; *tidak* is also used with adjectives.

I don't want to.
sai-yuh *tee*-dah(k) *mah*-hoo

Saya tidak mahu.
(lit: I no want)

Do not enter.
jah-*ngahn* mah-su(k)

Jangan masuk.
(lit: don't enter)

My car is not red.
ke-*reh*-tuh *sai*-yuh *tee*-dah(k) *meh*-rah(h)

Kereta saya tidak merah.
(lit: car my no red)

classifiers

When you use a number with a noun in Malay you must use a counter word (classifier) between the number and the noun. This classifier describes the category of thing you're counting. This also occurs in English all the time, when we talk about *slices* of toast or *pairs* of pants, although we don't call them classifiers. There are about 40 classifiers in Malay – too many to list – so here are the most common ones.

orang   for people

There are three women in that house.

ah-duh *tee*-guh o-rahng   *Ada tiga orang*
pe-*rem*-pwahn *dah*-lahm   *perempuan dalam*
roo-mah(h) *ee*-too   *rumah itu.*
                                   (lit: have three *orang* woman
                                   inside house that)

ekor   for other living things

I saw six fish.

sai-yuh *nahm*-pah(k)   *Saya nampak*
e-*nahm* eh-kor *ee*-kahn   *enam ekor ikan.*
                                   (lit: I see six *ekor* fish)

batang   for stick-like objects (eg, cigarettes, trees)

He bought two cigarettes.

dee-uh be-*lee* doo-uh   *Dia beli dua*
bah-tahng *ro*-ko(k)   *batang rokok.*
                                   (lit: he buy two *batang*
                                   cigarette)

biji   for small, easily moved objects (eg, fruit, eggs)

I ate one durian.

sai-yuh *mah*-kahn   *Saya makan*
sah-too *bee*-jee *doo*-ree-ahn *satu biji durian.*
                                   (lit: I to-eat one *biji* durian)

buah   for bulky objects and natural features (eg, houses, rive

I bought two houses.
*sai-*yuh be-*lee doo-*uh   *Saya beli dua*
*boo-*ah(h) *roo-*mah(h)   *buah rumah.*
     (lit: I buy two *buah* house)

prepositions

about	*ten-*tahng/	*tentang/*
	me-*nge-*nah-ee	*mengenai*
after	se-le-*pahs*	*selepas*
at (place)	dee	*di*
at (time)	*pah-*duh;	*pada;*
	*pah-*duh *poo-*kool	*pada pukul;*
	*wahk-*too; jahm	*waktu; jam*
between	dee ahn-*tah-*ruh	*di antara*
during	se-*mah-*suh	*semasa*
for	*oon-*tu(k)	*untuk*
for (time)	se-*lah-*muh	*selama*
if	*kah-*low	*kalau*
in	dee; dee dah-*lahm*	*di; di dalam*
inside	dah-*lahm*;	*dalam;*
	dee dah-*lahm*	*di dalam*
from	*dah-*ree	*dari*
(place & time)		
to/forward	ke	*ke*
(place)		
from (people)	dah-ree-*pah-*duh	*daripada*
to (people)	ke-*pah-*duh	*kepada*
on (time/person)	*pah-*duh	*pada*
on (place)	dee	*di*
since	se-*jahk*	*sejak*
through	me-*lah-*loo-ee	*melalui*
until	*sahm-*pai/	*sampai/*
	se-*hing-*guh	*sehingga*
with	de-ngahn	*dengan*
without	*tahn-*puh	*tanpa*
by	o-*leh*(h)	*oleh*

prepositions

Prepositions are used in the same way as English, eg:

I want rice with chilli sauce.

sai-yuh *mah*-hoo
nah-see de-*ngahn sahm*-bahl

*Saya mahu
nasi dengan sambal.*
(lit: I to-want rice with
   chilli-sauce)

She waited for three hours.

dee-uh *toong*-goo se-*lah*-muh
tee-guh jahm

*Dia tunggu selama
tiga jam.*
(lit: she wait for three hour)

conjunctions

and	dahn	*dan*
because	se-*bahb*/	*sebab*/
	ke-*rah*-nuh	*kerana*
but	te-*tah*-pee	*tetapi*
or	ah-*tow*	*atau*
so that	so-*pai*-yuh	*supaya*
(together) with	*ser*-tuh	*serta*
as if	se-*o*-lah(h)-*o*-lah(h)	*seolah-olah*

I want to eat because I am hungry.

sai-yuh nah(k) *mah*-kahn
se-*bahb sai*-yuh *lah*-pahr

*Saya nak makan
sebab saya lapar.*
(lit: I want-to to-eat
   because I hungry)

Bilangan & Jumlah

In Malay, numbers from 12 to 19 are comprised of the numbers one to nine plus *(-)belas*, *(-)be-lahs*. Numbers from 20 to 99 are counted with *(-)puluh*, *(-)poo-lu(h)*, '10'. The number 10 is *sepuluh*, *se-poo-lu(h)*, 20 is *dua puluh*, *doo-uh poo-lu(h)*, and so on.

In the hundreds, *(-)ratus*, *(-)rah-toos*, is used. So, *seratus*, *se-rah-toos*, is 100, *duaratus*, *doo-uh rah-toos*, is 200, and so on. For thousands, use *(-)ribu*, *(-)ree-boo*, and for millions, use *(-)juta*, *(-)joo-tuh*.

cardinal numbers

bilangan pokok

0	*ko*-song/see-*fahr*	*kosong/sifar*
1	*sah*-too	*satu*
2	*doo*-uh	*dua*
3	*tee*-guh	*tiga*
4	em-*paht*	*empat*
5	*lee*-muh	*lima*
6	e-*nahm*	*enam*
7	*too*-ju(h)	*tujuh*
8	*lah*-pahn	*lapan*
9	sem-*bee*-lahn	*sembilan*
10	se-*poo*-lu(h)	*sepuluh*
11	se-be-*lahs*	*sebelas*
12	*doo*-uh be-*lahs*	*dua belas*
13	*tee*-guh be-*lahs*	*tiga belas*
14	em-*paht* be-*lahs*	*empat belas*
15	*lee*-muh be-*lahs*	*lima belas*
16	e-*nahm* be-*lahs*	*enam belas*
17	*too*-ju(h) be-*lahs*	*tujuh belas*
18	*lah*-pahn be-*lahs*	*lapan belas*
19	sem-*bee*-lahn be-*lahs*	*sembilan belas*

20	*doo*-uh *poo*-lu(h)	*dua puluh*
21	*doo*-uh *poo*-lu(h) *sah*-too	*dua puluh satu*
22	*doo*-uh *poo*-lu(h) *doo*-uh	*dua puluh dua*
30	*tee*-guh *poo*-lu(h)	*tiga puluh*
40	em-*paht poo*-lu(h)	*empat puluh*
50	*lee*-muh *poo*-lu(h)	*lima puluh*
100	se-*rah*-toos	*seratus*
200	*doo*-uh *rah*-toos	*dua ratus*
268	*doo*-uh *rah*-toos e-*nahm*	*dua ratus enam*
	poo-lu(h) *lah*-pahn	*puluh lapan*
300	*tee*-guh *rah*-toos	*tiga ratus*
1000	se-*ree*-boo	*seribu*
2000	*doo*-uh *ree*-boo	*dua ribu*
3000	*tee*-guh *ree*-boo	*tiga ribu*
51,783	*lee*-muh *poo*-lu(h)	*lima puluh satu*
	sah-too *ree*-boo, *too*-ju(h)	*ribu, tujuh ratus*
	rah-toos *lah*-pahn	*lapan puluh tiga*
	poo-lu(h) *tee*-guh	
1 million	se-*joo*-tuh	*sejuta*
2 million	*doo*-uh *joo*-tuh	*dua juta*

ordinal numbers

bilangan tingkat

1st	per-*tah*-muh	*pertama*
2nd	ke-*doo*-uh	*kedua*
3rd	ke-*tee*-guh	*ketiga*
4th	ke-em-*paht*	*keempat*
5th	ke-*lee*-muh	*kelima*
6th	ke-e-*nahm*	*keenam*
7th	ke-*too*-ju(h)	*ketujuh*
8th	ke-*lah*-pahn	*kelapan*
9th	ke-sem-*bee*-lahn	*kesembilan*
10th	ke-se-*poo*-lu(h)	*kesepuluh*

the first bus
   bahs (yahng) per-*tah*-muh   *bas (yang) pertama*
the third building
   bah-*ngoo*-nahn (yahng) ke-*tee*-guh   *bangunan (yang) ketiga*

fractions

1/3	se-per-*tee*-guh	*sepertiga*
1/4	*soo*-koo	*suku*
1/2	se-te-*ngah(h)*	*setengah*
3/4	*tee*-guh pe-rem-*paht*	*tiga perempat*

quantity

Quantity can either be indicated by a number, or by a quantity word placed before a noun.

all	se-*moo*-uh	*semua*
both	ke-*doo*-uh-nyuh/	*keduanya/*
	ke-*doo*-uh-*doo*-uh-nyuh	*kedua-duanya*
double	*doo*-uh *kah*-lee *gahn*-duh	*dua kali ganda*
each	se-*tee*-ahp/	*setiap/tiap-tiap*
	tee-ahp-*tee*-ahp	
enough	*choo*-kup	*cukup*
every	se-*tee*-ahp/	*setiap/*
	mah-sing-*mah*-sing	*masing-masing*
few	be-be-*rah*-puh	*beberapa*
a little	se-*dee*-kit	*sedikit*
many (for things)	*bah*-nyah(k)	*banyak*
(for people)	rah-*mai*	*ramai*
much	*bah*-nyah(k)	*banyak*
one more	*sah*-too *lah*-gee	*satu lagi*

There are many people.

ah-duh rah-*mai* o-rahng	*Ada ramai orang.*
	(lit: there-are many person)

about	le-*bi(h)* koo-rahng/	*lebih kurang/*
	ki-*ruh*-ki-*ruh*	*kira-kira*
amount	jum-*lah(h)*	*jumlah*
to count	me-*ngi*-ruh	*mengira*
minus	*to*-lah(k)/*koo*-rahng	*tolak/kurang*

numbers & amounts

more	le-*bi*(h)	*lebih*
number	*nom*-bor/*ahng*-kuh/	*nombor/angka/*
	bee-*lah*-ngahn	*bilangan*
a pair	se-*pah*-sahng	*sepasang*
percent	pe-*rah*-toos	*peratus*
plus	*tahm*-bah(h)	*tambah*
quantity	bee-*lah*-ngahn/	*bilangan/*
	koo-*ahn*-ti-tee	*kuantiti*
some	be-be-*rah*-puh	*beberapa*

count down

Malay uses 'counters' before most numbers (see page 36, under Classifiers), like in English when we say 'a piece of paper'. However, in Malay these counters are used nearly all the time for specific numbers of things or people. Common counters include:

batang   bah-tahng
  long, roundish things such as pencils, rivers, trees, cigarettes

biji   bee-jee
  small round things such as fruit, sweets, beans

buah   boo-ah(h)
  large objects such as cars, houses, furniture, airplanes, buildings, mountains, planets

ekor   eh-kor
  animals

helai   heh-lai
  flat, thin, saggy things such as clothing and paper

keping   ke-ping
  flat, thin, hard things such as a sheet of metal or wood

kotak   ko-tah(k)
  box shaped things, like a cigarette carton or box

orang   o-rahng
  people

potong   po-tong
  a piece of something you can cut, eg, cake

I want to buy three shirts.

   sai-yuh nah(k) be-*lee* tee-guh   *Saya nak beli tiga*
   heh-lai bah-joo   *helai baju.*

Time, Dates & Festivals
Masa, Tarikh & Perayaan

Malaysians, especially in the big cities, tend to be punctual for business (although heavy rain and traffic jams may wreak havoc with schedules from time to time). However, for social functions, it's okay to be fashionably late.

telling the time

In Malay, 'am' and 'pm' are replaced by whole words.

8 am
poo-kool *lah*-pahn *pah*-gee   pukul lapan pagi
       (lit: hour eight morning)

8 pm
poo-kool *lah*-pahn *mah*-lahm   pukul lapan malam
       (lit: hour eight night)

morning (12 midnight – 12 noon)
pah-gee   pagi
afternoon (12 noon – 3 pm)
te-ngah-*hah*-ree   tengahari
evening (3 – 7 pm)
pe-*tahng*   petang
night (7 pm – 12 midnight)
mah-lahm   malam

o'clock	*poo*-kool	*pukul*
second	sa-*aht*/de-*ti(k)*	*saat/detik*
minute	*mi*-nit	*minit*
to	se-be-*lum*	*sebelum*

past	se-le-*pahs*	*selepas*
half	se-te-*ngah(h)*	*setengah*
quarter	*soo*-koo	*suku*
one hour	se-*jahm*	*sejam*
two hours	*doo*-uh *jahm*	*dua jam*

What time is it?

| *poo*-kool be-*rah*-puh | *Pukul berapa* |
| (se-*kah*-rahng)? | *(sekarang)?* |

It's three o'clock.

| *poo*-kool *tee*-guh | *Pukul tiga.* |

It's a quarter to four.

| *lah*-gee *soo*-koo jahm | *Lagi suku jam* |
| *poo*-kool em-*paht* | *pukul empat.* |

It's ten past three.

| se-*poo*-lu(h) *mi*-nit se-le-*pahs* | *Sepuluh minit selepas* |
| *poo*-kool *tee*-guh | *pukul tiga.* |

It's five-thirty.

| *poo*-kool *lee*-muh | *Pukul lima* |
| se-te-*ngah(h)* | *setengah.* |

Half past one.

| *poo*-kool *sah*-too se-te-*ngah(h)* | *Pukul satu setengah.* |

days

hari dalam seminggu

Monday	*hah*-ree *ees*-nin	*hari Isnin*
Tuesday	*hah*-ree se-*lah*-suh	*hari Selasa*
Wednesday	*hah*-ree *rah*-boo	*hari Rabu*
Thursday	*hah*-ree *khah*-mis	*hari Khamis*
Friday	*hah*-ree *joo*-mah-aht	*hari Jumaat*
Saturday	*hah*-ree *sahb*-too	*hari Sabtu*
Sunday	*hah*-ree *ah*-hahd	*hari Ahad*
on Monday	*pah*-duh *hah*-ree *ees*-nin	*pada hari Isnin*

BASICS

44

months

January	*jahn*-oo-ah-ree	*Januari*
February	*feh*-broo-ah-ree	*Februari*
March	mahch	*Mac*
April	*ah*-pril	*April*
May	may	*Mei*
June	joon	*Jun*
July	*joo*-lai	*Julai*
August	*o*-gos	*Ogos*
September	sehp-*tehm*-ber	*September*
October	ok-*to*-ber	*Oktober*
November	no-*vehm*-ber	*November*
December	dee-*sehm*-ber	*Disember*
during June	se-*mah*-suh *bu*-lahn joon	*semasa bulan Jun*

---

the night before

Nights refer to the following day – 'Saturday night' is expressed as 'the night before Sunday', rather like saying 'Christmas Eve'.

Thursday night
  mah-lahm *joo*-mah-aht   *malam Jumaat*
                              (lit: at-night Friday)

---

dates

Date order in Malaysia is expressed as day, month, year, eg:

17 August 1945
  too-ju(h) be-*lahs o*-gos   *Tujuh belas Ogos*
  sem-*bee*-lahn be-*lahs* em-*paht*   *sembilan belas*
  poo-lu(h) *lee*-muh   *empat puluh lima*

What date is it today?
  ah-puh *tah*-rikh *hah*-ree *ee*-nee?   *Apa tarikh hari ini?*

It's 28 June.
hah-ree *ee*-nee *doo*-uh *poo*-lu(h)   *Hari ini dua puluh lapan*
lah-pahn hah-ree-*bu*-lahn joon   *haribulan Jun.*

present

immediately	ser-*tah*-mer-*tah*	serta-merta
now	se-*kah*-rahng/*kee*-nee	sekarang/kini
currently	se-*dahng*	sedang
today	*hah*-ree *ee*-nee	hari ini
this morning	*pah*-gee *ee*-nee	pagi ini
during the day	*pah*-duh *hah*-ree *ee*-nee	pada hari ini
tonight	*mah*-lahm *ee*-nee;	malam ini;
	mah-lahm *nahn*-tee	malam nanti
this week	*ming*-goo *ee*-nee	minggu ini
this month	*boo*-lahn *ee*-nee	bulan ini
this year	*tah*-hoon *ee*-nee	tahun ini

past

just now	*bah*-roo *sah*-juh	baru saja
before	se-be-*lum*	sebelum
recently	*bah*-roo-*bah*-roo *ee*-nee	baru-baru ini
already	*soo*-dah(h)	sudah
yesterday	se-*mah*-lahm	semalam
yesterday morning	*pah*-gee se-*mah*-lahm	pagi semalam
yesterday afternoon	te-ngah-*hah*-ree se-*mah*-lahm	tengahari semalam
last night	*mah*-lahm se-*mah*-lahm	malam semalam
day before yesterday	kel-*mah*-rin	kelmarin
last week	*ming*-goo le-*pahs*	minggu lepas
two weeks ago	*doo*-uh *ming*-goo	dua minggu

	le-*pahs*	*lepas*
last month	*boo*-lahn le-*pahs*	*bulan lepas*
last year	*tah*-hoon le-*pahs*	*tahun lepas*
ago	yahng *lah*-loo; le-*pahs*	*yang lalu; lepas*
a while ago	se-*dee*-kit *mah*-suh	*sedikit masa*
	doo-*loo*	*dulu*
long ago	*lah*-muh doo-*loo*	*lama dulu*

future

		masa depan
as soon as	se-che-*paht*	*secepat*
** possible**	*moong*-kin	*mungkin*
soon	se-*geh*-ruh	*segera*
not yet	be-*lum lah*-gee	*belum lagi*
later	ke-*moo*-dee-ahn/	*kemudian/*
	nahn-tee	*nanti*
after	se-le-*pahs*/se-soo-dah(h)	*selepas/sesudah*
tomorrow	*eh*-so(k)	*esok*
** morning**	*eh*-so(k) *pah*-gee	*esok pagi*
** afternoon**	*eh*-so(k)	*esok*
	te-ngah-*hah*-ree	*tengahari*
** evening**	*eh*-so(k) pe-*tahng*	*esok petang*
day after	*loo*-suh	*lusa*
** tomorrow**		
next week	*ming*-goo de-*pahn*	*minggu depan*
next month	*boo*-lahn de-*pahn*	*bulan depan*
next year	*tah*-hoon de-*pahn*	*tahun depan*
forever	se-*lah*-muh-	*selama-*
	lah-muh-nyuh	*lamanya*
moment	se-*behn*-tahr	*sebentar*
minute	*mi*-nit	*minit*
hour	jahm	*jam*
day	*hah*-ree	*hari*
week	*ming*-goo	*minggu*
month	*boo*-lahn	*bulan*
year	*tah*-hoon	*tahun*

decade	*deh*-kahd	dekad
century	*ah*-bahd	abad
millennium	mi-*leh*-nee-um	milenium

during the day

dawn	*sen*-juh	senja
day	*hah*-ree	hari
early	*ah*-wahl	awal
early morning	*ah*-wahl *pah*-gee	awal pagi
midday	te-ngah-*hah*-ree	tengahari
midnight	te-*ngah(h)* *mah*-lahm	tengah malam
sunrise	mah-tuh-*hah*-ree ter-*bit*	matahari terbit
sunset	mah-tuh-*hah*-ree	matahari
	ter-*be*-nahm	terbenam

---

like a prayer

Malays sometimes refer to prayer times, rather than the time of day. If you hear a Malay saying the following, they mean:

Selepas zohor
following the midday prayers, which usually occur around 12:30 – 1:00 pm

Selepas asar
after the mid-afternoon prayers, which usually start around 3:30 – 4:30 pm

Selepas mahgrib
following the sunset prayers; sunset on the Peninsula usually falls between 7:00 – 7:30 pm

Selepas isyak
after the commencement of night prayers, which is usually about one hour after sunset. 'After isyak' could actually mean any time before dawn the next morning!

seasons

spring	*moo*-sim *boo*-nguh	*musim bunga*
summer	*moo*-sim *pah*-nahs	*musim panas*
autumn	*moo*-sim *loo*-ru(h); *goo*-gur	*musim luruh;* *gugur*
winter	*moo*-sim se-*joo(k)*	*musim sejuk*
dry season	*moo*-sim ke-*mah*-row/ ke-*ring*	*musim kemarau/* *kering*
rainy season	*moo*-sim *hoo*-jahn	*musim hujan*

holidays & festivals

percutian & perayaan

Malaysia loves a festival! There are many religious dates observed and celebrated by various communities. The dates on which Muslim holidays fall change from year to year, because they follow the (lunar) Islamic calendar.

Some festivals will affect your stay. Almost everything shuts down during Chinese New Year. For *Hari Raya Aidl Fitri*, there's a big parade and lots of flag waving in Kuala Lumpur. Travel before and during *Hari Raya Puasa* can be difficult, as the whole country endeavours to *balik kampung*, bah-li(k) kahm-pung, (lit: go-back village) get home for celebrations. Flights will be full, trains will be packed and traffic will be jammed.

chinese new year

Chinese New Year is a major national event which falls in January or February. Dragon dances are held and Chinese families have a reunion dinner on the eve of Chinese New Year, opening their homes for family and friends during the first two days of the festival. Children and unmarried relatives receive *ang pow*, ahng pow, (money in small red envelopes) and everyone wishes you *Gong Si Fatt Choy* (a happy and prosperous New Year). In a true overlapping of cultures, the Malays have adopted the use of a green *ang pow* envelope for giving money (also a Muslim tradition during *Hari Raya*, *hah-ree rai-yuh*). These envelopes are widely available for free at banks throughout Malaysia, before the festive periods.

deepavali

Deepavali, *dee-pah-vah-lee*, the Hindu 'Festival of Lights', celebrates *Rama's* victory over the demon *Ravana*. It's the most important of Hindu festivals in Malaysia. Oil lamps are lit to celebrate this victory and to invite *Lakshmi*, the goddess of wealth, into the home. The Malaysian Indians who celebrate *Deepavali* also hold open houses.

hari kebangsaan

Hari Kebahngsaan, *hah-ree ke-bahng-sah-ahn*, Malaysia's Independence Day, falls on 31 August and is marked with a national holiday.

hari raya aidil adha/hari raya haji

Hari Raya, *hah-ree rai-yuh*, literally means 'day celebration'. This Muslim festival commemorates Ibrahim's devotion to God. On being ordered by God to kill his son, Isaac, Ibrahim was about to do the deed when God put a stop to it and told him to kill a sheep instead. It's the day upon which the Muslim pilgrims to Mecca complete their pilgrimage. Almost every Muslim in Malaysia has some member of the family in Mecca every year.

The sacrifice – of a goat or a sheep – is re-eneacted throughout the Muslim areas of Malaysia on *Aidil Adha*, followed by great feasting. Muslims hold open houses, *rumah terbuka*, *roo-mah(h) ter-boo-kuh*, for friends and families, with a smorgasbord of delicious foods.

hari raya aidil fitri/hari raya puasa

The first day of the tenth month marks the end of *Ramadan*, *rah-mah-dahn*, and the celebration of *Hari Raya Puasa*, *hah-ree rai-yuh pwah-suh* – also known as *Aidil Fitri*, *ai-dil fee-tree*. It begins with mass prayers at mosques and in city squares, followed by two days of open houses, family visits and culinary engorgement.

ramadan

The ninth month of the Muslim calendar is the month of *Ramadan*, rah-mah-dahn, also known as *bulan puasa*, bu-lahn pwah-suh, 'the fasting month'. During *Ramadan*, most adult Muslims don't drink, eat, smoke, have sex or indulge in other pleasures during daylight hours. The fast is symbolic of a person's faith, and is also a way for Muslims to feel an affinity with those who are too poor to afford food.

Children, pregnant or menstruating women, and people who are sick or elderly aren't expected to fast. However, some women 'make up' for missed fasting days later in the year. No one is forced to fast, but it's best to eat indoors, out of sight. Many restaurants and food stalls remain open, with a shade-cloth over the door.

thaipusam

During *Thaipusam*, tai-*poo*-sahm, in January, Hindu devotees honor Lord *Subramaniam* with acts of physical endurance. The festival is celebrated primarily in Kuala Lumpur, at Batu Caves, and in Penang, at the Waterfall Hilltop Temple. The devotees march in a procession carrying *kavadi*, *kah*-vah-dee, heavy metal frames decorated with fruit, flowers and feathers. The *kavadi* are hung from their bodies with metal hooks and spikes driven through their flesh.

Selamat Hari   se-*lah*-maht *hah*-ree (lit: safe ... day)

If you arrive near a festival period, and express interest in the traditions and practices of any Malaysian, you might get a flag to an 'open house', a Malaysian tradition practised by all races and religions. Traditional foods are prepared, and every guest is treated to full hospitality. You're not expected to bring a gift – however it is appropriate to give small quantities of money to children and unmarried adults. Just feel free to go and enjoy the food and company.

This is one tradition during which racial tensions are often put aside. You'll see people of all origins at each other's homes. Chinese families who are expecting Muslim guests will often prepare food that is halal (allowed) for Muslims. If you don't get an invitation on Hari Raya Puasa, you can always go to the Prime Minister's house, where everyone in the nation is welcome!

Happy/Merry (festival name)!	se-*lah*-maht ...!	Selamat ...!
ang pow	ahng pow	ang pow
open house	*roo*-mah(h) ter-*boo*-kuh	rumah terbuka
Please come in.	see-luh mah-su(k)	Sila masuk.
Please help yourself.	see-luh mah-kahn/ mee-num	Sila makan/ minum. (lit: please eat/drink)
Thank you.	te-ree-muh kah-si(h)	Terima kasih.
What are these?	mah-kah-nahn ah-puh nee?	Makanan apa ni?

weddings

perkahwinan

Weddings are big business in Malaysia, often with hundreds of guests. Whole streets can be blocked off, tents set up and tables and decorations set on the road. Depending on the faith and/or wealth of the family, weddings can last for days. Even if you've never met the couple, it's not uncommon to be invited to the reception and wedding feast, *kenduri*, *ken-doo-ree*, rather than the actual religious ceremony, *nikah*, *nee-kah(h)*.

Although offering gifts is acceptable, it's customary to give money in an envelope to the parents who are hosting the reception.

Congratulations!	*tah(h)-nee-ah(h)!*	*Tahniah!*
wedding	*per-kah(h)-wi-nahn/*	*perkahwinan/*
	per-nee-kah(h)-ahn	*pernikahan*
reception	*ken-doo-ree*	*kenduri*

---

they say it's your birthday

Birthdays aren't a big deal once people have finished school. Malaysians sing the same happy birthday song that Westerners do – usually in English.

Happy Birthday!
 se-lah-maht hah-ree Selamat Hari
 jah-dee! Jadi!

When is your birthday?
 bee-luh hah-ree Bila hari
 jah-dee ahn-duh? jadi anda?

My birthday's on ...
 hah-ree jah-dee Hari jadi
 sai-yuh pah-duh ... saya pada ...

How old are you?
 oo-mur be-rah-puh-kah(h)? Umur berapakah?

---

funerals

pemakaman/perkebumian

Muslims believe that the corpse must be buried as soon as possible, and burial usually occurs within 24 hours of death.

Chinese and Indian funerals, which sometimes feature processions with professional mourners, tend to be more public.

My condolences.	*tahk*-zee-ah(h)	*Takziah.*
When did he/ she die?	*bee*-luh *dee*-uh me-*ning*-gahl?	*Bila dia meninggal?*

Jalan-Jalan

Kuala Lumpur's public transport system has undergone massive changes in the last 10 years, with the introduction of the LRT (light rapid transit), improved roadways and commuter trains. Travelling in other parts of the country requires a little more patience, and even in Kuala Lumpur a heavy downpour can bring things to a stop! Buses, trains and taxis are available throughout most of the country. Road maps of the cities can be found at hotels, bookstores and newsagents.

finding your way

cari jalan

Excuse me.	mah-*ahf*	Maaf.
I'm lost.	*sai*-yuh ter-*se*-saht	Saya tersesat.
Where's the ...?	dee *mah*-nuh ...?	Di mana ...?
airport	lah-*pahng*-ahn	lapangan
	ter-bahng	terbang
intercity	*steh*-sehn bahs	stesen bas
bus station	*bahn*-dahr	bandar
road to (Raub)	*jah*-lahn ke (rowb)	jalan ke (Raub)
train station	*steh*-sehn	stesen keretapi
	ke-reh-tuh-*ah*-pee	
What time does	... ber-*to*-lah(k)/*tee*-buh...	bertolak/tiba
the ... leave/arrive?	poo-kool be-*rah*-puh?	pukul berapa?
(inter) city bus	bahs *bahn*-dahr	Bas bandar
plane	*kah*-pahl ter-bahng	Kapal terbang
ship	*kah*-pahl	Kapal
train	ke-reh-tuh-*ah*-pee	Keretapi

How can I get to ...?
mah-chahm mah-nuh   *Macam mana*
sai-yuh bo-leh(h) per-gee ke ...?   *saya boleh pergi ke ...?*

Is it near/far?
de-kaht-kah(h)/jow(h)-kah(h)?   *Dekatkah/Jauhkah?*

Can we walk there?
bo-leh(h) jah-lahn kah-kee   *Boleh jalan kaki*
tah(k) ke sah-nuh?   *tak ke sana?*

Can you show me (on the map)?
to-long toon-joo(k)-kahn   *Tolong tunjukkan*
(dee peh-tuh)?   *(di peta)?*

Are there other means of getting there?
ah-duh chah-ruh   *Ada cara*
lain ke sah-nuh?   *lain ke sana?*

What street is this?
jah-lahn ee-nee   *Jalan ini*
jah-lahn ah-puh?   *jalan apa?*

What ... is this?	*ee-nee ... ah-puh?*	*Ini ... apa?*
city	*bahn-dahr*	*bandar*
village	*kahm-pong*	*kampung*

directions

arahan

(Go) Straight ahead!	*(jah-lahn) te-roos!*	*(Jalan) Terus!*
To the left/right.	ke *ki-ree/kah-nahn.*	*Ke kiri/kanan.*
Turn left/right	*beh-lo(k) ki-ree/*	*Belok kiri/*
at the ...	*kah-nahn dee ...*	*kanan di ...*
corner	*sim-pahng*	*simpang*
intersection	*sim-pahng*	*simpang*
next corner	*sim-pahng yang*	*simpang yang*
	ber-ee-koot-nyuh	*berikutnya*
T-junction	*sim-pahng tee*	*simpang T*

traffic lights	*lahm*-poo	*lampu*
	ee-*shah*-raht	*isyarat*
behind	dee be-lah-*kahng*	*di belakang*
far	jow(h)	*jauh*
in front of	dee de-*pahn*	*di depan*
next to	se-be-*lah(h)*	*sebelah*
opposite	ber-lah-*wah*-nahn	*berlawanan*
near	de-*kaht*	*dekat*
north	oo-*tah*-ruh	*utara*
south	se-*lah*-tahn	*selatan*
east	*tee*-mur	*timur*
west	*bah*-raht	*barat*

addresses

alamat

Common words that make up Malaysian addresses include:

jalan raya	**a bigger road, like a dual carriageway**
jalan	**road**
lorong	**smaller road**
pesiaran	**even smaller road**
lebuh raya	**a highway**
taman	**garden, as in 'Serenity Gardens' housing estate**
kampong	**village**

Malaysian city and town addresses look similar to this:

> Ali Abubakar
> 204, Jalan Air Hitam
> Taman Mewah
> 44300 Serdang, Selangor

This means Ali Abubakar lives at number 204, Air Hitam Street *(Jalan)*, Mewah Gardens *(Taman)*, a housing area, in the town/ city of Serdang in the state of Selangor, postcode 44300.

Addresses in rural areas may look something like this:

> Aishah Mohamed
> Lt 1445, Kampung Mangga
> Kubang Kerian, Kota Baru
> Kelantan

Lt means lot number, *kampung* means village. *Kubang Kerian* in this case is the name of a larger village area and *Kota Baru* is the name of the *daerah*, 'county', and *Kelantan* is the state.

buying tickets

Ticket prices are usually posted on noticeboards for ferry, LRT, bus and train travel. Commuter and LRT tickets can be bought from ticket machines or from employees at the stations. Fares on public transport are not negotiable.

How much does it cost to go to ...?
be-*rah*-puh *hahr*-guh-nyuh
oon-tu(k) ke ...?
Berapa harganya
untuk ke ...?

How much is it from Johor to Ipoh?
be-*rah*-puh *hahr*-guh tee-*keht*
dah-ree *jo*-hor ke *ee*-po(h)?
Berapa harga tiket
dari Johor ke Ipoh?

Where can I buy a ticket?
tee-*keht* dee-*joo*-ahl
dee *mah*-nuh?
Tiket dijual
di mana?

We want to go to ...
kah-mee nah(k) ke ...
Kami nak ke ...

Do I need to book?
ah-duh-kah(h) *hah*-roos peh-*sahn*?
Adakah harus pesan?

I'd like to book a seat to ...
sai-yuh nah(k) me-*me*-sahn
tem-*paht* doo-du(k) ke ...
Saya nak memesan
tempat duduk ke ...

I'd like (a) ...	*sai*-yuh nah(k) ...	*Saya nak ...*
one-way ticket	tee-*keht* se-*hah*-luh	*tiket sehala*
return ticket	tee-*keht*	*tiket*
	per-gee-*bah*-li(k)	*pergi-balik*
two tickets	*doo*-ah tee-*keht*	*dua tiket*
student's fare	*hahr*-guh pe-*lah*-jahr	*harga pelajar*

1st class	ke-*lahs* per-tah-muh	*kelas pertama*
2nd class	ke-*lahs* ke-*doo*-ah/	*kelas kedua/*
	bis-nis	*bisnis*
economy class	ke-*lahs* ee-ko-*no*-mee	*kelas ekonomi*
child's/pensioner's	*hahr*-guh *ah*-nah(k)/	*harga anak/pesara*
fare	pe-*sah*-ruh	

What about my change?
   doo-it *bah*-li(k) *mah*-nuh?   *Duit balik mana?*

confirmation	kon-fir-*mah*-see	*konfirmasi*
destination	de-sti-*nah*-see	*destinasi*
seat	tem-*paht doo*-du(k)	*tempat duduk*
ticket	tee-*keht*	*tiket*
ticket counter	*kown*-ter tee-*keht*	*kaunter tiket*
timetable	ja-*doo*-al	*jadual*

air

Malaysian Airlines (MAS) and Pelangi Air offer services within the country to most locations. Both airlines have a good safety record.

Is there a flight to Penang on (Monday)?
   ah-duh-kah(h)   *Adakah*
   pe-ner-*bah*-ngahn ke   *penerbangan ke*
   pe-*nahng pah*-duh   *Penang pada*
   (*hah*-ree *ees*-nin)?   (*hari Isnin*)?

What time is the flight to Penang on (Monday)?

poo-kool be-*rah*-puh
pe-ner-*bahng*-ahn
ber-*to*-lah(k) ke pe-*nahng*
pah-duh (*hah*-ree *ees*-nin)?

*Pukul berapa
penerbangan
bertolak ke Penang
pada (hari Isnin)?*

What time do I have to be at the airport?

poo-kool be-*rah*-puh
sai-yuh *hah*-roos *ah*-duh dee
lah-*pahng*-ahn ter-*bahng*?

*Pukul berapa
saya harus ada di
lapangan terbang?*

When's the next flight to ...?

bee-luh pe-ner-*bahng*-ahn
ke ... yahng se-te-*roos*-nyuh?

*Bila penerbangan
ke ... yang seterusnya?*

I'd like to reconfirm my ticket to Perlis.

sai-yuh nah(k) me-mas-*tee*-kahn
tee-*keht sai*-yuh ke *per*-lees

*Saya nak memastikan
tiket saya ke Perlis.*

How long does the flight take?

per-jah-lah-*nahn*-nya
be-*rah*-puh *lah*-muh?

*Perjalanannya
berapa lama?*

Where's the baggage claim?

bah-*gah*-see dee *mah*-nuh?

Bagasi di mana?

customs   kastam

Customs officers are generally friendly (unless you're a smuggler) and are impressed if you greet them in Malay and make an attempt to speak the language.

I have nothing to declare.

bah-*rahng sai*-yuh *tee*-dah(k)
per-*loo* dee-lah-*por*-kahn

*Barang saya tidak
perlu dilaporkan.*

I have something to declare.

sai-yuh *ah*-duh bah-*rahng*
yahng per-*loo* dee-lah-*por*-kahn

*Saya ada barang
yang perlu dilaporkan.*

Do I have to declare this?

ah-duh-kah(h) *sai*-yuh per-*loo*
me-lah-*por*-kahn *ee*-nee?

*Adakah saya perlu
melaporkan ini?*

barang hilang	**lost property**
pertolakan	**departures**
ketibaan	**arrivals**
pendaftaran	**check-in**
imigrasi	**passport control**

This is all my luggage.

ee-nee se-*moo*-uh   *Ini semua barang saya.*
bah-*rahng sai*-yuh

I didn't know I had to declare it.

sai-yuh *tee*-dah(k) *tah*-hoo   *Saya tidak tahu*
bah-*rahng ee*-nee *hah*-roos   *barang ini harus*
dee-lah-*por*-kahn.   *dilaporkan.*

| **aeroplane** | *kah*-pahl *ter*-bahng | *kapal terbang* |
| **airport** | lah-*pahng*-ahn *ter*-bahng | *lapangan terbang* |

bus

bas

Malaysia's buses are usually fast, economical and comfortable. Local and city buses can be hailed at bus stops, which usually are well signposted. You may need to make reservations for long distance buses, especially around festive times. In rural areas buses tend to be older and without air-con. For sightseeing and really experiencing local life, these are ideal. Just pay your fare to the conductor or driver.

Most city buses have complete air-con. Check when you purchase your tickets by asking: *Bas ini ada air-con tak?*, bahs *ee*-nee *ah*-duh *air*-con tah(k)?, 'Does this bus have air-con or not?'. Long distance buses have toilets and usually stop to let passengers off for meals; some will also combine a meal-stop with a prayer-stop for the Muslim passengers.

Which bus goes to ...?

bahs yahng *mah*-nuh   *Bas yang mana*
nahk ke ...?   *nak ke ...?*

Does this bus go to ...?
bahs *ee*-nee *per*-gee ke ...?   *Bas ini pergi ke ...?*

Do buses come often?
bahs *ee*-nee *dah*-tahng   *Bas ini datang*
se-*lah*-loo kahn?   *selalu, kan?*

Often./Rarely.
se-*lah*-loo/*jah*-rahng   *Selalu./Jarang.*

Where do I get the bus for ...?
bahs ke ... dee *mah*-nuh?   *Bas ke ... di mana?*

What time's	*poo*-kool be-*rah*-puh	*Pukul berapa*
the ... bus (to ...)?	bahs ... (ke ...)?	*bas ... (ke ...)?*
first	per-*tah*-muh	*pertama*
last	ter-*ah*-khir	*terakhir*
next	ber-ee-*koot*-nyuh	*berikutnya*

Will the bus stop at a restaurant?
bahs *ee*-nee ber-*hen*-tee   *Bas ini berhenti*
dee *res*-to-rahn?   *di restoran?*

Could you let me know when
we arrive at ...?
to-long ber-ee-*tah*-hoo   *Tolong beritahu*
sai-yuh *bee*-luh *kee*-tuh   *saya bila kita*
soo-dah(h) *sahm*-pai dee ...?   *sudah sampai di ...?*

Where are we now?
kee-tuh *mah*-nuh   *Kita mana*
se-*kah*-rahng?   *sekarang?*

I want to get off.
sai-yah nah(k) *too*-roon   *Saya nak turun.*

train

keretapi

Train travel in Malaysia is fun, cheap, easy and trains are generally on time. Express trains only stop at the main stations, but
some of the local services, especially on the east coast, offer a
colourful experience, stopping in small towns and even in the
jungle to let passengers off.

I want to go by express train to ...
sai-yuh nah(k) nai(k)
ke-reh-tuh-*ah*-pee
ehk-sprehs ke ...

Saya nak naik
keretapi
ekspres ke ...

Which platform does the train leave from?
dah-ree *lahn*-dah-sahn
mah-nuh ke-reh-tuh-*ah*-pee
ber-*ahng*-kaht?

Dari landasan
mana keretapi
berangkat?

Where do I need to change trains?
sai-yuh ber-*too*-kahr
ke-reh-tuh-*ah*-pee dee *mah*-nuh?

Saya bertukar
keretapi di mana?

Does this train stop at Kuala Pilah?
ah-duh-kah(h) ke-reh-tuh-*ah*-pee
ee-nee ber-*hen*-tee dee
kwah-luh *pee*-lah(h)?

Adakah keretapi
ini berhenti di
Kuala Pilah?

Can I get off at Kuala Pilah?
bo-*leh(h)* *sai*-yuh *too*-roon
dee *kwah*-luh *pee*-lah(h)?

Boleh saya turun
di Kuala Pilah?

Is this seat free?
ke-*roo*-see *ee*-nee
ko-song-kah(h)?

Kerusi ini kosongkah?

This seat's taken.
soo-dah(h) *ah*-duh o-rahng

Sudah ada orang.

Would you mind if I open the window?
bo-*leh(h)* *sai*-yuh
boo-kuh *ting*-kahp?

Boleh saya
buka tingkap?

---

they may say

ke-reh-tuh *ah*-pee *ee*-nee/*ee*-too ...	**This/That train is ...**
	departures
dee-bah-*tahl*-kahn	**cancelled**
lahm-baht	**delayed/late**
te-*paht*	**on time**

What's ... station?	*ah*-puh *nah*-muh-nyuh	*Apa namanya*
	steh-sehn ...?	*stesen ...?*
this	*ee*-nee	*ini*
the next	*yahng*	*yang*
	ber-ee-*koot*-nyuh	*berikutnya*

Do I need to change trains?
    ah-duh-kah(h) *sai*-yuh   *Adakah saya*
    hah-*roos* ber-*too*-kahr   *harus bertukar*
    ke-reh-tuh-*ah*-pee?   *keretapi?*

You must change at ...
    ahn-dah hah-*roos*   *Anda harus bertukar di ...*
    ber-*too*-kahr dee ...

I want to get off at ...
    sai-yuh nah(k) *too*-roon dee ... *Saya nak turun di ...*

How long will it be delayed?
    be-*rah*-puh *lahm*-baht-nyuh? *Berapa lambatnya?*

taxi

teksi

Taxis in most big cities now operate with meters – if not, it's best to sort out the fare before getting in! Long distance taxis are a convenient way to get around, and still cheap. These taxis take up to four passengers, and will often wait around to find the full number bound for the same destination. You can pay a little more and have the whole vehicle to yourself.

Is this taxi available?
    tehk-see *ee*-nee *ko*-song-kah(h)? *Teksi ini kosongkah?*

finding your religion

Be forewarned, the drivers of long distance taxis often drive at high speeds. Malaysian drivers will overtake almost anywhere, and the motto in the cities seems to be 'if there's a space, fill it'. There aren't as many accidents as you might imagine, so just close your eyes and hang on.

Please use the meter.
  to-long *pah*-kai *mee*-ter

Tolong pakai meter.

How much is the fare?
  be-*rah*-puh *hahr*-guh
  per-jah-*lah*-nahn?

*Berapa harga
perjalanan?*

Please take me   *to*-long *hahn*-tahr   *Tolong hantar*
to ...   *sai*-yuh ke ...   *saya ke ...*
  this address   *ah*-lah-maht *ee*-nee   *alamat ini*
  the airport   lah-*pahng*-ahn *ter*-bahng   *lapangan terbang*

instructions   **arahan**

Here's fine, thanks.
  ber-*hen*-tee dee
  see-nee *sah*-juh

*Berhenti di
sini saja.*

The next street, please.
  jah-lahn ber-ee-*koot*-nyuh

Jalan berikutnya.

The next street (to the left/right).
  jah-lahn (dee se-be-*lah(h)*
  ki-ree/*kah*-nahn)
  yahng ber-ee-*koot*-nyuh

*Jalan (di sebelah
kiri/ kanan)
yang berikutnya.*

Continue/Straight on!   te-*roos*-kahn!   *Teruskan!*
Please slow down.   per-lah-*hahn*-kahn   *Perlahankan*
                            se-*dee*-kit   *sedikit.*
Please hurry.   *to*-long che-*paht*   *Tolong cepat*
                            se-*dee*-kit   *sedikit.*
Stop here!   ber-*hen*-tee dee   *Berhenti di sini!*
                            see-nee!
Stop at the corner.   ber-*hen*-tee dee   *Berhenti di*
                            soo-dut *ee*-too   *sudut itu.*
Please wait here.   *to*-long *toong*-goo   *Tolong tunggu*
                            dee *see*-nee   *di sini.*

I'll be right back.
  sai-yuh *ah*-kahn kem-*bah*-lee
  se-ke-*jahp* lah-gee

*Saya akan kembali
sekejap lagi.*

boat

Some isolated areas in Sabah and Sarawak can only be reached by small river boats. Ferries are commonly used to reach islands off the coast. Some local operators are lax about observing safety rules; if you think a boat is overloaded or otherwise unsafe, don't board it. Speedboat ferries are faster but the journey can be rough.

boat	bot/*kah*-pahl/ *sahm*-pahn	bot/kapal/ sampan
cabin	*bee*-li(k)	bilik
dock	*jeh*-tee	jeti
harbour/port	pe-lah-*boo*-hahn	pelabuhan
river	*soo*-ngai	sungai
sail	*lai*-yahr	layar
sea	lowt	laut

Where does the boat leave from?
  kah-pahl *ee*-too
  ber-*ahng*-kaht dee *mah*-nuh?

*Kapal itu
berangkat di mana?*

What time does the boat arrive at ...?
  poo-kool be-*rah*-puh
  kah-pahl *ee*-too *tee*-buh dee ...?

*Pukul berapa
kapal itu tiba di ...?*

car

Car hire is possible throughout Malaysia; you can also hire a driver, although this is much more expensive. Most petrol stations are self-service. Look for a *layanan-penuh*, *lai-yah*-nahn-pe-*nu(h)*, sign if you want your car filled for you.

Where can I hire a car?
  dee *mah*-nuh *sai*-yuh
  bo-*leh(h)* men-*yeh*-wuh
  ke-reh-tuh?

*Di mana saya
boleh menyewa
kereta?*

How much is it daily/weekly?

be-rah-*puh*-kah(h) *hahr*-guh
seh-*wah*-nyuh *oon*-tu(k)
se-*hah*-ree/se-*ming*-goo?

*Berapakah harga
sewanya untuk
sehari/seminggu?*

Does that include insurance?

ah-duh-kah(h) *hahr*-guh-nyuh
ter-*mah*-su(k) in-soo-*rahns*-kah(h)?

*Adakah harganya
termasuk insuranskah?*

Can we get a driver?

bo-*leh(h)*-kah(h) *kah*-mee
men-*dah*-paht pe-*mahn*-doo?

*Bolehkah kami
mendapat pemandu?*

Where's the next petrol station?

steh-sehn *min*-yah(k)
ber-ee-*koot*-nyuh dee *mah*-nuh?

*Stesen minyak
berikutnya di mana?*

I want ... litres of petrol.

sai-yuh nah(k) ...
lee-ter *min*-yah(k)

*Saya nak ...
liter minyak.*

Please fill up the tank.

to-long pe-*nu(h)*-kahn
tahng-kee

*Tolong penuhkan
tangki.*

Please check the ...   *to*-long pe-*rik*-suh ... *Tolong periksa ...*
  oil   *min*-yahk *hee*-tahm *minyak hitam*
  tyre pressure   te-*kahn*-an *tai*-yahr *tekanan tayar*
  water   air   *air*

---

road signs

beri jalan	**give way**
dilarang ...	**no ...**
masuk	**entry**
letak kereta	**parking**
jalan tol	**toll way**
kerja raya	**roadworks**
sehala	**one way**
tempat	**car park**

Is this the road to ...?
ee-nee-kah(h) *jah*-lahn ke ...? — *Inikah jalan ke ...?*

Can I park here?
bo-*leh(h)* leh-tah(k) — *Boleh letak*
ke-*reh*-tuh dee *see*-nee? — *kereta di sini?*

How much does it cost to park here?
be-*rah*-puh *hahr*-guh — *Berapa harga*
me-*leh*-tah(k) ke-*reh*-tuh — *meletak kereta*
dee *see*-nee? — *di sini?*

air	oo-*dah*-ruh	udara
automatic	oh-toh-*mah*-tik	otomatik
battery	bah-*te*-ree	bateri
brakes	brehk	brek
car	ke-*reh*-tuh	kereta
clutch	klahch	klac
driver	pe-*mahn*-doo	pemandu
drivers licence	*leh*-sen me-*mahn*-doo	lesen memandu
engine	*ehn*-jin	enjin
garage	*gah*-rahj	garaj
horn	hon	hon
indicator	pe-*noon*-joo(k)	penunjuk
lights	*lahm*-poo	lampu
main road	*jah*-lahn rai-yuh/	jalan raya/utama
	oo-*tah*-muh	
oil	*min*-yah(k) *hee*-tahm	minyak hitam
petrol (gas)	*min*-yah(k)/*peh*-trol	minyak/petrol
diesel	*dee*-sel	disel
premium	pre-*mee*-um *tahn*-puh	premium tanpa
unleaded	*ploom*-boom	plumbum
unleaded	*tahn*-puh	tanpa
	ploom-boom	plumbum
puncture	ke-bo-*cho*-rahn	kebocoran
radiator	rah-dee-*ah*-tor	radiator
roadmap	*peh*-tuh *jah*-lahn	peta jalan
seatbelt	*tah*-lee *ping*-gahng	tali pinggang
	ke-*reh*-dahr	keledar
self-service	*lai*-yahn *dir*-ree	layan diri

PRACTICAL

speed limit	hahd *lah*-joo	*had laju*
tyres	*tai*-yahr	*tayar*
windscreen	*kah*-chuh de-*pahn*	*kaca depan*
distance	*jah*-rah(k)	*jarak*
length of time	*lah*-muh	*lama*

car problems

masalah kereta

We need a mechanic.
  kah-mee me-mer-*loo*-kahn
  me-*ka*-nik

*Kami memerlukan
mekanik.*

What make is it?
  ke-*reh*-tuh je-*nis*
  ah-puh *ee*-nee?

*Kereta jenis
apa ini?*

Our car broke down at ...
  ke-*reh*-tuh *kah*-mee
  ro-sah(k) dee ...

*Kereta kami
rosak di ...*

The car isn't working.
  ke-*reh*-tuh *ee*-nee *ro*-sah(k)

Kereta ini rosak.

---

a country mile

With traffic jams in bigger cities, confusing signs in smaller towns, and some poor maintenance on out-of-the-way roads, you might be better off asking 'how long' rather than 'how far' your destination is!

**How long (time/distance)
is the journey?**
  be-*rah*-puh (lah-*muh*/jow(h))
  ber-*jah*-lah-nahn *ee*-nee?

*Berapa (lama/jauh)
perjalanan ini?*

It's 50km away.
  jah-rah(k)-nyah *lee*-mah
  poo-lu(h) ki-lo-*mee*-ter

*Jaraknya lima
puluh kilometer.*

The trip takes two hours.
  per-*jah*-lah-nahn *ee*-nee
  me-*ngahm*-bil *doo*-uh jahm

*Perjalanan ini
mengambil dua jam.*

The engine's dead.
ehn-jin *mah*-tee   *Enjin mati.*

The engine is overheating.
ehn-jin ter-*lah*-loo *pah*-nahs   *Enjin terlalu panas.*

I've run out of petrol
min-yah(k) *soo*-dah(h) *hah*-bees   *Minyak sudah habis.*

The battery's flat.
bah-*ter*-ee *ee*-nee *mah*-tee   *Bateri ini mati.*

The radiator's leaking.
rah-dee-*ah*-tor *bo*-chor   *Radiator bocor.*

I have a flat tyre.
tai-yahr-nyuh *kem*-pis   *Tayarnya kempis.*

I've lost my car keys.
koon-chee ke-*reh*-tuh   *Kunci kereta*
sai-yuh *hee*-lahng   *saya hilang.*

bicycle

Bike hire is becoming popular throughout the region and is a
great way to get around resort areas. Serious cyclists will need
to buy or bring their own bikes.

Where can I hire a bicycle?
dee *mah*-nuh *sai*-yuh bo-*leh*(h)   *Di mana saya boleh*
me-*nyeh*-wuh bah-*see*-kahl?   *menyewa basikal?*

I have a flat tyre.
tai-yahr *sai*-yuh *kem*-pis   *Tayar saya kempis.*

How much is it ...?	be-*rah*-puh	*Berapa*
	hahr-guh-nyuh ...?	*harganya ...?*
per hour	*oon*-tu(k) se-*jahm*	*untuk sejam*
until (3 o'clock)	*sahm*-pai	*sampai*
	(*poo*-kool *tee*-guh)	*(pukul tiga)*
the day	*oon*-tu(k)	*untuk*
	se-*hah*-ree	*sehari*

bike	bah-*see*-kahl	*basikal*
brakes	brayk	*brek*
to cycle	ber-bah-*see*-kahl	*berbasikal*
gears	*gee*-gee	*gigi*
handlebars	*gah*-gahng bah-*see*-kahl	*gagang basikal*
helmet	*to*-pee ke-*leh*-dahr	*topi keledar*
inner tube	*tee*-oob dah-*lah*-mahn	*tiub dalaman*
lights	*lahm*-poo	*lampu*
lock	*koon*-chee	*kunci*
pump	pahm	*pam*
puncture	ke-bo-*cho*-rahn	*kebocoran*
saddle	ke-*roo*-see	*kerusi*
wheel	*ro*-duh	*roda*

local transport

kendaraan tempatan

Beca, *beh*-chuh, bicycle-rickshaws, used to be found in many towns and cities across the nation, but these days they are only common in some northern towns.

Wait!	toong-*goo*!	*Tunggu!*
I want to get off!	*sai*-yuh nah(k) *too*-roon!	*Saya nak turun!*
Careful!	ber-*hah*-ti-*hah*-ti *see*-kit!	*Berhati-hati sikit!*
Danger!	bah-*hai*-yuh!	*Bahaya!*
Stop!	ber-*hen*-tee!	*Berhenti!*

baby you can guard my car

When you park on the streets in larger towns and cities, you may be helped into your parking space by a smiling character, madly waving his arms. He is a *jaga kereta* boy, *jah-guh ke-reh-tuh* (lit: guard car). Although some cities have tried to eradicate this freelance job, it is best to give him a small amount of money, one or two *ringgit*, for helping you. You can pay up before leaving the car, or say 'Guard my car well', *Jaga kereta saya baik-baik*, *jah-guh ke-reh-tuh sai-yuh bai(k)-bai(k)*, and pay when you come back.

Accommodation

Penginapan

Accommodation choices in Malaysia run from cheap as chips to very expensive, from no-frills *rumah tumpangan*, *roo*-mah(h) toom-*pahng*-ahn, to government-run 'rest houses', *rumah rihat*, *roo*-mah(h) *ree*-haht, to 5-star hotels. Guest houses, which can be little huts or dorm-like accommodation, are available at beach centres and in major tourist cities. Homestays are still possible in some towns.

finding accommodation

mencari penginapan

I'm looking for a ...	*sai*-yuh men-*chah*-ree ...	*Saya mencari ...*
camping ground	tem-*paht*	*tempat*
	per-kheh-*mah*-hahn	*perkhemahan*
guesthouse	*roo*-mah(h) te-*tah*-moo	*rumah tetamu*
upmarket hotel	*ho*-tehl *meh*-wah(h)	*hotel mewah*
Where's a ... hotel?	*ho*-tehl yahng ...	*Hotel yang ...*
	dee *mah*-nuh?	*di mana?*
cheap	ter-moo-*rah*	*termurah*
clean	*ber*-si(h)	*bersih*
good	bah-*gus*	*bagus*
nearby	de-*kaht*	*dekat*

I've already found a hotel.
sai-yuh *soo*-dah(h) *joom*-puh   *Saya sudah jumpa*
se-*boo*-ah(h) *ho*-tehl   *sebuah hotel.*

Please take me to the ... hotel.
to-long *hahn*-tahr   *Tolong hantar*
sai-yuh ke *ho*-tehl …   *saya ke hotel ...*

What's the address?
ah-puh-kah(h) *ah*-lah-maht-nyuh?   *Apakah alamatnya?*

Could you write down the address, please?
to-long too-*lis*-kahn
ah-lah-*maht ee*-too

Tolong tuliskan alamat itu?

The hotel is near the ...	*ho*-tehl-nyuh de-*kaht* ...	*Hotelnya dekat ...*
alley	lo-*rong*	*lorong*
beach	*pahn*-tai	*pantai*
shop	ke-*dai*	*kedai*
street	*jah*-lahn	*jalan*
town square	*dah*-tah-rahn	*dataran*

booking ahead

Can I book a room?
bo-*leh*(h) mem-*boo*-aht
tem-*pah*-hahn *bee*-li(k)?

Boleh membuat tempahan bilik?

My name's ...
nah-muh *sai*-yuh ...

Nama saya ...

For (three) nights.
se-*lah*-muh (*tee*-guh) *mah*-lahm

Selama (tiga) malam.

How much for ...?	be-*rah*-puh hahr-gah-nyuh ...?	*Berapa harganya ...?*
one night	*oon*-tu(k) *sah*-too *mah*-lahm	*untuk satu malam*
a week	*oon*-tu(k) se-*ming*-goo	*untuk seminggu*
two people	*oon*-tu(k) *doo*-uh o-rahng	*untuk dua orang*

I'll/We'll be arriving ...	*sai*-yuh/*kah*-mee ah-*kahn* tee-buh ...	*Saya/Kami akan tiba ...*
on the (3rd)	*pah*-duh (*tee*-guh hah-ree-*bu*-lahn)	*pada (tiga haribulan)*

later tonight	*mah*-lahm *ee*-nee *nahn*-tee	malam ini nanti

checking in

No matter how long you're staying, you may be able to arrange a *diskaun*, *dis*-kown, 'discount'. An easy way to get cheaper room rates is to exclaim *Mahalnya!*, mah-*hal*-nyuh!, 'So expensive!' in mock horror, and act like you're going elsewhere. See what offer comes up then, but be sure you look at the room before you decide to take it.

I'd like a room for ...	*sai*-yuh men-*chah*-ree *bee*-li(k) *oon*-tu(k) ...	Saya mencari bilik untuk ...
one person	*se*-o-rahng	seorang
two people	*doo*-uh o-rahng	dua orang

I'd like a room with a ...	*sai*-yuh men-*chah*-ree *bee*-li(k) yahng mem-*poon*-yah-ee ...	Saya mencari bilik yang mempunyai ...
bathroom	*bee*-li(k) air	bilik air
fan	*kee*-pahs	kipas
shower	tem-*paht* mahn-dee	tempat mandi
TV	tee vee	TV
window	*ting*-kahp	tingkap

I'm going to stay for (one) ...	*sai*-yuh ah-*kahn* ber-*mah*-lahm se-*lah*-muh (*sah*-too) ...	Saya akan bermalam selama (satu) ...
day	*hah*-ree	hari
week	*ming*-goo	minggu

I'd like to share a dorm.
sai-yuh nah(k) ber-*kong*-see *bee*-li(k) *hos*-tehl

Saya nak berkongsi bilik hostel.

Is there a room available?
ah-duh *bee*-li(k) yahng *ko*-song?

Ada bilik yang kosong?

Can I see the room?
bo-*leh(h)* sai-*yuh* me-*lee*-haht
bee-li(k) *ee*-too?

Boleh saya melihat bilik itu?

Is there a discount for ...?
ah-duh dis-kown oon-tu(k) ...?

Ada diskaun untuk ...?

  children   *ah*-nah(k)   *anak*

  students   pe-*lah*-jahr   *pelajar*

I'm not sure how long I'm staying.
sai-*yuh* be-*lum* tah-hoo
be-*rah*-puh la-muh sai-*yuh*
ah-kahn ber-*mah*-lahm
dee *see*-nee

Saya belum tahu berapa lama saya akan bermalam di sini.

I (don't) like this room.
sai-*yuh* (tah(k)) *soo*-kuh
bee-li(k) *ee*-nee

Saya (tak) suka bilik ini.

Do you have a better room?
ah-duh *bee*-li(k) yahng
le-*bi(h)* bai(k)?

Ada bilik yang lebih baik?

Do you have a room with ..?
ah-duh tah(k) *bee*-li(k) yahng *ah*-duh ...?

Ada tak bilik yang ada...?

  two beds   *doo*-uh *kah*-til   *dua katil*

  a double bed   *kah*-til be-*sahr*   *katil besar*

Where's the bathroom?
bee-li(k) *mahn*-dee
dee *mah*-nuh?

Bilik mandi di mana?

Is there hot water all day?
ah-duh-kah(h) air *pah*-nahs
se-*pahn*-jahng hah-ree?

Adakah air panas sepanjang hari?

Is breakfast included?
mah-kahn *pah*-gee
ter-*mah*-su(k)-kah(h)?

Makan pagi termasukkah?

This room's fine.
bee-li(k) *ee*-nee se-*swai*

Bilik ini sesuai.

paying   pembayaran

How much does it cost per day?
be-*rah*-puh *hahr*-guh-nyuh
oon-tu(k) se-*hah*-ree?   *Berapa harganya*
untuk sehari?

What's the daily rate?
be-*rah*-puh *hahr*-guh
hah-ree-*ahn*-nyuh?   *Berapa harga*
hariannya?

Does the price include breakfast/tax?
hahr-guh-nyuh ter-*mah*-su(k)
sah-rah-pahn-kah(h)/
choo-kai-kah(h)?   *Harganya termasuk*
sarapankah/
cukaikah?

Do you allow children?
bo-*leh(h) sai*-yuh
bah-wah *ah*-nah(k)?   *Boleh saya*
bawa anak?

Is there an extra charge for children?
ah-duh *hahr*-guh tahm-*bah*-hahn
oon-tu(k) *ah*-nah(k)?   *Ada harga tambahan*
untuk anak?

Can I pay by ...?   bo-*leh(h) bai*-yahr   *Boleh bayar*
de-*ngahn* ...?   *dengan ...?*
credit card   kahd *kreh*-dit   *kad kredit*

---

they may say ...

soo-dah(h) pe-*nu(h)*	**We're full.**
be-*rah*-puh *lah*-muh?	**For how long?**
be-*rah*-puh	**How many**
mah-lahm/o-rahng?	**nights/people?**
ter-*mah*-su(k)	**It includes**
teh(h)/*ko*-pee	**tea/coffee.**
bai-*yahr* doo-loo	**Please pay now.**
bai-*yahr* ke-*moo*-dee-ahn	**Pay later.**

travellers cheque	chehk	*cek pelancong*
	pe-*lahn*-chong	

requests & complaints

Do you have a safe where I can leave my valuables?
ah-duh pe-*tee keh*-bahl
oon-tu(k) men-*yim*-pahn
bah-rahng ber-*hahr*-guh?

*Ada peti kebal
untuk menyimpan
barang berharga?*

Could I have a receipt for them?
ah-duh *reh*-seet
oon-tu(k) me-*reh*-kuh?

Ada resit untuk mereka?

Where can I wash my clothes?
dee *mah*-nuh *sai*-yuh
bo-*leh(h)* men-*choo*-chee
pah-kai-ahn?

*Di mana saya
boleh mencuci
pakaian?*

Do you have a laundry service?
ah-duh *ser*-vis *choo*-chee
pah-kai-ahn?

*Ada servis cuci
pakaian?*

When will they be ready?
bee-luh *see*-ahp?

Bila siap?

Can I use the telephone?
bo-*leh(h) pah*-kai
teh-*leh*-fon tah(k)?

Boleh pakai telefon tak?

There are mosquitoes.
ah-duh *nyah*-mu(k)-lah(h)

Ada nyamuklah.

Do you have (a) ...?	*ah*-duh ...?	*Ada ...?*
insect repellant	*oo*-baht	*ubat nyamuk*
	nyah-mu(k)	
mosquito net	ke-*lahm*-boo	*kelambu*

I need another ...	*sai*-yuh	*Saya*
	me-mer-*loo*-kahn	*memerlukan*
	lah-gee *sah*-too ...	*lagi satu ...*

blanket	se-*lee*-moot	*selimut*
pillow	*bahn*-tahl	*bantal*
pillowcase	sah-*rong bahn*-tahl	*sarung bantal*
sheet	*chah*-dahr	*cadar*
towel	too-*ah*-lah	*tuala*

Please change it/them.
to-long *too*-kahr-kahn *ee*-nee   *Tolong tukarkan ini.*

Please clean my room.
to-long *ber*-si(h)-kahn   *Tolong bersihkan*
bee-li(k) *sai*-yuh   *bilik saya.*

Excuse me, I have a problem.
mah-*ahf*, ah-duh mah-*sah*-lah(h)   *Maaf, ada masalah.*

The (window) is broken.
(*ting*-kahp) *ee*-too ro-*sah(k)*   *(Tingkap) itu rosak.*

I can't open/	*sai*-yuh tah(k) bo-*leh(h)*	*Saya tak boleh*
close the ...	*boo*-kuh/too-*tup* ...	*buka/tutup ...*
door	*peen*-too	*pintu*
window	*ting*-kahp	*tingkap*

I can't lock the door.
sai-yuh *tee*-dah(k)   *Saya tidak*
bo-*leh(h)* koon-chee *pin*-too   *boleh kunci pintu.*

I've locked myself out.
koon-chee *sai*-yuh   *Kunci saya*
ter-*ting*-gahl *dah*-lahm *bee*-li(k)   *tertinggal dalam bilik.*

Can you get it fixed?
bo-*leh(h) bai*-kee tah(k)?   *Boleh baiki tak?*

The room is	*bee*-li(k) *ee*-nee	*Bilik ini*
too ...	ter-*lah*-loo ...	*terlalu ...*
cold	se-*joo(k)*	*sejuk*
dark	ge-*lahp*	*gelap*
hot	*pah*-nahs	*panas*
noisy	bee-*sing*	*bising*
smelly	boo-*soo(k)*	*busuk*

candle	*li*-leen	lilin
chair	ke-*roo*-see	kerusi
door	*pin*-too	pintu
electricity	eh-*lehk*-trik	elektrik
key	*koon*-chee	kunci
lamp	*lahm*-poo	lampu
lock	*koon*-chee	kunci
mattress	tee-*lahm*	tilam
mosquito coil	*oo*-baht *nyah*-mu(k)	ubat nyamuk
quiet	sen-*yahp*	senyap
roof	*ah*-tahp; *boom*-boong	atap; bumbung
soap	*sah*-bon	sabun
toilet paper	ti-soo; ti-soo *tahn*-dahs	tisu; tisu tandas
towel	*twah*-lah	tuala
to wake	*bah*-ngoon	bangun
wardrobe	ahl-*mah*-ree	almari
... water	air ...	air ...
drinking	*mee*-num	minum
hot	*pah*-nahs	panas

time after time

Malaysians divide up their day this way:

morning (from dawn until noon)
  pah-gee   pagi

midday (from noon until about three o'clock)
  te-ngah-*hah*-ree   tengahari

afternoon/evening (from about three o'clock until sunset)
  pe-*tahng*   petang

night (from sunset until dawn)
  mah-lahm   malam

checking out

I'm leaving today.
sai-yuh ber-*ahng*-kaht
hah-ree *ee*-nee
Saya berangkat hari ini.

Please prepare my/our bill.
to-long se-*dee*-ah-kahn
bil *sai*-yuh/*kah*-mee
*Tolong sediakan
bil saya/kami.*

There's a mistake in the bill.
bil *ee*-nee *sah*-lah(h)
Bil ini salah.

Please call me a taxi.
to-long *pahng*-gil-kahn *tehk*-see
Tolong panggilkan teksi.

Can I leave my	bo-*leh(h)* tah(k)	*Boleh tak*
things here	*sai*-yuh *sim*-pahn	*saya simpan*
until ...?	*bah*-rahng dee	*barang di*
	see-nee *sahm*-pai ...?	*sini sampai ...?*
this afternoon	te-ngah-*hah*-ree/	*tengahari/*
	pe-*tahng ee*-nee	*petang ini*
this evening	pe-*tahng ee*-nee	*petang ini*
tonight	*mah*-lahm	*malam*

longer stays

Some guesthouses offer cheaper rates for longer stays. Also look into homestays, available in Kota Baru, Kuala Lumpur and Johor Baru.

to rent
me-*nyeh*-wuh
menyewa

Is there a room available?
ah-duh *bee*-li(k) ko-song?
Ada bilik kosong?

I'm looking for a room near the beach/city-centre.

sai-yuh *chah*-ree *bee*-li(k)
de-*kaht pan*-tai/
poo-saht *bahn*-dahr

*Saya cari bilik
dekat pantai/
pusat bandar.*

I want to rent a room/house for (three) months.

sai-yuh nah(k) me-*nyeh*-wuh
bee-li(k)/*roo*-mah(h)
se-*lah*-muh (*tee*-guh) *bu*-lahn

*Saya nak menyewa
bilik/rumah
selama (tiga) bulan.*

How much per month?

be-*rah*-puh *hahr*-guh-nyuh
oon-tu(k) se-*bu*-lahn?

*Berapa harganya
untuk sebulan?*

Around Town
Di Bandar

The atmosphere on the streets of Malaysia is action-packed. People are out and about from early morning long into the night. Shops are usually open until 9 or 10pm, restaurants much later, and roadside stalls later still. Night markets, *pasar malam*, *pah*-sahr *mah*-lahm, are a must for the visitor who wants a taste of the Malaysian way of life.

looking for ...

	mencari ...	
How far is a/an/ the ...?	be-*rah*-puh jow(h) ...?	*Berapa jauh ...?*
I'm going to a/an/ the ...	*sai*-yuh *per*-gee ke ...	*Saya pergi ke ...*
I'm looking for a/an/the ...	*sai*-yuh men-*chah*-ree ...	*Saya mencari ...*
bank	bank	*bank*
barber shop	ke-*dai goon*-ting *rahm*-boot	*kedai gunting rambut*
consulate	*kon*-soo-laht	*konsulat*
crossroad	sim-*pahng* em-*paht*	*simpang empat*
embassy	ke-*doo*-tah-ahn be-*sahr*	*kedutaan besar*
hairdresser; hair salon	sa-*lon*; ke-*dai goon*-ting *rahm*-boot	*salon; kedai gunting rambut*
hospital	*hos*-pee-tahl	*hospital*
hotel	ho-*tehl*	*hotel*
money changer	tem-*paht* pe-*noo*-kahr-ahn wahng	*tempat penukaran wang*
museum	moo-*zee*-um	*muzium*
police station	*bah*-lai po-lis	*balai polis*
post office	pe-*jah*-baht pos	*pejabat pos*
public telephone	teh-*leh*-fon *ah*-wahm	*telefon awam*

public toilet	*tahn*-duhs *ah*-wahm	*tandas awam*
restaurant	*res*-to-rahn	*restoran*
school	se-*ko*-lah(h)	*sekolah*
temple	*chan*-dee/*poo*-rah	*candi/pura*
town square	dah-*tah*-rahn	*dataran*
traditional market	*pah*-sahr	*pasar*
village	*kahm*-pong	*kampong*
zoo	zoo	*zoo*

What time does it open/close?

poo-kool be-*rah*-puh	*Pukul berapa*
boo-kuh/*too*-tup	*buka/tutup?*

Is it still open?

boo-kuh *lah*-gee tah(k)?	*Buka lagi tak?*

at the bank

di bank

All tourist areas and large towns have money changers as well as banks. Money changers, *tempat penukaran wang*, tem-*paht* pe-*noo*-kahr-ahn wahng, usually have longer opening hours and exchange rates are generally better than banks. Hotels and some department stores will also change money for you, but the rates aren't as good.

Can I exchange money here?

bo-*leh(h)* *too*-kahr wahng	*Boleh tukar wang*
dee *see*-nee?	*di sini?*

Can I use my credit card to withdraw money?

bo-*leh(h)* *sai*-yuh	*Boleh saya*
meng-*goo*-nah-kahn kahd	*menggunakan kad*
kreh-dit *oon*-tu(k)	*kredit untuk*
me-nge-*loo*-ahr-kahn *doo*-it?	*mengeluarkan duit?*

Please write it down.

to-long *too*-lis-kahn	*Tolong tuliskan.*

Can I have smaller notes?
  ah-duh *doo*-it ke-*chil* tah(k)?   *Ada duit kecil tak?*

The ATM swallowed my card.
  kahd *sai*-yuh dee-*teh*-lahn   *Kad saya ditelan*
  ay tee em   *ATM.*

Where can I cash a travellers cheque?
  dee *mah*-nuh *sai*-yuh bo-*leh(h)*   *Di mana saya boleh*
  me-*noo*-kahr-kahn chehk   *menukarkan cek*
  kem-*bah*-ruh *ee*-nee ke-*pah*-duh   *kembara ini kepada*
  wahng *too*-nai?   *wang tunai?*

I want to	*sai*-yuh nah(k)	*Saya nak*
change ...	me-*noo*-kahr-kahn ...	*menukarkan ...*
Australian dollars	*do*-lahr os-*trah*-lee-ah	*dolar Australia*
cash	wahng *too*-nai	*wang tunai*
Pounds Sterling	paun stuh-*ling*	*Pounds Stirling*
travellers cheques	chehk kem-*bah*-ruh	*cek kembara*
US dollars	*do*-lahr ah-*mehr*-ree-kah	*dolar Amerika*

What's the exchange rate?
  ah-puh-kah(h) *kah*-dahr   *Apakah kadar*
  pe-*noo*-kahr-ahn?   *penukaran?*

Has any money arrived for me?
  ah-duh-kah(h) *hahn*-tahr-ahn   *Adakah hantaran wang*
  wahng *oon*-tu(k) *sai*-yuh?   *untuk saya?*

Can I transfer money
from my bank to here?
  bo-*leh(h)*-kah(h) bank   *Bolehkah bank*
  sai-yuh meng-*hahn*-tahr   *saya menghantar*
  doo-it ke bank *ee*-nee?   *duit ke bank ini?*

How long will it take?
  be-*rah*-puh *lah*-muh?   *Berapa lama?*

Do I have to pay commission?
  ah-duh-kah(h) ko-*mi*-shen   *Adakah komisyen perlu*
  per-*loo* dee-*bai*-yahr?   *dibayar?*

branch	chah-*wah*-gahn	*cawangan*
cash	wahng *too*-nai	*wang tunai*
cashier	*joo*-roo-wahng	*juruwang*
cashier's window	*ting*-kahp	*tingkap*
	joo-roo-wahng	*juruwang*
cheque	chehk	*cek*
coins	*doo*-it *shi*-ling	*duit syiling*
commission	ko-*mi*-shen	*komisyen*
credit card	kahd *kreh*-dit	*kad kredit*
ID card	kahd pe-nge-*nah*-lahn	*kad pengenalan*
main office	ee-boo pe-*jah*-baht	*ibu pejabat*
letter of credit	soo-*raht kreh*-dit	*surat kredit*
manager	pe-*ngoo*-rus	*pengurus*
money	wahng/*doo*-it	*wang/duit*
money order	wahng *ki*-ree-mahn	*wang kiriman*
note (bill)	*doo*-it *ker*-tahs	*duit kertas*
signature	*tahn*-duh *tah*-ngahn	*tanda tangan*
teller	*teh*-ler	*teler*

at the post office

Post offices, *pejabat pos*, pe-*jah*-baht pos, with their bright red facades, can be found in all towns.

I want to	*sai*-yuh nah(k)	*Saya nak*
buy ...	mem-be-*lee* ...	*membeli ...*
envelopes	*sahm*-pul soo-raht	*sampul surat*
postcards	*pos*-kahd	*poskad*
stamps	se-*tehm*	*setem*

I want to	*sai*-yuh nah(k)	*Saya nak*
send a/an ...	meng-*hahn*-tahr ...	*menghantar ...*
aerogram	*ehr*-o-gram	*aerogram*
letter	soo-*raht*	*surat*
parcel	*boong*-koo-sahn	*bungkusan*
telegram	*teh*-le-gram	*telegram*

Please send it (by) ... mail.	to-long hahn-tar de-ngahn ...	Tolong hantar dengan ...
air	mehl oo-dah-ruh	mel udara
express	pos lah-joo	pos laju
registered	soo-raht ber-dahf-tahr	surat berdaftar
surface	pos bee-ah-suh	pos biasa

signs

awas	caution
bahaya	danger
berhenti	stop
buka	open
dilarang ...	no ...
masuk	entry
merokok	smoking
dingin	cold
halal	allowed for muslim consumption
keluar	exit
lelaki	men
masuk	entrance
panas	hot
tandas	toilets
tarik	pull
tolak	push
tutup	closed

around town

87

How much does it cost to send this to ...?
be-*rah*-puh *hahr*-guh peng-hahn-*tah*-rahn ee-nee ke ...?

Berapa harga penghantaran ini ke ...?

How much is an airmail letter to (the US)?
be-*rah*-puh ki-*ree*-mahn soo-*raht* pos oo-*dah*-ruh ke (ah-*mehr*-ee-kah)?

Berapa kiriman surat pos udara ke (Amerika)?

Please send this parcel to ... by surface mail.
to-long *ki*-reem-kahn *boong*-koo-sahn ee-nee ke ... de-*ngahn* pos bee-*ah*-suh

Tolong kirimkan bungkusan ini ke ... dengan pos biasa.

Please weigh this letter.
to-long *tim*-bahng soo-*raht* ee-nee

Tolong timbang surat ini.

glue	gahm	*gam*
mailbox	pe-*tee* soo-*raht*	*peti surat*
pen	pen	*pen*
postcode	*pos*-kod	*poskod*
receiver	pe-ner-*ree*-muh	*penerima*
sender	pen-*gee*-rim	*pengirim*
string	*tah*-lee	*tali*

telecommunications

Making domestic telephone calls in Malaysia is easy. You can direct-dial local and long-distance calls using coins and there are card telephones operated by Telecom Malaysia and Uniphone. The cards are widely available at small shops, 7-Eleven stores, post offices and newsagents. Calling Singapore is not considered an international call. All operators speak English, although you may need to speak slowly.

Could I please use the telephone?
bo-*leh(h)* pah-kai teh-*leh*-fon? *Boleh pakai telefon?*

What's the area code for ...?
kod kah-*wah*-sahn teh-*leh*-fon *Kod kawasan telefon*
... be-*rah*-puh? *... berapa?*

I want to call ...
sai-yuh nah(k) me-neh-*leh*-fon ... *Saya nak menelefon ...*

The number is ...
nom-bor-nyuh ee-*ah*-lah(h) ... *Nombornya ialah ...*

I want to speak for (three) minutes.
sai-yuh nah(k) ber-*chah*-kahp *Saya nak bercakap selama*
se-*lah*-muh (*tee*-guh) mi-nit *(tiga) minit.*

How much is a
(three)-minute call to ...?
be-*rah*-puh *ring*-git *Berapa ringgit panggilan*
pang-*gil*-ahn (*tee*-guh) *(tiga) minit ke ...?*
mi-nit ke ...?

I want to make a
reverse-charge phone call.
sai-yuh nah(k) me-neh-*leh*-fon *Saya nak menelefon*
poong-*oo*-tahn *pungutan.*

When's a cheap time to call?
poo-kool be-*rah*-puh *mah*-suh *Pukul berapa masa*
moo-rah(h) *oon*-tu(k) *murah untuk*
meng-*goo*-nuh-kahn *menggunakan telefon?*
teh-*leh*-fon?

Operator, I've been cut off.
o-pe-*ray*-tor pang-*gil*-ahn *Operator, panggilan saya*
sai-yuh ter-*poo*-toos *terputus.*

The line is busy.
tah-lee-ahn ee-too see-bu(k)/ *Talian itu sibuk/engage.*
ehn-*gehj*

Sorry, you've got the wrong number.
mah-*ahf* sah-lah(h) *nom*-bor *Maaf, salah nombor.*

Hello, do you speak English?
   heh-lo bo-*leh(h)* chah-kahp
   bah-*hah*-suh *ing*-ge-ris?

Helo, boleh cakap bahasa
Inggeris?

making a call

membuat panggilan

Hello.
   heh-lo

Helo.

May I speak to ...?
   bo-*leh(h) sai*-yuh
   ber-*chah*-kahp de-*ngahn* ...?

Boleh saya
bercakap dengan ...?

Who's calling?
   see-*ah*-puh nee?

Siapa ni?

This is ... speaking.
   ee-nee ...

Ini ...

Yes, she's/he's here.
   yah *dee*-uh *ah*-duh dee *see*-nee

Ya, dia ada di sini.

One moment, please.
   toong-goo se-ke-*jahp*

Tunggu sekejap.

I'm sorry, they're not here.
   mah-*ahf* me-*reh*-kah tah(k)
   ah-duh dee *see*-nee

Maaf, mereka tak
ada di sini.

What time will she/he be back?
   poo-kool be-*rah*-puh *dee*-uh
   poo-*lahng*?

Pukul berapa dia pulang?

Can I leave a message?
   bo-*leh(h)* ting-*gahl*-kahn
   pe-*sah*-nahn?

Boleh tinggalkan
pesanan?

Please tell him/her I called.
   to-long be-ree-*ta*-hoo *dee*-uh
   sai-yuh teh-*leh*-fon

Tolong beritahu dia saya
telefon.

I'll call back later.
   sai-yuh teh-*leh*-fon
   ke-*moo*-dee-ahn

Saya telefon kemudian.

operator	o-pe-*ray*-tor	operator
phone book	*boo*-koo teh-*leh*-fon	buku telefon

phone box	teh-*leh*-fon *ah*-wahm	*telefon awam*
phone call	pahng-*gil*-ahn teh-*leh*-fon	*panggilan telefon*
phonecard	kad teh-*leh*-fon	*kad telefon*
reverse charges	*poong*-oo-tahn	*pungutan*
telephone	teh-*leh*-fon	*telefon*
to telephone	me-neh-*leh*-fon	*menelefon*
urgent call	pahng-*gil*-ahn *pen*-ting	*panggilan penting*

internet   internet

Internet cafes have sprung up all over Malaysia in the past few
years, offering cheap – yet sometimes slow – email access.

Is there a local Internet cafe?
ah-duh *sai*-ber ka-*fay* tah(k)   *Ada cyber cafe tak di*
dee kah-*wah*-sahn *ee*-nee?   *kawasan ini?*

**Where can I get access
to the Internet?**
dee *mah*-nuh *sai*-yuh bo-*leh*(h)   *Di mana saya boleh*
pah-kai *in*-ter-neht?   *pakai internet?*

What's the rate per hour?
kah-dahr se-*jahm* be-*rah*-puh?   *Kadar sejam berapa?*

sightseeing

bersiar-siar

Malaysians love to go sightseeing, *makan angin*, *mah*-kahn
ah-ngin (lit: to-eat air). You don't have to visit the big sights
to enjoy Malaysia – the local markets and shopping areas are

just as interesting. Notice the differences in multilingual signs, smells and sounds of the predominantly Chinese, Indian or Malay neighbourhoods.

Where's the tourist office?
pe-*jah*-baht pe-*lahn*-chong-ahn dee *mah*-nuh? — *Pejabat pelancongan di mana?*

What's that building?
bahn-*goo*-nahn *ah*-puh ee-too? — *Bangunan apa itu?*

What's this monument?
too-goo *ah*-puh ee-too? — *Tugu apa itu?*

Who lived there?
see-*ah*-puh per-nah(h) *ting*-gahl dee *sah*-nuh? — *Siapa pernah tinggal di sana?*

Do you have a local map?
ah-duh pe-*tuh* tem-*pah*-tahn tah(k)? — *Ada peta tempatan tak?*

Can I take (your) photo(s)?
bo-*leh(h)* sai-yuh *ahm*-bil *fo*-to/*gahm*-bahr (*ahn*-dah)? — *Boleh saya ambil foto/gambar (anda)?*

I'll send you the photograph.
nahn-tee sai-yuh *hahn*-tahr *fo*-to/*gahm*-bahr ee-nee ke-*pah*-duh *ahn*-dah — *Nanti saya hantar foto/gambar ini kepada anda.*

Could you take a photo of (me)?
to-long *ahm*-bil *fo*-to/*gahm*-bahr (*sai*-yuh)? — *Tolong ambil foto/gambar (saya)?*

I want to see a/the ...	sai-yuh nah(k) me-*lee*-haht ...	*Saya nak melihat ...*
I'd like to go to a/the ...	sai-yuh nah(k) per-gee ke ...	*Saya nak pergi ke ...*
church	ge-*reh*-juh	*gereja*
garden	*tah*-mahn	*taman*
(botanical)	bo-*tahn*-i-kahl	*botanikal*
mosque	*mahs*-jid	*masjid*
museum	moo-*zee*-um	*muzium*

nightclub	ke-*lahb mah*-lahm	*kelab malam*
palace	ees-*tah*-nuh	*istana*
park	*tah*-mahn	*taman*
performance	per-*toon*-joo(k)-kahn	*pertunjukan*
public square	dah-*tah*-rahn	*dataran*
royal palace	ees-*tah*-nuh dee-*rah*-juh	*istana diraja*
statue	*pah*-tung	*patung*
university	yoo-ni-*ver*-si-tee	*universiti*

paperwork

mengisi borang

If you need to deal with the Malaysian government for any reason, you'll get further if you dress neatly and do your best to be polite and soft-spoken. Most government officials are Malays, who can be easily offended by obvious displays of impatience or anger, or what they define as loud voices or any form of arrogance. Many printed forms in Malaysia are in Malay and English, so you shouldn't have a lot of trouble.

forms   borang

name	*nah*-muh	*nama*
address	*ah*-lah-maht	*alamat*
date/place of birth	*tah*-rikh/tem-*paht* lah-*hir*	*tarikh/tempat lahir*
age	*oo*-moor	*umur*
sex	jahn-*tee*-nuh	*jantina*
nationality	*bahng*-suh	*bangsa*
religion	ah-*gah*-muh	*agama*
profession	pe-*ker*-jah-ahn	*pekerjaan*
marital status	tah-rahf	*taraf*
	per-*kah(h)*-wi-nahn	*perkahwinan*
single	be-*lum kah(h)*-win	*belum kahwin*
married	ber-*kah(h)*-win	*berkahwin*
divorced	ber-*che*-rai	*bercerai*
widow	*jahn*-duh	*janda*
widower	*doo*-duh	*duda*

around town

93

identification	pe-*nge*-nahl-ahn	*pengenalan*
passport number	*nom*-bor pahs-port	*nombor pasport*
visa	*vee*-suh	*visa*
birth certificate	soo-*raht* ber-*ah*-nah(k)	*surat beranak*
drivers licence	*leh*-sehn me-*mahn*-doo	*lesen memandu*
purpose of visit	se-*bahb* lah-*wah*-tahn	*sebab lawatan*
business	pe-*ker*-jah-ahn	*pekerjaan*
holiday	per-*choo*-tee-ahn	*percutian*
visiting	me-*lah*-waht	*melawat*
relatives	ke-loo-*ahr*-guh	*keluarga*

Shopping
Membeli Belah

looking for ...

mencari ...

Malaysians are big on shopping, and you can join the frenzy in a variety of shops, malls, traditional markets and stalls throughout the country. Whether you're shopping for electronic goods, handicrafts, antiques, brand name clothes or something that's excitingly near the real thing, everything's a bargain, so get going!

Where's a/the ...?	... dee *mah*-nuh?	... *di mana*?
bakery	ke-*dai* ro-tee	*Kedai roti*
barber	ke-*dai goon*-ting *rahm*-but	*Kedai gunting rambut*
bookshop	ke-*dai boo*-koo	*Kedai buku*
camera shop	ke-*dai ka*-me-ruh	*Kedai kamera*
chemist	*fahr*-mah-see; ke-*dai oo*-baht	*Farmasi; Kedai ubat*
clothing store	ke-*dai* pah-*kai*-ahn	*Kedai pakaian*
general store	ke-*dai roon*-chit	*Kedai runcit*
market	*pah*-sahr	*Pasar*
music store	ke-*dai moo*-zi(k)	*Kedia muzik*
night market	*pah*-sahr *mah*-lahm	*Pasar malam*
shopping centre	*poo*-saht mem-be-*lee*-be-*lah(h)*	*Pusat membeli-belah*
souvenir shop	ke-*dai* chehn-de-rah-*mah*-tuh	*Kedai cenderamata*
supermarket	pah-sah-*rai*-yuh	*Pasaraya*
tailor	*too*-kahng *jah*-hit	*Tukang jahit*

shopping

95

making a purchase

Shopkeepers might assume that you'll want a foreign product – set them straight if you're looking for locally made things *barang tempatan*, *bah*-rahng tem-*pah*-tahn.

Where can I buy ...?
   ... dee-*joo*-ahl dee *mah*-nuh?   *... dijual di mana?*

Do you have any ...?
   ... *ah*-duh tah(k)?   *... ada tak?*

I'm looking for (a) ...
   sai-yuh nah(k) *chah*-ree ...   *Saya nak cari ...*

I'm just looking.
   sai-yuh nah(k) te-*ngo(k)* sah-juh   *Saya nak tengok saja.*

How much is it?
   be-*rah*-puh *hahr*-guh-nyuh?   *Berapa harganya?*

Can you write down the price?
   to-long *too*-lis-kahn   *Tolong tuliskan*
   hahr-guh-nyuh   *harganya.*

Can I try this on?
   bo-*leh(h) sai*-yuh *choo*-buh?   *Boleh saya cuba?*

Can I pay by credit card?
   bo-*leh(h)* bai-yahr   *Boleh bayar*
   de-*ngahn* kahd *kreh*-dit?   *dengan kad kredit?*

Do you have others?
   ah-duh yahng lain?   *Ada yang lain?*

Where are these made?
   bah-rahng-*bah*-rahng *ee*-nee   *Barang-barang ini*
   dee-*boo*-aht dee *mah*-nuh?   *dibuat di mana?*

Can I see it?
   bo-*leh(h) sai*-yuh te-*ngo(k)*?   *Boleh saya tengok?*

I don't like it.
   sai-yuh tah(k) *soo*-kuh *ee*-nee   *Saya tak suka ini.*

It's beautiful!
   in-dah(h)/*chahn*-ti(k) se-*kah*-lee!   *Indah/Cantik sekali!*

I'll take it.
    sai-yuh nah(k) be-*lee ee*-nee   *Saya nak beli ini.*

bargaining

Bargaining is something of a game to Malaysians. Be good-humoured in your bargaining: steady, but not aggressive pressure is the best. If you don't like the price, or think you can do better, there are usually other places to try.

It's too expensive.
    mah-*hahl*-nyuh!   *Mahalnya!*

Can you lower the price?
    bo-*leh(h) koo*-rahng-kahn   *Boleh kurangkan*
    hahr-guh tah(k)?   *harga tak?*

they may say ...	
bo-*leh(h) sai*-yuh *to*-long *ahn*-duh?	Can I help you?
chah-ree *ah*-puh?	What are you looking for?
ah-duh, se-ke-*jahp*	We've got that, just a moment
wahr-nuh *ah*-puh?	What colour?
ee-nee-kah(h) *bah*-rahng yahng *ah*-wah(k) *chah*-ree	Is this what you're looking for?
hahr-guh-nyuh *lee*-muh *poo*-lu(h) *ring*-git	The price is RM50.
tee-dah(k)/tah(k) *ah*-duh	We don't have any.

How much discount?
be-*rah*-puh-kah *dis*-kown? *Berapakah diskaun?*

I'll give you ...
sai-yuh bah-gee *ahn*-duh ... *Saya bagi anda ...*

No more/less than ...
tah(k) le-*bi(h)*/ *Tak lebih/*
koo-rahng dah-ree-*pah*-duh ... *kurang daripada ...*

This is my final offer.
ee-nee tah-*wahr*-ahn *Ini tawaran*
te-*rah*-khi(r) *sai*-yuh *terakhir saya.*

cheap	*moo*-rah(h)	*murah*
discount	*dis*-kown	*diskaun*
expensive	mah-*hahl*	*mahal*

essential items

I'm looking for (a) ...	*sai*-yuh *chah*-ree ...	*Saya cari ...*
batteries	*bah*-te-ree	*bateri*
bread	*ro*-tee	*roti*
butter	men-*teh*-guh	*mentega*
cheese	*keh*-joo	*keju*
chocolate	*chok*-laht	*coklat*
eggs	te-*lur*	*telur*
flour	te-*pung*	*tepung*
ham	*dah*-ging *bah*-bee	*daging babi*
honey	*mah*-doo	*madu*

margarine	men-*teh*-guh	*mentega*
matches	*mahn*-chis	*mancis*
milk	*soo*-soo	*susu*
toilet paper	*tee*-soo	*tisu*
toothpaste	oo-baht *gee*-gee	*ubat gigi*
torch (flashlight)	*lahm*-poo *soo*-lu(h)	*lampu suluh*
towel	*twah*-luh	*tuala*
washing powder	*ser*-bu(k) *choo*-chee	*serbuk cuci*
yogurt	*yo*-gurt	*yogurt*

souvenirs

cendera hati

Traditional handicraft production has declined due to changes in national lifestyle, so arty items you see may often be from Indonesia. The east coast, Sabah and Sarawak still have some excellent crafts; Melaka is a centre for antiques, as is Penang.

basket	*bah*-kool	*bakul*
... batik	*bah*-ti(k) ...	*batik* ...
hand painted	*loo*-kis *tah*-ngahn	*lukis tangan*
printed	chahp	*cap*
bracelet	ge-*lahng*	*gelang*
cane ware	*bah*-rahng-ahn *ro*-tahn	*barangan rotan*
... carving	oo-ki-rahn	*ukiran* ...
stone	*bah*-too	*batu*
wood	*kai*-yoo	*kayu*
earrings	*soo*-bahng	*subang*
handcrafts	krahf-*tah*-ngahn	*kraftangan*

---

the real mccoy

When looking for souvenirs or items made in Malaysia, ask:

'Is this made in Malaysia?'
ee-nee *bah*-rahng
boo-ah-tahn mah-*lay*-see-ah?

Ini barang
buatan Malaysia?

jewellery	*bah*-rahng ke-*mahs*	barang kemas
machete	*pah*-rahng	parang
carved masks	*to*-peng yahng dee-*oo*-kir	topeng yang diukir
material (fabric)	kain	kain
necklace	*rahn*-tai *leh*-hehr	rantai leher
Malay knives	ke-*ris*	keris
paintings	loo-*kee*-sahn	lukisan
pottery	tem-*bee*-kahr	tembikar
shadow puppets	*wai*-yahng *koo*-lit	wayang kulit
ring	*chin*-chin	cincin
sarong	*sah*-rung	sarung
statue	*pah*-tung	patung

clothing

pakaian

bra	*cho*-lee	coli
cardigan	*bah*-joo se-*joo(k)* yahng ber-*boo*-tahng de-*pahn*	baju sejuk yang berbutang depan
dress	*bah*-joo gown	baju gaun
gloves	*sah*-rung tah-*ngahn*	sarung tangan
hat	*to*-pee	topi
jacket	jah-*keht*	jaket
jeans	jeens	jeans
jumper	*bah*-joo se-ju(k)	baju sejuk
pants	se-*loo*-ahr *pahn*-jahng	seluar panjang
raincoat	*bah*-joo *hoo*-jahn	baju hujan

hot and cold

Think hot, hot, hot. It simply never cools down, except during the rainy season on the east coast. You'll need cotton clothes that breathe, and protect you from the sun (and any eager eyes checking you out). If you head into the highlands you may need to rug up, so take waterproof gear or a light jumper.

sandals	se-*lee*-pahr	*selipar*
shirt	*bah*-joo/ke-*meh*-juh	*baju/kemeja*
shoelaces	*tah*-lee *kah*-sut	*tali kasut*
shoes	*kah*-sut	*kasut*
shorts	se-*loo*-ahr *pehn*-deh(k)	*seluar pendek*
skirt	sket	*skirt*
socks	*sto*-king	*stoking*
swimsuit	pah-*kai*-ahn/	*pakaian/*
	bah-joo reh-nahng	*baju renang*
tie	*tah*-lee *leh*-hehr	*tali leher*
trousers	se-*loo*-ahr *pahn*-jahng	*seluar panjang*
T-shirt	*bah*-joo tee	*baju T*
underwear	se-*loo*-ahr *dah*-lahm	*seluar dalam*

materials

bahan

The *Jalan Masjid India* and *Jalan Tuanku Abdul Rahman* areas of Kuala Lumpur have a huge variety of shops selling material.

bone	*too*-lahng	*tulang*
cotton	*kah*-pahs	*kapas*
gold	e-*mahs*	*emas*
jackfruit wood	*kai*-yoo *nahng*-kuh	*kayu nangka*
leather	*koo*-lit	*kulit*
rattan/cane	*ro*-tahn	*rotan*
sandalwood	chehn-*dah*-nuh	*cendana*
shell	*koo*-lit *see*-put	*kulit siput*

shopping

101

silk	*soo*-te-ruh	*sutera*
silver	*peh*-rah(k)	*perak*
wood	*kai*-yoo	*kayu*
wool	*boo*-loo *bi*-ree-*bi*-ree	*bulu biri-biri*

colours

warna

black	*hee*-tahm	*hitam*
blonde/tan	*peh*-rahng	*perang*
blue	*bee*-roo	*biru*
brown	*chok*-laht	*coklat*
dark ...	... *too*-uh	... *tua*
green	*hee*-jow	*hijau*
grey	ke-*lah*-boo/*ah*-sahp	*kelabu/asap*
light ...	... *moo*-duh	... *muda*
multicoloured	ber-*wahr*-nah-*wahr*-nee	*berwarna-warni*
orange	o-rehn/*jing*-guh	*oren/jingga*
pink	*meh*-rah(h) *jahm*-boo	*merah jambu*
purple	*oon*-goo	*ungu*
red	*meh*-rah(h)	*merah*
white	*poo*-ti(h)	*putih*
yellow	*koo*-ning	*kuning*

toiletries

barangan bilik air

In smaller towns you may find some of these items in traditional Chinese medicine shops.

comb	*see*-kaht	*sikat*
condoms	*kon*-dom	*kondom*
contraceptive ...	*oo*-baht/	*ubat/*
device/	*ah*-laht pe-*rahn*-chang	*alat perancang*
medicine	ke-loo-*ahr*-guh	*keluarga*
deodorant	dee-*o*-do-rahn	*deodoran*

laxative	*joo*-lahp	*julap*
lip balm	bahm *bee*-bir	*bam bibir*
lipstick	*gin*-choo/chaht *bee*-bir	*gincu/cat bibir*
moisturising	kreem	*krim*
cream	pe-*lehm*-bahb *koo*-lit	*pelembab kulit*
mosquito repellent	*oo*-baht *nyah*-mu(k)	*ubat nyamuk*
razor	pen-*choo*-kur	*pencukur*
razor blade	*pee*-sow *choo*-kur	*pisau cukur*
sanitary napkins	*twah*-luh wah-*nee*-tuh	*tuala wanita*
shampoo	*shahm*-poo	*syampu*
shaver	pen-*choo*-kur	*pencukur*
shaving cream	kreem *choo*-kur	*krim cukur*
soap	*sah*-bun	*sabun*
sunblock cream	kreem pe-*lin*-dung	*krim pelindung*
	chah-*hai*-yuh	*cahaya*
	mah-tuh-*hah*-ree	*matahari*
tampons	*tahm*-pohn	*tampon*
tissues	*ti*-soo	*tisu*
toothbrush	be-*roos gee*-gee	*berus gigi*

for the baby

untuk bayi

baby's bottle	bo-tol *bah*-yee	*botol bayi*
baby clothes	pah-*kai*-ahn *bah*-yee	*pakaian bayi*
(children's)	(*kah*-nah(k)-*kah*-nah(k))	*(kanak-kanak)*
baby food	*mah*-kah-nahn *bah*-yee	*makanan bayi*
baby powder	be-*dahk bah*-yee	*bedak bayi*
bib	bib	*bib*
boiled water	air *mah*-sah(k)	*air masak*

lukewarm	swahm	suam
disposable nappies	kain *lahm*-pin yahng	kain lampin yang
(diapers)	bo-*leh*(h) dee-*boo*-ahng	boleh dibuang
dummy (pacifier)	*poo*-ting	puting
nappy rash cream	kreem *roo*-ahm *bah*-yee	krim ruam bayi
powdered milk	*soo*-soo ser-bu(k)	susu serbuk

music

I'm looking for a ... CD.
sai-yuh nah(k)
men-*chah*-ree CD ...

*Saya nak
mencari CD ...*

Do you have ...?
ah-duh ...?

Ada ...?

I heard a band/singer called ...
sai-yuh *per*-nah(h)
men-*deh*-ngahr *koom*-poo-lahn/
pe-*nyah*-nyee ber-*nah*-muh ...

*Saya pernah
mendengar kumpulan/
penyanyi bernama ...*

Can I listen to this CD here?
bo-*leh*(h) tah(k) *sai*-yuh
men-*deh*-ngahr CD *ee*-nee
dee *see*-nee?

*Boleh tak saya
mendengar CD ini
di sini?*

I want a blank tape.
sai-yuh nah(k) *ka*-seht *ko*-song

Saya nak kaset kosong.

stationery & publications

alat tulis-menulis & penerbitan

There are many bookstores and newsagents in the larger cities
that carry English titles. Stock up before you head out.

**Is there an English-language
bookshop here?**
ah-duh ke-*dai* boo-koo
bah-*hah*-suh *ing*-ge-ris tah(k)
dee *see*-nee?

*Ada kedai buku
bahasa Inggeris
tak di sini?*

Is there an English-language section?
ah-duh bah-hah-gee-ahn   *Ada bahagian*
bah-hah-suh ing-ge-ris tah(k)?   *bahasa Inggeris tak?*

Do you sell ...?	ah-duh-kah(h) ...	*Adakah ...*
	dee-joo-ahl?	*dijual?*
envelopes	sahm-pool soo-raht	*sampul surat*
magazines	mah-jah-luh(h)	*majalah*
newspapers	soo-raht khah-bahr	*surat khabar*
(English-	(bah-hah-suh	*(bahasa*
language)	ing-ge-ris)	*Inggeris)*
novels	no-vel/boo-koo	*novel/buku*
	che-ree-tuh	*cerita*
pens	pehn	*pen*
postcards	pos-kahd	*poskad*
stamps	se-tehm	*setem*
writing paper	ker-tahs too-lis	*kertas tulis*
... dictionaries	kah-moos ...	*kamus ...*
bilingual	dwee-bah-hah-suh	*dwibahasa*
pocket	po-keht	*poket*
... maps	peh-tuh ...	*peta ...*
city	bahn-duh-rai-yuh	*bandaraya*
regional	dah-eh-rah(h)/	*daerah/*
	rahn-tow	*rantau*
road	jah-lahn	*jalan*

photography

There are film and processing shops all over Malaysia, which also take passport photos. Photo processing is good quality and it's much cheaper than many places overseas. You can bargain for cameras and other equipment, unless you're buying them in a department store.

I'd like a film for this camera.
sai-yuh nah(k) fee-lem   *Saya nak filem*
oon-tu(k) ka-me-ruh ee-nee   *untuk kamera ini.*

How much is it for processing and developing?
be-*rah*-puh *hahr*-guh pen-*choo*-chee-ahn *fee*-lem *ee*-nee? — *Berapa harga pencucian filem ini?*

When will it be ready?
bee-luh see-*ahp*? — *Bila siap?*

Do you repair cameras here?
bo-*leh(h) bai*-kee *ka*-me-ruh tah(k) dee *see*-nee? — *Boleh baiki kamera tak di sini?*

battery	*ba*-te-ree	*bateri*
B&W (film)	(fee-lem) hee-tahm poo-ti(h)	*(filem) hitam putih*
camera	*ka*-me-ruh	*kamera*
colour (film)	(fee-lem) ber-*wahr*-nuh	*(filem) berwarna*
to develop	men-*choo*-cee	*cuci*
film	(*fee*-lem)	*filem*
flash(bulb)	pahn-*chah*-rahn (*mehn*-tul)	*pancaran (mentul)*
lens	*lehn*-suh	*lensa*
light meter	*mee*-ter chah-*hai*-yuh	*meter cahaya*
photograph	fo-to/*gahm*-bahr	*foto/gambar*
to print	men-*choo*-chee	*mencuci*
(make) reprints	(*boo*-aht) *sah*-lee-nahn	*(buat) salinan*
slides	slaid	*slaid*
videotape	*pee*-tuh *vi*-dee-o	*pita video*

smoking

merokok

Some cigarettes in Malaysia have a higher tar/nicotine content than they do in other countries. If you're smoking 'lights' they may not be as 'light' as you think! The intense spicy aroma of the imported Indonesian 'clove cigarettes', *kretek*, kreh-teh(k), will be the smell of your Malaysian memories. Smuggling kretek into Malaysia is a big but illegal business.

A packet of cigarettes, please.
to-long *bah*-gee   *Tolong bagi*
se-*ko*-tah(k) *ro*-ko(k)   *sekotak rokok.*

Do you have a light?
ah-duh *mahn*-chis?   *Ada mancis?*

Are these cigarettes strong or mild?
ah-duh-kah(h) ro-ko(k)   *Adakah rokok*
ee-nee ke-*rahs* ah-*tow* ri-*ngahn*?   *ini keras atau ringan?*

Can I smoke here?
bo-*leh(h)* tah(k)   *Boleh tak*
me-*ro*-ko(k) dee *see*-nee?   *merokok di sini?*

Do you have an ashtray?
ah-duh-kah(h) be-*kahs*   *Adakah bekas*
ah-boo ro-ko(k)?   *abu rokok?*

Please don't smoke.
to-long jah-*ngahn* me-*ro*-ko(k)   *Tolong jangan merokok.*

I'm trying to give up smoking.
sai-yuh se-*dahng* men-*choo*-buh   *Saya sedang mencuba*
ber-*hen*-tee me-*ro*-ko(k)   *berhenti merokok.*

cigarette papers	*ker*-tahs ro-ko(k)	kertas rokok
cigarettes	*ro*-ko(k)	rokok
clove cigarette	*kreh*-teh(k)	kretek
filter	*fil*-ter	filter
lighter	*mahn*-chis *ah*-pee	mancis api
matches	*mahn*-chis	mancis
menthol	*mehn*-tol	mentol

pipe	paip	*paip*
smoke	*ah*-sahp	*asap*
to smoke	me-*ro*-ko(k)	*merokok*
tobacco	tehm-*bah*-kow	*tembakau*

sizes & comparisons

a little bit	se-*dee*-kit	*sedikit*
big	be-*sahr*	*besar*
bigger	le-*bi(h)* be-*sahr*	*lebih besar*
biggest	*pah*-ling be-*sahr*	*paling besar*
enough	*choo*-kup	*cukup*
heavy	be-*raht*	*berat*

---

street life

You are unlikely to be harassed by people on the streets, even in the rougher parts of town:

Come here!
see-nee-lah(h)/*mah*-ree   *Sinilah/Mari*
see-nee-lah(h)   *sinilah.*

Go away!!
per-gee!/be-*lah(h)!*   *Pergi/Belah!*

I don't have any money.
tah(k) *ah*-duh *doo*-it   *Tak ada duit.*

alley	*lo*-rong	*lorong*
footpath	*ping*-gir *jah*-lahn	*pinggir jalan*
hawker	pen-*joo*-ahl	*penjual*
homeless person	*o*-rahng *gee*-luh	*orang gila*
thief	pen-*choo*-ree	*pencuri*
street	*jah*-lahn	*jalan*
street stall (food)	ge-*rai/wah*-rung	*gerai/warung*
traffic lights	*lahm*-poo	*lampu*
	ee-*shah*-raht	*isyarat*

too much/many	ter-*lah*-loo *bah*-nyah(k)	*terlalu banyak*
less	koo-*rahng*	*kurang*
light	ri-*ngahn*	*ringan*
long	pahn-*jahng*	*panjang*
many	*bah*-nyah(k)	*banyak*
more	le-*bi(h)* *bah*-nyah(k)	*lebih banyak*
narrow	sem-*pit*	*sempit*
short	*pehn*-deh(k)	*pendek*
small	ke-*chil*	*kecil*
smaller	le-*bi(h)* ke-*chil*	*lebih kecil*
smallest	*pah*-ling ke-*chil*	*paling kecil*
spacious	loo-*ahs*	*luas*
tall	*ting*-gee	*tinggi*
too big	ter-*lah*-loo be-*sahr*	*terlalu besar*
very big	*sah*-ngaht be-*sahr*	*sangat besar*
wide	le-*bahr*	*lebar*

weights & measures

		berat & ukuran
millimetre	*mi*-li-*mee*-ter	*milimeter*
centimetre	*sen*-ti-*mee*-ter	*sentimeter*
metre	*mee*-ter	*meter*
kilometre	*ki*-lo-*mee*-ter	*kilometer*
litre	*lee*-ter	*liter*
gram	gram	*gram*
kilogram	*ki*-lo-gram	*kilogram*

useful words

		perkataan yang berguna
to buy	mem-be-*lee*	*membeli*
cheap	*moo*-rah(h)	*murah*
to export	meng-*ehk*-sport	*mengeksport*
to import	meng-*im*-port	*mengimport*
made in	dee-per-*boo*-aht dee	*diperbuat di*

old	*too*-uh/*lah*-muh	*tua/lama*
to order	me-*nehm*-pah(h)	*menempah*
quality	*moo*-too/*kwah*-li-tee	*mutu/kualiti*
quantity	*joom*-lah(h)	*jumlah*
to sell	men-*joo*-ahl	*menjual*
type (of product)	je-*nis*/*mah*-chahm	*jenis/macam*

Specific Needs
Keperluan Khusus

disabled travellers

orang cacat

Few facilities cater to the disabled in Malaysia. In most cities and towns there are seldom any sidewalks, and if there are, the curbs tend to be high and uneven. Toilets for the disabled are few and far between. Some of the newer mass transit and train systems in Kuala Lumpur have more accessibility. Malays in particular tend to stare at any one who looks different (this includes most non-Asian travellers) so be prepared to be gawked at.

I'm disabled.
sai-yuh *chah*-chaht | *Saya cacat.*

I need assistance.
sai-yuh per-*loo*-kahn bahn-*too*-ahn | *Saya perlukan bantuan.*

What services do you have for disabled people?
ah-duh per-*kheed*-mah-tahn oon-tu(k) o-rahng *chah*-chaht? | *Ada perkhidmatan untuk orang cacat?*

Is there wheelchair access?
ah-duh *jah*-lahn *mah*-su(k) oon-tu(k) ke-*roo*-see be-*ro*-duh? | *Ada jalan masuk untuk kerusi beroda?*

I'm deaf.
sai-yuh pe-*kah(k)* | *Saya pekak.*

I can lipread.
sai-yuh *dah*-paht mem-*bah*-chuh ge-*rah*-kahn *bee*-bir | *Saya dapat membaca gerakan bibir.*

Does anyone here know sign language?
ah-duh o-rahng yahng *tah*-hoo bah-*hah*-suh ee-*shah*-raht? | *Ada orang yang tahu bahasa isyarat?*

I have a hearing aid.
  sai-yuh *ah-*duh *ah*-laht
  bahn-too de-*ngahr*
                                            Saya ada alat bantu
                                            dengar.

Speak more loudly please.
  to-long *chah*-kahp
  kwaht see-*kit*
                                            Tolong cakap
                                            kuat sikit.

Are guide dogs permitted?
  bo-*leh(h)*-kah(h) *sai*-yuh
  mem-*bah*-wuh *mah*-su(k)
  ahn-jing pe-*mahn*-doo?
                                            Bolehkah saya membawa
                                            masuk anjing pemandu?

Braille library	per-poos-tah-*kah*-ahn brehl	*perpustakaan Braille*
disabled person	o-rahng *chah*-chaht	*orang cacat*
guide dog	*ahn*-jing pe-*mahn*-doo	*anjing pemandu*
wheelchair	ke-roo-see be-*ro*-duh	*kerusi beroda*

gay travellers

                                       orang homoseksual

Despite negative views of homosexuality and laws which allow for the punishment of homosexual acts by imprisonment or caning, Malaysia is amazingly tolerant of transvestites, *pondan*, *pon*-dahn. Public displays of affection are not okay, however.

    There is a gay scene in Kuala Lumpur. The word 'gay', pronounced geh, will be understood.

Where are the gay hangouts?
  dee *mah*-nuh tem-*paht*
  ber-*koom*-pool o-rahng geh/
  ho-mo-*sek*-soo-ahl?
                                            Di mana tempat
                                            berkumpul orang
                                            gay/homoseksual?

Where are the gay clubs?
  ke-*lahb* mah-lahm *oon*-tu(k)
  o-rahng geh dee *mah*-nuh?
                                            Kelab malam untuk
                                            orang gay di mana?

[Are we; Am I] likely to be harassed?
  ah-duh-kah o-rahng geh
  se-*ring* de-*gahng*-goo dee
  see-nee?
                                            Adakah orang gay
                                            sering diganggu di sini?

Is there a gay organisation in Kuala Lumpur?

ah-duh or-gahn-i-*sah*-see geh
dee *kwah*-luh *loom*-pur tah(k)?

Ada organisasi gay di Kuala Lumpur tak?

travelling with the family

perjalanan dengan keluarga

Malaysians love children, and if you have some it can be a real icebreaker. Discounts are available for children at most attractions and on public transport. You will see children eating out with adults, even in pricey restaurants, at almost any time of day.

Are there facilities for babies?

ah-duh ke-moo-*dah(h)*-ahn
oon-tu(k) *bah*-yee tah(k)?

Ada kemudahan untuk bayi tak?

Do you have a childminding service?

ah-duh per-*kheed*-mah-tahn
pen-*jah*-gah-ahn ah-nah(k) tah(k)?

Ada perkhidmatan penjagaan anak tak?

Where can I find a/an (English-speaking) babysitter?

dee *mah*-nuh *sai*-yuh bo-*leh(h)*
men-*chah*-ree pen-*jah*-guh
ah-*nah(k)* (yahng *tah*-hoo
ber-*chah*-kahp *dah*-lahm
bah-*hah*-suh *ing*-ge-ris)?

Di mana saya boleh mencari penjaga anak (yang tahu bercakap dalam Bahasa Inggeris)?

Can you put an (extra) bed/cot in the room?

bo-*leh(h) sai*-yuh *min*-tuh
sah-too (*lah*-gee) *kah*-til *oon*-tu(k)
bee-li(k) *kah*-mee?

Boleh saya minta satu (lagi) katil untuk bilik kami?

I need a car with a child seat.

sai-yuh *per*-loo-kahn ke-*reh*-tuh
de-*ngahn* ke-*roo*-see
kah-nah(k)-*kah*-nah(k)

Saya perlukan kereta dengan kerusi kanak-kanak.

Is it suitable for children?
ah-duh-kah(h) *ee*-nee se-*swai*
oon-tu(k) *kah*-nah(k)-*kah*-nah(k)?
Adakah ini sesuai untuk kanak-kanak?

Are there any activities for children?
ah-duh ke-gee-*ah*-tahn oon-tu(k)
kah-nah(k)-*kah*-nah(k)?
Ada kegiatan untuk kanak-kanak?

Is there a family discount?
ah-duh *dis*-kown oon-tu(k)
ke-loo-*ahr*-guh?
Ada diskaun untuk keluarga?

Are children allowed?
ah-duh-kah(h)
kah-nah(k)-*kah*-nah(k)
dee-be-*nahr*-kahn *mah*-su(k)?
Adakah kanak-kanak dibenarkan masuk?

Do you have a children's menu?
ah-duh *meh*-nyoo oon-tu(k)
kah-nah(k)-*kah*-nah(k) tah(k)?
Ada menu untuk kanak-kanak tak?

on business

perjalanan perniagaan

We're attending a ...	*kah*-mee meng-hah-*di*-ree ...	*Kami menghadiri ...*
conference	per-*see*-dah-ngahn/ kon-fer-*ehn*-see	*persidangan/ konferensi*
meeting	me-shoo-*ah*-raht	*mesyuarat*
trade fair	*pehs*-tuh per-*toon*-joo-kahn per-*dah*-gah-ngahn	*pesta pertunjukan perdagangan*

I'm on a course.
sai-yuh se-*dahng* ber-*koor*-sus
Saya sedang berkursus.

I have an appointment with ...
sai-yuh *ah*-duh te-moo-*jahn*-jee de-*ngahn* ...
Saya ada temujanji dengan ...

Here's my business card.
ee-nee kahd *nah*-muh *sai*-yuh
Ini kad nama saya.

I need an interpreter.
  sai-yuh per-*loo*
  pen-ter-*jeh*-mah(h)

  Saya perlu penterjemah.

I'd like to use a computer.
  sai-yuh per-*loo* meng-*goo*-nuh
  kom-*poo*-ter

  Saya perlu mengguna komputer.

I'd like to send [a fax; an email].
  sai-yuh nah(k) meng-*hahn*-tahr
  fahks/*ee*-mehl

  Saya nak menghantar faks/e-mel.

client	pe-*lahng*-gahn/*klai*-ehn	pelanggan/klien
colleague	*rah*-kahn se-*ker*-juh	rakan sekerja
distributor	pe-*ngeh*-dahr	pengedar
email	*ee*-mehl	e-mel
exhibition	*pah*-meh-rahn	pameran
manager	pe-*ngoo*-roos	pengurus
mobile phone	teh-*leh*-fon *bim*-bit	telefon bimbit
profit	*oon*-tung	untung
proposal	*oo*-sool/*chah*-dah-ngahn	usul/cadangan

film & TV crews

kru filem & televisyen

Can we film here?
  bo-*leh(h) kah*-mee
  me-rah-*kahm*-kahn
  fee-lem dee *see*-nee?

  Boleh kami merakamkan filem di sini?

We're filming!
  kah-mee se-*dahng*
  mem-*boo*-aht *fee*-lem!

  Kami sedang membuat filem!

We're making a ...	*kah*-mee mem-*boo*-aht ...	Kami membuat ...
film	*fee*-lem	filem
documentary	do-koo-*mehn*-tah-ree	dokumentari
TV series	*si*-ree *rahn*-chah-ngahn teh-le-vi-shen	siri rancangan televisyen

specific needs

pilgrimage & religion

Malaysian Muslims can be a little touchy about discussing religion. Approach Islam with great respect. If you're asking questions it's better to ask a Chinese or Indian Malaysian who is less likely to be a Muslim. Talking too much to a Malay about religions other than Islam might be perceived as trying to convert them, which is against the law. Remember that in order to enter a mosque, a man must wear a shirt, preferably with sleeves, and pants (or a *sarong*) falling below the knees. Women must wear clothing that covers their head and body with the exception of their hands and face – usually a skirt rather than pants. Don't walk in front of people who are performing their prayers.

Can I attend this service?
bo-*leh(h)* meng-hah-*di*-ree
oo-pah-*chah*-ruh *ee*-nee?

*Boleh menghadiri
upacara ini?*

Can I pray here?
bo-*leh(h)* sai-yuh
ber-sehm-*bai*-yahng dee *see*-nee?

*Boleh saya
bersembayang di sini?*

Where can I pray/worship?
dee *mah*-nuh tem-*paht* yahng
sai-yuh bo-*leh(h)*
ber-sehm-*bai*-yahng?

*Di mana tempat yang
saya boleh
bersembayang?*

**Where can I make confession
(in English)?**
pe-*ngah*-koo-ahn (*dah*-lahm
bah-*hah*-suh *ing*-ge-ris)
dee-lah-*koo*-kahn dee *mah*-nuh?

*Pengakuan (dalam
Bahasa Inggeris)
dilakukan di mana?*

barefoot & fancy free

All Malaysians take off their shoes before entering accommodation of any kind, so remember to remove yours and put them next to the pile. Footwear must also be removed when visiting mosques and some temples, and beware – expensive shoes can walk off on their own.

May I enter this mosque?
bo-*leh(h)* tah(k) *sai*-yuh *Boleh tak saya*
mah-su(k) *mahs*-jid ee-nee? *masuk masjid ini?*

Where may I stand/
walk in the mosque?
dee *mah*-nuh *sai*-yuh bo-*leh(h)* *Di mana saya boleh*
ber-*di*-ree/*jah*-lahn *dah*-lahm *berdiri/jalan dalam*
mahs-jid? *masjid?*

baptism	*bahp*-tis	baptis
christening	*bahp*-tis	baptis
church	ge-*reh*-juh	gereja
communion	per-*jah*-moo-ahn *soo*-chee	perjamuan suci
confession	pe-*ngah*-koo-ahn	pengakuan
fasting month	*rah*-mah-dahn	Ramadhan
Friday prayers	sem-*bah(h)*-yahng *joo*-mah-aht	sembahyang Jumaat
funeral	pe-*mah*-kah-mahn	pemakaman
God (Muslim)	*too*-hahn/*ahl*-lah(h)	Tuhan/Allah
monk	*rah*-hib	rahib
mosque	*mahs*-jid	masjid
pilgrim (Muslim) (m/f)	*hah*-jee/*haj*-jah(h)	haji/hajjah
pilgrimage to Mecca	hahj	hajj
prayer	*do*-ah/*sem*-bah(h)-yahng	doa/sembahyang
priest (Catholic)	*pah*-dree	padri
pastor (Protestant)	*pah*-dree/*pahs*-tor	padri/pastor
relic	pe-*ning*-gah-lahn	peninggalan
religious procession	pe-*rah*-rah-kahn *ah*-gah-muh	perarakan agama
religious tax	*zah*-kaht	zakat
saint	o-rahng *soo*-chee/*wah*-lee	orang suci/wali
shrine	tem-*paht soo*-chee	tempat suci
... temple	*to*-kong ...	tokong ...
Buddhist	*boo*-dah	Buddha
Chinese	*chee*-nah	Cina
Hindu	*koo*-il	kuil

tracing roots & history

I think my ancestors came from this area.
sai-yuh *rah*-suh neh-*neh(k)*
mo-yahng *sai*-yuh ber-*ah*-sahl
dah-ree *kah*-wah-sahn ee-nee

Saya rasa nenek
moyang saya berasal
dari kawasan ini.

I'm looking for my relatives.
sai-yuh men-*chah*-ree *ah(h)*-lee
ke-loo-ahr-guh sai-yuh

Saya mencari ahli
keluarga saya.

I have/had a relative who lives around here.
doo-loo ke-loo-*ahr*-guh *sai*-yuh
ting-gahl dee *kah*-wah-sahn ee-nee

Dulu keluarga saya
tinggal di kawasan ini.

Is there anyone here by the name of ...?
ah-duh *o*-rahng dee *see*-nee
yahng ber-*nah*-muh ...?

Ada orang di sini
yang bernama ...?

I'd like to go to the cemetery/ burial ground.
sai-yuh *i*-ngin me-*lah*-waht
per-*koo*-bu-rahn

Saya ingin melawat
perkuburan.

My father used to work here.
ai-yah(h) *sai*-yuh per-*nah(h)*
ber-*ker*-juh dee *see*-nee

Ayah saya pernah
berkerja di sini.

SOCIAL > Meeting People
Perkenalan

Malaysians are very interested in meeting foreigners, and they'll be happy if you even attempt to speak their language. *Lepak*, leh-pah(k), 'hanging out' is a national pastime and since chatting to a stranger is considered normal, you'll have plenty of opportunity to practise.

First conversations tend to include questions about family, nationality, and whether you like spicy food. People will often question what you're doing, or where you're going. The 32nd person who asks *Berasal dari mana?*, ber-ah-sahl dah-ree mah-nuh?, 'Where are you from?' may think they're the first, so go with the flow and try asking a few questions of your own.

you should know

anda patut tahu

Yes.	yah	*Ya.*
No.	tee-dah(k)	*Tidak.*
Excuse me.	mah-*ahf*	*Maaf.*
Hello.	heh-lo	*Helo.*

Goodbye. (if you're staying)
se-*lah*-maht *jah*-lahn   *Selamat jalan.*

Goodbye. (if you're leaving)
se-*lah*-maht *ting*-gahl   *Selamat tinggal.*

Please sit down.
see-*lah*-kahn doo-du(k)   *Silakan duduk.*

Thank you (very much).
te-*ree*-muh kah-si(h)   *Terima kasih (banyak-*
(*bah*-nyah(k)-*bah*-nyah(k))   *banyak).*

You're welcome.
sah-muh-*sah*-muh   *Sama-sama.*

Excuse me; Sorry.
mah-*ahf*; *min*-tuh mah-*ahf*   *Maaf; Minta maaf.*

meeting people

119

May I?; Do you mind?
    bo-*leh(h)*?   *Boleh?*

That's fine; No problem.
    bo-*leh(h)*; tah(k) *ah*-puh   *Boleh; Tak apa.*

What did you say?
    ah-puh-*dee*-uh?   *Apadia?*

I'm (very) sorry. (apology)
    (*min*-tuh) mah-*ahf*   *(Minta) Maaf.*

There are two Malay words for 'please'. Use *tolong*, to-long, 'help', if making a request or asking someone to do something for you.

Please open the window.
    to-long *boo*-kah ting-kahp   *Tolong buka tingkap.*

Or, if you're offering something to somebody, use the word *silakan*, see-*lah*-kahn (lit: be-my-guest).

greetings & goodbyes

Malay greetings can range from a 'Hey, you!' to a lengthy and formal exchange. Not to worry, since there are across-the-board greetings that are fine to use almost anywhere. The word *selamat*, se-*lah*-maht, comes from the Arabic word *salam*, meaning 'peace'. Putting this word together with 'morning' or 'evening' means something like 'Have a nice morning/evening'.

As in English, Malay greetings are based on the time of day – and also on routine or prayer times. While you may think the day's just begun, the person you're speaking to may have already been to market and prepared lunch.

Good morning. (sunrise – 10 am)
    se-*lah*-maht *pah*-gee   *Selamat pagi.*

Before 10 is the best time to be out and about, watching kids in starched uniforms off to school, people carrying produce to market, or drivers digging into a bowl of *bubur ayam*, *boo-*bur *ai-*yahm, 'chicken porridge.'

Good day. (10 am – 4 pm)
se-*lah-*maht te-ngah-*hah-*ree   *Selamat tengahari.*

By this time the heat and the traffic have really kicked in.

Good afternoon. (4 – sunset)
se-*lah-*maht pe-*tahng*   *Selamat petang.*

The sun is beyond the danger zone and children's kites are filling the sky, or the punctual tropical downpour has begun.

Good night. (goodbye at night – a farewell)
se-*lah-*maht *mah-*lahm   *Selamat malam.*

There's not really a term for good evening – instead you can just say hello as you would in English (also used as an informal greeting between friends):

Hello.   *heh-*lo   *Helo*

See you later.
*joom-*pah *lah-*gee *nahn-*tee   *Jumpa lagi nanti.*

I'm going home now.
*sai-*yuh *bah-*li(k) *doo-*loo   *Saya balik dulu.*

Bye. (pronounced as in English)   *Bye.*

forms of address

It's a good idea to use 'Sir' or 'Ma'am' when talking to someone older or deserving of respect.

Mrs; Ma'am	pwahn	*Puan*
Mr	en-*chi(k)*	*Encik*
Sir	twahn	*Tuan*
Miss	chi(k)	*Cik*

first encounters

pertemuan pertama

What's your name?
see-ah-puh nah-muh ahn-duh?   Siapa nama anda?

My name's ...
nah-muh sai-yuh ...   Nama saya ...

I'd like to introduce ...
to you.
sai-yuh nah(k)   Saya nak
mem-per-ke-nahl-kahn ...   memperkenalkan ...
ke-pah-duh ahn-duh   kepada anda.

I'm pleased to meet you.
sai-yuh gem-bi-ruh ber-te-moo   Saya gembira bertemu
de-ngahn ahn-duh   dengan anda.

making conversation

perbualan

Greetings aside, many people will launch straight into the guts of a conversation. Don't be surprised if you're quickly quizzed on topics 'Are you married?', 'Are your teeth real?' If you're asked 'How much money do you make?' you can just answer *cukup,* choo-kup, 'enough' with a smile. Common starters include:

How are you?; How's it going?
ah-puh khah-bahr?   Apa khabar?

Fine. And you?
  khah-bahr bai(k).   *Khabar baik.*
  ah-puh *khah*-bahr?   *Apa khabar?*

Where are you going?
  nah(k) ke *mah*-nuh?   *Nak ke mana?*

Asked most often as an ice-breaker, the response *jalan-jalan*, *jah*-lahn-*jah*-lahn, 'travelling around', is perfect. Other easy answers include:

To (Petaling Jaya).
  ke (pe-*tah*-ling *jah*-yuh)   *Ke (Petaling Jaya).*

Out and about.
  mah-kahn *ah*-ngin   *Makan angin.*
                             (lit: eating the breeze)

Some of the things people will want to know about you are:

How long have you been in Malaysia?
  soo-dah(h) be-*rah*-puh *lah*-muh   *Sudah berapa lama di*
  dee mah-*lay*-see-ah?   *Malaysia?*

I've been here for two weeks.
  sai-yuh *soo*-dah(h) *doo*-uh   *Saya sudah dua minggu*
  ming-goo dee *see*-nee   *di sini.*

How long will you be in Malaysia?
  be-*rah*-puh *lah*-muh *ahn*-duh   *Berapa lama anda di*
  dee mah-*lay*-see-ah?   *Malaysia?*

I'll be in Malaysia for (one month).
  sai-yuh *ah*-kahn ber-*ah*-duh   *Saya akan berada di*
  dee mah-*lay*-see-ah se-*lah*-muh *Malaysia selama*
  (se-*boo*-lahn)   *(sebulan).*

Where have you been so far?
  soo-dah(h) ke *mah*-nuh?   *Sudah ke mana?*

I've been to Penang and Ipoh.
sai-yuh soo-dah(h) ke pee-*nahng*   Saya sudah ke Penang
dan *ee*-po(h)   dan Ipoh.

Have you been to Mersing?
soo-dah(h) ke *mer*-sing?   Sudah ke Mersing?

Not yet.
be-*lum*   Belum.

Yes, I have.
soo-dah(h)   Sudah.

Are you here on holiday?
ahn-duh *choo*-tee dee *see*-nee?   Anda cuti di sini?

I'm here ...	*sai*-yuh ...	Saya ...
for a holiday	ber-*choo*-tee	bercuti
on business	ber-*ker*-juh	bekerja
to study	be-*lah*-jahr	belajar

How long are you here for?
be-*rah*-puh *lah*-muh *ahn*-duh   Berapa lama anda di sini?
dee *see*-nee?

I'm/We're here for ... weeks/days.
sai-yuh/*kah*-mee dee   Saya/Kami di
see-nee se-*lah*-muh   sini selama
... *ming*-goo/*hah*-ree   ... minggu/hari.

Do you like it here?
ah-duh-kah(h) *ahn*-duh   Adakah anda
soo-kuh dee *see*-nee?   suka di sini?

I/We like it here very much.
sai-yuh/*kah*-mee *sah*-ngaht   Saya/Kami sangat
soo-kuh dee *see*-nee   suka di sini.

Can you eat spicy food?
bo-*leh*(h) *mah*-kahn   Boleh makan
mah-kah-nahn pe-*dahs*?   makanan pedas?

I (don't) like spicy food.
sai-yuh (tah(k)) *soo*-kuh   Saya (tak) suka
mah-kah-nahn pe-*dahs*   makanan pedas.

useful words & phrases

English	Pronunciation	Malay
Sure.	be-*tul*	Betul.
It's OK.	tah(k) *ah*-puh	Tak apa.
Are you ready?	soo-dah(h) see-**ahp**?	Sudah siap?
Just a minute.	se-*ben*-tahr/ se-ke-*jahp*	Sebentar/ Sekejap.
Wait!	*toong*-goo!	Tunggu!
Look!	*lee*-haht!	Lihat!
Listen!	de-*ngahr*-lah(h)!	Dengarlah!
I'm ready.	*sai*-yuh see-*ahp*	Saya siap.
Slow down!	per-lah-*hahn* see-*kit*!	Perlahan sikit!
Hurry up!	che-*paht* see-*kit*!	Cepat sikit!
Go away!	per-*gee*-lah(h)!	Pergilah!
Watch out!	ber-*hah*-ti-*hah*-ti!	Berhati-hati!
It's (not) possible.	(*tee*-dah(k)/tah(k)) bo-*leh*(h)	(Tidak/Tak) Boleh.
I forgot.	*sai*-yuh *loo*-puh	Saya lupa.
It's (not) important.	(*tee*-dah(k)/tah(k)) pen-*ting*	(Tidak/Tak) Penting.
It doesn't matter.	tah(k) *ah*-puh	Tak apa.
Let's go!	*joom*-lah(h)!	Jumlah!

What are you doing?
    ahn-duh *boo*-aht *ah*-puh?   *Anda buat apa?*

Are you waiting too?
    ahn-duh me-*noong*-goo   *Anda menunggu juga?*
    joo-guh?

Do you live here?
    ahn-duh *ting*-gahl dee   *Anda tinggal di sini?*
    see-nee?

---

lean on me

Physical contact between the same sex is considered normal in Malaysia. You'll see boys hanging out with their arms around each other's shoulders, and women holding hands with their close friends or relatives.

What's your opinion about ...?
ah-puh-kah(h)
pen-*dah*-paht
ahn-duh ten-tahng ...?

Apakah pendapat anda tentang ...?

It's hot!
pah-nahs kahn!

Panas, kan!

Beautiful, isn't it!
chahn-ti(k) boo-*kahn*!

Cantik, bukan!

That's strange!
pe-*li(k)*-nyuh!

Peliknya!

That's funny! (amusing)
lah-*wah(k)*-nyuh!

Lawaknya!

nationalities

In Malay, you'll find that many names of countries are similar to the English names, but pronounced slightly differently.

Where are you from?
ahn-duh ber-*ah*-sahl *dah*-ree mah-nuh?

Anda berasal dari mana?

I'm from ...	sai-yuh ber-*ah*-sahl dah-ree ...	Saya berasal dari ...
Australia	*	Australia
Canada	*	Kanada
England	*ing*-ge-ris	Inggeris
Europe	e-*ro*-pah(h)	Eropah
India	*	India
Ireland	*	Ireland
Japan	*jeh*-poon	Jepun
New Zealand	*	New Zealand
Scotland	*	Scotland
the USA	*	Amerika
Wales	*	Wales
(* as in English)		

SOCIAL

126

I'm ...	*sai*-yuh *o*-rahng ...	*Saya orang ...*
Australian	*	*Australia*
Dutch	be-*lahn*-duh	*Belanda*
English	*ing*-ge-ris	*Inggeris*

I live in a/the ...	*sai*-yuh *ting*-gahl dee ...	*Saya tinggal di ...*
city	*bahn*-dahr	*bandar*
countryside	loo-*ahr bahn*-dahr	*luar bandar*
seaside	*pahn*-tai	*pantai*
suburbs of ...	*ping*-geer	*pinggir*
	bahn-dahr ...	*bandar ...*
village	*kahm*-pung	*kampung*

cultural differences

perbezaan kebudayaan

How do you do this in your country?
bah-gai-*mah*-nuh *ee*-nee
dee-*boo*-aht dee ne-*gah*-ruh
ahn-duh?

Bagaimana ini dibuat di negara anda?

Is this a local or national custom?
ah-daht *ee*-nee *ah*-daht
dah-*eh*-rah(h) ah-*tow ah*-daht
nah-see-*o*-nahl?

Adat ini adat daerah atau adat nasional?

I don't want to offend you.
sai-yuh tah(k) nah(k)
me-*nying*-goong pe-*rah*-sah-ahn
ahn-duh

Saya tak nak menyinggung perasaan anda.

I'm sorry, it's not the custom in my country.
    mah-*ahf*, *ah*-daht *ee*-nee tah(k)
    bee-*ah*-suh dee ne-*gah*-ruh
    sai-yuh

Maaf, adat ini tak biasa di negara saya.

I don't mind watching, but I'd prefer not to participate.
    sai-yuh le-*bi(h)* se-nahng
    me-*non*-ton dah-ree-*pah*-duh
    me-*lee*-baht-kahn *di*-ree

Saya lebih senang menonton daripada melibatkan diri.

age

umur

It's not off-limits to ask someone's age in Malaysia, so expect it often. One response could be *Cuba teka*, *choo*-buh *teh*-kuh, 'Guess!'

How old are you?	be-*rah*-puh oo-moor *ahn*-duh?	*Berapa umur anda?*
I'm ... years old.	oo-moor *sai*-yuh ... *tah*-hoon	*Umur saya ... tahun.*
20	*doo*-uh *poo*-lu(h)	*dua puluh*
35	*tee*-gah *poo*-lu(h) *lee*-muh	*tiga puluh lima*

(See **Numbers & Amounts** on page 39 for your age.)

occupations

pekerjaan

What's your occupation?
    ah-puh pe-*ker*-jah-ahn *ahn*-duh?

Apa pekerjaan anda?

What do you do?
    ahn-duh ber-*ker*-jah se-*bah*-gai *ah*-puh?

Anda bekerja sebagai apa?

I'm (a/an) ...	sai-yuh ...	Saya ...
artist	ahr-tees	artis
businessperson	pe-nee-ah-gah	peniaga
chef	too-kahng mah-sah(k)	tukang masak
doctor	dok-tor	doktor
engineer	joo-roo-te-rah	jurutera
factory worker	pe-ker-jah kee-lahng	pekerja kilang
farmer	pe-tah-nee	petani
journalist	wahr-tah-wahn	wartawan
lawyer	pe-gwahm	peguam
lecturer (university)	pen-shah-rah(h)	pensyarah
mechanic	me-kan-ik	mekanik
musician	pe-main	pemain
	moo-zi(k)	muzik
nurse	joo-roo-rah-waht	jururawat
office worker	pe-gah-wai	pegawai
retired	pe-sah-ruh	pesara
scientist	sain-tees	saintis
secretary	joo-roo-taip	jurutaip
student (school)	moo-rid/pe-lah-jahr	murid/pelajar
student (uni)	pe-lah-jahr	pelajar
teacher (school)	goo-roo/chi(k)-goo	guru/cikgu
unemployed	pe-ngahng-goor	penganggur
waiter	pe-lai-ahn	pelayan
writer	pe-noo-lees	penulis

What are you studying?	ahn-duh be-lah-jahr ah-puh?	Anda belajar apa?
I'm studying ...	sai-yuh be-lah-jahr ...	Saya belajar ...
art	ke-se-nee-ahn	kesenian
business	per-nee-ah-gah-ahn	perniagaan
engineering	ke-joo-te-rah-ahn	kejuteraan
languages	bah-hah-suh	bahasa
law	oon-dahng-oon-dahng	undang-undang
literature	sahs-ter-ah	sastera
medicine	per-oo-bah-tahn	perubatan
science	sains	sains
teaching	pen-gah-jahr-ahn	pengajaran

You may offer to help prepare food or clean up, but as a guest, your host will insist you sit and do nothing:

'Don't bother yourself.'
jah-ngahn soo-sah(h)-soo-sah(h)
Jangan susah-susah.

If the host asks you what you'd like to eat or drink, you may reply with the same phrase. When you get to the table, you'll hear:

'Please drink/eat.'
see-luh mee-num/*mah*-kahn
Sila minum/makan.

Decline an offer when it's first made – this is good manners. Then go for it!

religion

agama

Most Malays are Muslim; Malaysians of other backgrounds may also be Muslim, Christian, Hindu or Buddhist. Religion is considered essential in everyone's life, and you'll maintain better relations by claiming to have one, or by saying your parents belong to one.

What's your religion?	*ahn*-duh ber-ah-*gah*-muh *ah*-puh?	Anda beragama apa?
My religion is ...	ah-*gah*-muh *sai*-yuh ...	Agama saya ...
Buddhist	*boo*-duh	Buda
Catholic	*kah*-to-lik	Katolik
Christian	*kris*-ti-ahn	Kristian
Hindu	*hin*-doo	Hindu
Jewish	yah-*hoo*-dee	Yahudi
Muslim	*is*-lahm	Islam
Protestant	*pro*-tes-tahn	Protestan

I'm ... but not practising.
   sai-yuh ber-ah-*gah*-muh ...   *Saya beragama ...*
   tah-pee jah-*rahng* ke ge-*reh*-jah   *tapi jarang ke gereja.*

My parents are ...
   ee-boo *bah*-puh *sai*-yuh   *Ibu bapa saya*
   ber-ah-*gah*-muh …   *beragama ...*

I think I believe in God.
   sai-yuh *rah*-suh *sai*-yuh   *Saya rasa saya*
   per-*chah*-yuh ke-*pah*-duh   *percaya kepada*
   too-hahn   *Tuhan.*

I'm not religious.
   sai-yuh *tee*-dah(k)   *Saya tidak*
   ber-ah-*gah*-muh   *beragama.*

---

the sisterhood

Considering that the official religion of Malaysia is Islam, women in general have a great deal of freedom and rights. There's a strong female presence in the working world, both in government – several cabinet ministers are women – and the private sector.

Civil laws generally cover all Malaysians, except in the area of family law, in which Muslims must follow Syariah court rulings. These laws are discriminatory against women, and many are working towards addressing these inequities. For example, it is very easy for a Muslim man to divorce his wife: he simply says, "I divorce you." A woman, on the other hand, must go through the Syariah courts to get a divorce.

Since 1979, many Malay women have made the personal decision to wear clothing that covers their whole body, except for their face and hands. Women travelling in Malaysia will need to have a think about what is appropriate in a Muslim country. Wearing short skirts, skimpy shorts or beach gear in public will only reinforce negative stereotypes and may be seen to encourage harassment. Covering up more than you usually would, and even covering your head with a scarf in rural areas or on the east coast, will help.

I believe in destiny/fate.
> sai-yuh per-chah-yuh
> ke-pah-duh tah(k)-dir

*Saya percaya
kepada takdir.*

**I'm interested in astrology/
philosophy.**
> sai-yuh ter-tah-ri(k) ke-pah-duh
> ahs-tro-lo-gee/fahl-sah-fah(h)

*Saya tertarik kepada
astrologi/falsafah.*

I'm an atheist.
> sai-yuh ay-thee-is

Saya atheis.

I'm agnostic.
> sai-yuh ahg-nos-tik

Saya agnostik.

family

Family is all-important to Malaysians. Family ties are expressed in everyday conversations through the use of words like abang, ah-bahng, 'big brother' and makcik, mah(k)-chi(k), 'auntie'. Whether at the market or in someone's home, you'll almost certainly be asked questions about yourself and the members of your family.

Are you married?   soo-dah(h) kah(h)-win?   *Sudah kahwin?*

Unless you have tied the knot, in which case you reply soo-dah(h) 'already', the best answer is:

Not yet.   be-lum lah-gee   *Belum lagi.*

Saying tidak, tee-dah(k), 'no', would be grammatically fine, b|
many Malaysians might think it's weird if you're not marrie|
or at least thinking about it. Also, the word for 'friend', kawa|
kah-wahn, often implies a romantic relationship. Ada kawan?, d|
duh kah-wahn?, may actually mean:

Do you have a boyfriend/girlfriend?
> ah-duh pah(k)-we/mah(k)-we?

Ada pakwe/makwe?

Is your husband/wife here?
> swah-mee/ees-te-ree ahn-duh
> dee see-nee?

Suami/Isteri anda di sin|

Do you have any brothers and sisters?
  ah-duh ah-*di(k)*-be-*rah*-di(k)?　　　*Ada adik-beradik?*
Do you have any children?
  soo-dah(h) *ah*-duh *ah*-nah(k)?　　　*Sudah ada anak?*
How many children do you have?
  be-*rah*-puh o-rahng *ah*-nah(k)?　　　*Berapa orang anak?*

I'm not married yet.
  sai-yuh be-*lum*　　　　　　　　*Saya belum*
  kah(h)-win/*nee*-kah(h)　　　　　*kahwin/nikah.*
I'm still single.
  sai-yuh *mah*-si(h) *boo*-jahng　　*Saya masih bujang.*
I'm married.
  sai-yuh *soo*-dah(h) *kah(h)*-win　*Saya sudah kahwin.*
I don't have any children (yet).
  sai-yuh *tee*-dah(k) (be-*lum*)　　*Saya tidak (belum)*
  ah-duh *ah*-nah(k)　　　　　　　*ada anak.*

This is my ...	*ee*-nee ... *sai*-yuh	*Ini ... saya.*
I have ...	*sai*-yuh *ah*-duh ...	*Saya ada ...*
one son	se-*o*-rahng *ah*-nah(k) le-*lah*-kee	*seorang anak lelaki*
three sons	*tee*-guh o-rahng *ah*-nah(k) le-*lah*-kee	*tiga orang anak lelaki*
one daughter	se-*o*-rahng *ah*-nah(k) pe-*rem*-pwahn	*seorang anak perempuan*

---

heart-warming

You'll find that many people, especially the Malays, follow the handshake with a touch of the heart, a habit worth forming. In cases where respect is called for, such as when a young child greets an elder, the child will kiss the elder's hand and then sometimes touch it to their own forehead.

family members

Brothers and sisters are always referred to as older or younger.

aunt	*mah(k)-chi(k)*	makcik
boyfriend	*pah(k)-we/te-mahn*	pakwe/teman
	le-lah-kee	lelaki
child(ren)	*ah-nah(k)(-ah-nah(k))*	anak(-anak)
cousin	*se-poo-poo*	sepupu
daughter	*ah-nah(k)*	anak
(unmarried)	*pe-rem-pwahn*	perempuan
	ah-nah(k) dah-ruh	anak dara
eldest	*soo-long*	sulong
family	*ke-loo-ahr-guh*	keluarga
father	*bah-pah(k)/ai-yah(h)*	bapak/ayah
friend	*kah-wahn*	kawan
girlfriend	*mah(k)-we/te-mahn*	makwe/teman
	wah-nee-tuh	wanita
grandchild	*choo-choo*	cucu
grandfather	*dah-tu(k)*	datuk
grandmother	*neh-neh(k)*	nenek
husband	*swah-mee*	suami
mother	*mah(k)/ee-boo*	mak/ibu
older brother	*ah-bahng le-lah-kee*	abang lelaki
older sister	*kah-kah(k)*	kakak
	pe-rem-pwahn	perempuan
partner	*pah-sahng-ahn*	pasangan

no means no

Malaysians have a variety of ways of avoiding a direct answer, especially when it's a negative one. If you feel uncomfortable answering a particular question try some of the following (a smile works too!):

I don't know.	*sai-yuh tah(k) tah-hoo*	Saya tak tahu.
I'm busy.	*sai-yuh see-bu(k)*	Saya sibuk.
It's not appropriate.	*ee-nee tah(k) se-swai*	Ini tak sesuai.

134

son	*ah*-nah(k) le-*lah*-kee	*anak lelaki*
uncle	*pah(k)*-chi(k)	*pakcik*
wife	*ees*-te-ree	*isteri*
younger brother	ah-*di(k)* le-*lah*-kee	*adik lelaki*
younger sister	ah-*di(k)* pe-*rem*-pwahn	*adik perempuan*
youngest	*bong*-soo	*bongsu*

body language

bahasa badan

A growing number of Malays feel that handshaking, or any casual physical contact between the sexes is inappropriate and against the teachings of Islam. Particularly in the more conservative northern states, or in rural areas, it's better to smile instead when meeting someone of the opposite sex. If they extend their hand, then by all means, shake it! Handshaking is otherwise widely accepted: a gentle brush of the palms rather than a knuckle-crusher is what you should aim for. It's appropriate to shake hands when being introduced, when visiting somebody in their home, or when you haven't seen someone for a while.

Touching someone's head is generally considered rude. If someone is sitting on the floor in a home, stepping over their legs is not the thing to do either. Walk around their legs, no matter how inconvenient it is. It's also considered polite to bow your body slightly and extend your right arm straight downwards towards the floor when crossing the path of someone who's seated, or when interrupting people. At the same time you can say *maaf*, mah-ahf, 'excuse me'.

feelings

I'm ...	sai-yuh ...	Saya ...
Are you ...?	ah-duh-kah(h) ahn-duh ... ?	Adakah anda ...?
afraid	tah-kut	takut
angry	mah-rah(h)	marah
bored	bo-sahn	bosan
cold	se-joo(k)	sejuk
disgusted	men-yahm-pah(h)	menyampah
full	ken-yahng	kenyang
grateful	ber-shoo-koor	bersyukur
happy	gem-bee-ruh	gembira
hot	pah-nahs	panas
hungry	lah-pahr	lapar
in a hurry	ter-ge-suh-ge-suh	tergesa-gesa
keen	ber-soong-guh soong-guh	bersungguh-sungguh
alright (content)	pwahs	puas
sad	se-di(h)	sedih
sick	sah-kit	sakit
sleepy	meng-ahn-to(k)	mengantuk
sorry (condolence)	ta(k)-zee-ah(h)	takziah
sorry (regret)	me-nye-sahl	menyesal
thirsty	hows	haus
tired	le-ti(h)	letih
well	bai(k)	baik
worried	bim-bahng	bimbang

breaking the language barrier

Do you speak English?
ah-duh-kah(h) ahn-duh
ber-bah-hah-suh ing-ge-ris?

Adakah anda
berbahasa Inggeris?

Yes./No.
  yah/tah(k) bo-*leh(h)*   Ya./Tak boleh.

I can only speak a little Malay.
  sai-yuh *hahn*-yuh
  ber-bah-*hah*-suh me-*lah*-yoo   Saya hanya
  se-*dee*-kit *sah*-juh   berbahasa Melayu
     sedikit saja.

Do you understand?
  ah-duh-kah(h) *ahn*-duh   Adakah anda
  fah-hahm?   faham?

I (don't) understand.
  sai-yuh (tah(k)) *fah*-hahm   Saya (tak) faham.

How do you say ... in Malay?
  mah-chahm *mah*-nuh   Macam mana
  chah-kahp ... dah-*lahm*   cakap ... dalam
  bah-*hah*-suh me-*lah*-yoo?   Bahasa Melayu?

What's this called?
  ah-puh nee?   Apa ni?

What does this mean?
  ah-puh *mah(k)*-sud-nyuh?   Apa maksudnya?

Please speak slowly.
  to-long *chah*-kahp   Tolong cacap
  per-*lah*-hahn *see*-kit   perlahan sikit.

**Please write that word
down for me.**
  to-long *too*-lis-kahn   Tolong tuliskan
  per-kah-*tah*-ahn *ee*-too   perkataan itu
  oon-tu(k) *sai*-yuh   untuk saya.

Please repeat that.
  to-long oo-*lah*-ngee   Tolong ulangi.

Please translate for me.
  to-long ter-je-*mah(h)*-kahn   Tolong terjemahkan
  oon-tu(k) *sai*-yuh   untuk saya.

staying in touch

Where are you staying?
ahn-duh *doo*-du(k) dee
mah-nuh?

Anda duduk di mana?

What's your address?
ah-puh-kah(h) *ah*-lah-maht
ahn-duh?

Apakah alamat anda?

I'm staying at ...
sai-yuh *doo*-du(k) dee ...

Saya duduk di ...

Can we meet again?
bo-*leh(h)*-kah(h) *kee*-tuh
ber-*joom*-puh *lah*-gee?

*Bolehkah kita
berjumpa lagi?*

Let's meet at (6 o'clock) at ...
kee-tuh ber-*te*-moo *pah*-duh
(*poo*-kool e-*nahm*) dee ...

*Kita bertemu
(pukul enam) di ...*

Come to my house any time.
dah-tahng ke *roo*-mah(h)
sai-yuh *bee*-luh-*bee*-luh
sah-juh

*Datang ke rumah
saya bila-bila
saja.*

going out

When the hot sun goes down over Malaysia, the air cools and activity picks up! Bustling night markets open just before sunset, offering myriad food, goods and people-watching opportunities. Shopping malls are packed and the big cities have plenty of coffee shops, clubs, pubs and bars.

Where's a ...?	... dee *mah*-nuh?	... *di mana?*
I'd like to go	*sai*-yuh nah(k)	*Saya nak*
to a ...	*per*-gee ke ...	*pergi ke ...*
bar	bahr	*bar*
cafe	ka-*fay*	*cafe*

SOCIAL

138

food stalls	ge-*rai*	*gerai*
nightclub	ke-*lahb mah*-lahm	*kelab malam*
night market	*pah*-sahr *mah*-lahm	*pasar malam*
I feel like ...	*sai*-yuh nah(k) ...	*Saya nak ...*
dancing	me-*nah*-ree	*menari*
eating	*mah*-kahn	*makan*
watching a film	me-*non*-ton *fee*-lem	*menonton filem*
I feel like going to a/the ...	*sai*-yuh nah(k) ke ...	*Saya nak ke ...*
cinema	*pahng*-gung	*panggung*
	wai-yahng	*wayang*
concert	*kon*-sert	*konsert*
shadow	per-*toon*-joo(k)-ahn	*pertunjukan*
puppet show	*wai*-yahng *koo*-lit	*wayang kulit*
theatre	*tee*-ah-ter; *chan*-dee	*teater; candi*
	wah-rah	*wara*

common interests

Malaysians undertake leisure time with gusto. The worst feeling for many is boringlah, *boh*-reeng-lah(h), an adaption of the English word boring. The opposite feeling is shiok, *shee*-oh(k), 'delicious and wonderful'.

Do you like ...?	*ahn*-duh *soo*-kuh ...?	*Anda suka ...?*
I (don't) like ...	*sai*-yuh (tah(k))	*Saya (tak)*
	soo-kuh ...	*suka ...*
art	ke-se-*nee*-ahn	*kesenian*
cooking	me-*mah*-sah(k)	*memasak*
dancing	me-*nah*-ree	*menari*
traditional)	trah-di-see-o-nahl	*tradisional*
discos	*dis*-ko	*disko*
film	*fee*-lem;	*filem;*
	wai-yahng	*wayang*
	gahm-bahr	*gambar*
going out	ber-*jah*-lahn-*jah*-lahn	*berjalan-jalan*

going shopping	mem-be-*lee*-be-*lah(h)*	*membeli-belah*
music	*moo*-zi(k)	*muzik*
photography	fo-to-*grah*-fee	*fotografi*
playing sport	ber-*soo*-kahn	*bersukan*
reading books	mem-*bah*-chuh	*membaca*
	boo-koo	*buku*
the theatre	*tee*-ah-ter;	*teater*;
	sahn-dee-*wah*-rah	*sandiwara*
travelling	men-gem-*bah*-ruh	*mengembara*
travel	kem-*bah*-ruh	*kembara*
watching TV	me-*non*-ton tee vee	*menonton TV*
writing	me-*noo*-lis	*menulis*

sport

sukan

Malaysians are into sport, especially badminton and *bola sepak*, *bo*-luh *seh*-pah(k), 'soccer'. Malaysian badminton players rank among the best in the world. The national soccer league *Liga Malaysia* also has a passionate following. *Sepak takraw*, *seh*-pah(k) *tah*-kraw, is an impressive game, common in Malaysia, Indonesia and Thailand. Balls made of *rotan*, *ro*-tahn, 'rattan' are used like volleyballs. Players can only use their heads and feet to get the ball back and forth over the net, without letting it touch the ground.

Do you like sport?
ahn-duh *soo*-kuh	*Anda suka*
ber-*soo*-kahn?	*bersukan?*

I like playing sport.
sai-yuh *soo*-kuh	*Saya suka*
ber-*soo*-kahn	*bersukan.*

Do you play ...? — *ahn*-duh main ... tah(k)? — *Anda main ... tak?*
Would you like — *ahn*-duh nah(k) — *Anda nak*
to play/go/do ...? main ...? — *main ...?*

badminton	*bahd*-min-ton	*badminton*
basketball	*bo*-luh ke-*rahn*-jahng	*bola keranjang*

boxing	*teen*-joo	*tinju*
diving	me-nye-*lahm*	*menyelam*
soccer	*bo*-luh seh-pah(k)	*bola sepak*
gymnastics	jim-*nahs*-tik	*gimnastik*
hockey	*ho*-kee	*hoki*
martial arts	se-*nee* mem-per-*tah*-hahn-kahn *di*-ree	*seni memperta-hankan diri*
rugby	*rahg*-bee	*ragbi*
water skiing	main skee air	*main ski air*
soccer	*bo*-luh seh-pah(k)	*bola sepak*
surfing	ber-se-*lahn*-chahr	*berselancar*
swimming	be-re-*nahng*	*berenang*
table tennis	*ping*-pong	*ping-pong*
tennis	*teh*-nis	*tenis*
takraw	*seh*-pah(k) *tah*-kraw	*sepak takraw*
top (spinning)	*gah*-sing	*gasing*

homestays

Hospitality on a formal level is the norm when you're invited into a Malaysian home. If you stay in a rural or small town setting, you'll probably be treated like a star! Don't be surprised to see the neighbourhood children peering in a door or window to gawk at the *orang asing*, o-rahng *ah*-sing, 'foreigner'.

It's good to bring a small gift *buah tangan*, *boo*-ah(h) *tah*-ngahn, (lit: fruit hand): a bag of fruit such as oranges or apples, or a small souvenir from your country. It's considered polite to greet and shake hands with every adult present – remember to wait for the hand extended from the opposite sex – and sometimes the children, too. Bringing photos of your home or family, or a map of your country, is a good idea.

Savoury and sweet cakes and tidbits are common fare in Malaysian homes. If they're not to your liking, just take a few bites. It's considered rude to refuse to eat or drink what is served. If you're unable to eat certain things, it's best to tell your host or hostess early.

I'm sorry, I can't eat wheat flour;
I have an allergy.

mah-*ahf, sai*-yuh tah(k) bo-*leh(h)*
mah-kahn te-*pong gahn*-doom
se-*bahb sai*-yuh *ah*-duh *ah*-ler-jee

Maaf, saya tak boleh
makan tepong gandum,
sebab saya ada alergi.

(the English word 'allergy' is also widely understood)

I have diabetes so I can't have sugar.

sai-yuh *ah*-duh dai-ah-*bee*-tees
jah-dee tah(k) bo-*leh(h)*
mah-kahn *goo*-luh

Saya ada diabetes,
jadi tak boleh
makan gula.

Sorry, I've just eaten.

mah-*ahf sai*-yuh bah-*roo*
mah-kahn

Maaf, saya baru
makan.

When you feel it's time to go, say *Saya nak balik dulu, sai*-yuh
nah(k) bah-*li(k)* doo-loo, 'I'm going home first'. The family will
undoubtedly urge you to stay, but take your leave with *Terima*
kasih banyak-banyak!, te-*ree*-muh *kah*-si(h) *bah*-nyah(k)-*bah*-
nyah(k), 'thanks very, very much'.

In the Country

Di Luar Bandar

camping

berkhemah

Malaysia offers cheap camping options: many of the national parks have camping grounds, and you can set up anywhere in the country. Sites near waterfalls and other jungle areas easily accessible by road are popular, so they can be crowded and a bit messy. Men and women can camp together, but again, it's best to say you're married to avoid any hassles.

The weather is wet, warm and humid and there are plenty of bugs. Make sure your tent has mosquito netting.

Can we camp here?
bo-*leh(h)* ber-*kheh*-mah(h)   *Boleh berkhemah di sini?*
dee *see*-nee?

How much is it per person/tent?
be-*rah*-puh *hahr*-guh-nyuh   *Berapa harganya*
oon-tu(k) *sah*-too o-rahng/   *untuk satu orang/*
kheh-mah(h)?   *khemah?*

Where can I hire a tent?
kheh-mah(h) dee-*seh*-wuh   *Khemah disewa di mana?*
dee *mah*-nuh?

Are there shower facilities?
ah-duh tem-*paht*   *Ada tempat*
mahn-dee tah(k)?   *mandi tak?*

backpack	behg *sahn*-dahr	*beg sandar*
campground	kah-*wah*-sahn	*kawasan*
	per-*kheh*-mah(h)-ahn	*perkhemahan*
camping	ber-*kheh*-mah(h)	*berkhemah*
campsite	*tah*-pah(k)	*tapak*
	per-*kheh*-mah(h)-ahn	*perkhemahan*
firewood	*kai*-yoo *ah*-pee	*kayu api*

143

mat	*tee-*kahr	*tikar*
mosquito net	ke-*lahm-*boo	*kelambu*
national park	*tah-*mahn ne-*gah-*ruh	*taman negara*
penknife	*pee-*sow *lee-*paht	*pisau lipat*
sleeping bag	*kahn-*tung *tee-*dur	*kantung tidur*
stove (burner)	*dah-*pur	*dapur*
tent	*kheh-*mah(h)	*khemah*
torch (flashlight)	*lahm-*poo *soo-*luh	*lampu suluh*

hiking

Are there any tourist attractions near here?
   *ah-*duh tem-*paht tah-*ree-kahn
   pe-*lahn-*cong de-*kaht see-*nee?

*Ada tempat tarikan
pelancong dekat sini?*

Where's the nearest village?
   dee *mah-*nuh *kahm-*pung
   yahng *pah-*ling de-*kaht?*

*Di mana kampung
yang paling dekat?*

Is it safe to climb this mountain?
   se-*lah-*maht-kah(h) *oon-*tu(k)
   men-*dah-*kee *goo-*nung *ee-*nee?

*Selamatkah untuk
mendaki gunung ini?*

Is there a hut up there?
   *ah-*duh *pon-*do(k)-kah(h) dee *ah-*tahs?

Ada pondokkah di atas?

Do I need a guide?
   *ah-*duh-kah(h) *sai-*yuh per-*loo*
   pe-*mahn-*doo pe-*lahn-*chong?

*Adakah saya perlu
pemandu pelancong?*

**Where can I find out about hiking
trails in the region?**
   dee *mah-*nuh *ah-*duh*
   *mah(k)-*loo-maht *tehn-*tahng
   je-*jah-*kahn me-*rehn-*tahs
   *hoo-*tahn dee dah-*eh-*rah(h) *ee-*nee?

*Di mana ada
maklumat tentang
jejakan merentas
hutan di daerah ini?*

**I'd like to talk to someone who
knows this area.**
   *sai-*yuh nah(k) ber-*chah-*kahp*
   de-*ngahn se-se-*o-*rahng

*Saya nak bercakap
dengan seseorang*

yahng *tah*-hoo *tehn*-tahng
dah-*eh*-rah(h) *ee*-nee

yang tahu tentang
daerah ini.

How long is the trail?
be-*rah*-puh *pahn*-jahng
lo-rong me-*rehn*-tahs
hoo-tahn *ee*-nee?

Berapa panjang
lorong merentas
hutan ini?

Is the track well marked?
ah-duh-kah(h) *trehk*-nyuh
dee-*tahn*-duh de-ngahn bai(k)?

Adakah treknya
ditanda dengan baik?

How high is the climb?
be-*rah*-puh *ting*-gee
pen-dah-*kee*-ahn *ee*-nee?

Berapa tinggi
pendakian ini?

Which is the shortest/easiest route?
yahng *mah*-nuh
lah-loo-ahn yahng
pah-ling che-*paht*/*moo*-dah(h)?

Yang mana
laluan yang
paling cepat/mudah?

When does it get dark?
bee-luh-kah(h)
hah-ree *moo*-luh ge-*lahp*?

Bilakah
hari mula gelap?

Is it very scenic?
pe-*mahn*-dahng-ahn-nyuh
in-dah(h) se-*kah*-lee tah(k)?

Pemandangannya
indah sekali tak?

Where can I hire mountain gear?
ah-laht men-*dah*-kee
goo-nung dee-*seh*-wuh
dee *mah*-nuh?

Alat mendaki
gunung disewa
di mana?

Where can we buy supplies?
be-*kah*-lahn dee-*joo*-ahl
dee *mah*-nuh?

Bekalan dijual
di mana?

on the path

dalam perjalanan

Where have you come from?
ahn-duh *dah*-tahng
dah-ree *mah*-nuh?

Anda datang
dari mana?

How long did it take you?
be-*rah*-puh *lah*-muh
per-*jah*-lah-nahn *ah*-wah(k)?

*Berapa lama
perjalanan awak?*

Does this path go to ...?
ah-duh-kah(h) *jah*-lahn
ee-nee me-*noo*-joo ke ...?

*Adakah jalan
ini menuju ke ...?*

Where can we spend the night?
dee *mah*-nuh *kah*-mee
bo-*leh(h)* ber-*mah*-lahm?

*Di mana kami
boleh bermalam?*

**Can I leave some things
here for a while?**
bo-*leh(h)* sim-pahn bah-*rahng*
dee *see*-nee se-ke-*jahp*?

*Boleh simpan barang
di sini sekejap?*

There's a cave here.
ah-duh *goo*-ah dee *see*-nee

Ada gua di sini.

I'm lost.	*sai*-yuh ter-*seh*-saht	*Saya tersesat.*
altitude	ke-*ting*-gee-ahn	*ketinggian*
binoculars	te-*ro*-pong	*teropong*
candles	*lee*-lin	*lilin*
to climb	men-*dah*-kee/	*mendaki/*
	me-*nai*-kee	*menaiki*
compass	*kom*-pahs	*kompas*
downhill	*too*-roon *boo*-kit	*turun bukit*
first-aid kit	*ko*-tah(k)	*kotak*
	ke-che-*mah*-sahn	*kecemasan*
gloves	*sah*-rung tah-*ngahn*	*sarung tangan*
guide	pe-mahn-doo	*pemandu*
guided trek	trehk yahng	*trek yang*
	ber-*pahn*-doo	*berpandu*

hiking	me-*rehn*-tahs *hoo*-tahn	*merentas hutan*
hiking boots	*kah*-sut me-*rehn*-tahs *hoo*-tahn	*kasut merentas hutan*
hunting	ber-*boo*-roo	*berburu*
ledge	*bi*-rai	*birai*
lookout	tem-*paht* me-*mahn*-dahng	*tempat memandang*
map	*peh*-tuh	*peta*
mountain climbing	men-*dah*-kee *goo*-nung	*mendaki gunung*
pick	be-*lee*-ung	*beliung*
provisions	be-*kah*-lahn	*bekalan*
rock climbing	me-*mahn*-jaht *bah*-too	*memanjat batu*
rope	*tah*-lee	*tali*
short cut	*jah*-lahn *pin*-tahs	*jalan pintas*
signpost	*tahn*-duh *jah*-lahn	*tanda jalan*
steep	*choo*-rahm	*curam*
track	trehk; *jah*-lahn ke-*chil*; *lo*-rong	*trek; jalan kecil; lorong*
trek	trehk	*trek*
uphill	nai(k) *boo*-kit	*naik bukit*
to walk	ber-*jah*-lahn *kah*-kee	*berjalan kaki*

at the beach

Can we swim here?
bo-*leh(h)* be-re-*nahng* dee *see*-nee?
Boleh berenang di sini?

Is it safe to swim here?
se-lah-*maht*-kah(h) be-re-*nahng* dee *see*-nee?
Selamatkah berenang di sini?

What time is high/low tide?
poo-kool be-*rah*-puh air *pah*-sahng *ting*-gee/*rehn*-dah(h)?
Pukul berapa air pasang tinggi/rendah?

147

coast	*pahn*-tai	*pantai*
diving	me-nye-*lahm*	*menyelam*
fishing	me-*mahn*-ching	*memancing*
marine reserve	*tah*-mahn	*taman*
	sim-pah-nahn lowt	*simpanan laut*
reef	*bah*-too *kah*-rahng	*batu karang*
sand	*pah*-sir	*pasir*
sea	lowt	*laut*
snorkelling	*snor*-kel	*snorkel*
sunblock	pe-*lin*-dung	*pelindung*
	chah-*hai*-yuh	*cahaya*
	mah-tuh-*hah*-ree	*matahari*
sunglasses	cher-*min mah*-tuh	*cermin*
	hee-tahm	*mata hitam*
surf	*om*-bah(k)	*ombak*
surfboard	*pah*-pahn se-*lahn*-chahr	*papan selancar*
surfing	ber-se-*lahn*-chahr	*berselancar*
swimming	be-re-*nahng*	*berenang*
tide	air *pah*-sahng	*air pasang*
towel	*twah*-luh	*tuala*
waterski	skee air	*ski air*
waves	*om*-bah(k)	*ombak*
windsurfing	ber-se-*lahn*-chahr	*berselancar*
	ah-ngin	*angin*

diving   penyelaman

Are there good diving sites here?
ah-duh tem-*paht*   *Ada tempat*
pe-nye-*lah*-mahn   *penyelaman*
yahng bah-*gus* dee *see*-nee?   *yang bagus di sini?*

Can we hire a diving boat/guide?
bo-*leh*(h)-kah(h) *kah*-mee   *Bolehkah kami*
me-*nyeh*-wuh bot/   *menyewa bot/*
pe-*mahn*-doo *oon*-tu(k)   *pemandu untuk*
me-nye-*lahm*?   *menyelam?*

We'd like to hire diving equipment.
kah-mee nah(k) me-*nyeh*-wuh   *Kami nak menyewa*
ke-leng-*kah*-pahn   *kelengkapan*
pe-nye-*lah*-mahn   *penyelaman.*

I'm interested in exploring wrecks.
sai-yuh ber-*mee*-naht   *Saya berminat*
oon-tuk men-*chah*-ree   *untuk mencari*
kah-pahl *kah*-rahm   *kapal karam.*

weather

Weather reports in Malaysia are always the same. Rain in some places, dry in others. Hot during the day, slightly cooler at night. Humidity: high. In the Klang Valley (Kuala Lumpur and surrounding area) afternoon thunderstorms are common.

What's the weather like?
bah-gai-*mah*-nuh   *Bagaimana*
choo-*ah*-chuh-nyuh?   *cuacanya?*

Today it's ...	choo-*ah*-chuh	*Cuaca hari ini ...*
	hah-ree ee-nee ...	
cloudy	*men*-dung/	*mendung/*
	be-*rah*-wahn	*berawan*
cold	se-*joo*(k)	*sejuk*
flooding	*bahn*-jir	*banjir*
hot	*pah*-nahs	*panas*

blame it on the rain

Malaysia is monsoonal, but only the east coast has a clear season of rain, when it buckets down for days and days. The driest part of the Peninsula is Kuala Pilah, Negeri Sembilan.

| *musim hujan* | the rainy (monsoon) season, October to March |
| *musim kemarau* | the dry season, April to September |

149

humid/wet	lem-*bahb*	*lembab*
raining heavily	hoo-jahn leh-*baht*	*hujan lebat*
raining lightly	ge-*ree*-mis	*gerimis*
warm	koo-*rahng pah*-nahs	*kurang panas*
windy	be-*rah*-ngin	*berangin*
What time is ...?	*poo*-kool be-*rah*-puh ...?	*Pukul berapa ...?*
sunrise	mah-tuh-*hah*-ree ter-*bit*	*matahari terbit*
sunset	mah-tuh-*hah*-ree ter-be-nahm	*matahari terbenam*
cloud	*ah*-wahn	*awan*
fog	*kah*-boos	*kabus*
moon	*bu*-lahn	*bulan*
mud	*loom*-pur	*lumpur*
rain	hoo-*jahn*	*hujan*
sky	lah-*ngit*	*langit*
smoke	*ah*-sahp	*asap*
storm	*ree*-but	*ribut*
sun	mah-tuh-*hah*-ree	*matahari*
typhoon	*tow*-fahn	*taufan*

geographical terms

istilah geografi

atoll	*poo*-low *chin*-chin	*pulau cincin*
beach	*pahn*-tai	*pantai*
bridge	*jahm*-bah-tahn	*jambatan*
cave	*goo*-uh	*gua*
city	*bahn*-dahr	*bandar*

SOCIAL

150

cliff	te-*bing ting*-gee	*tebing tinggi*
earth	*boo*-mee	*bumi*
earthquake	*gehm*-puh *boo*-mee	*gempa bumi*
estuary	moo-*ah*-ruh	*muara*
farm	*lah*-dahng/	*ladang/*
	ke-*bun*	*kebun*
footpath	*lo*-rong ber-*jah*-lahn	*lorong berjalan*
	kah-kee	*kaki*
forest	*hoo*-tahn/*rim*-buh	*hutan/rimba*
gap (narrow pass)	*lah*-loo-ahn sem-*pit*	*laluan sempit*
harbour	pe-*lah*-boo-hahn	*pelabuhan*
hill	*boo*-kit	*bukit*
hot spring	*mah*-tuh air *pah*-nahs	*mata air panas*
jungle	*hoo*-tahn/*rim*-buh	*hutan/rimba*
island	*poo*-low	*pulau*
lake	*tah*-si(k)	*tasik*
mountain (path)	(*lah*-loo-ahn)	*(laluan)*
	goo-nung	*gunung*
pass	*lah*-loo-ahn	*laluan*
peak	*poon*-chah(k)	*puncak*
plain	dah-*tah*-rahn	*dataran*
river	*soo*-ngai	*sungai*
rock	*bah*-too	*batu*
town	*ko*-tuh	*kota*
valley	*lehm*-bah(h)	*lembah*
village	*kahm*-pung/*deh*-suh	*kampung/desa*
volcano	*goo*-nung ber-*ah*-pee	*gunung berapi*
waterfall	air ter-*joon*	*air terjun*

fauna

dunia binatang

bird	*boo*-rung	*burung*
buffalo	ker-*bow*	*kerbau*
cat	*koo*-ching	*kucing*
chicken	*ai*-yahm	*ayam*
civet cat	*moo*-sahng	*musang*

cow	*lehm*-boo	lembu
crocodile	boo-*ai*-yuh	buaya
dog	*ahn*-jing	anjing
fish	*ee*-kahn	ikan
frog	*kah*-tah(k)/*ko*-do(k)	katak/kodok
gecko	*chi(k)*-chah(k)	cikcak
goat	*kahm*-bing	kambing
horse	*koo*-duh	kuda
monitor lizard	bee-*ah*-wah(k)	biawak
monkey	*mo*-nyeht	monyet
mouse deer	*kahn*-chil	kancil
pig	*bah*-bee	babi
python	*sah*-wah(h)	sawah
rooster	*ai*-yahm *jahn*-tahn	ayam jantan
sheep	*bi*-ree-*bi*-ree	biri-biri
(poisonous) snake	*oo*-lahr (ber-*bee*-suh)	ular (berbisa)
tiger	*hah*-ree-mow	harimau

insects   serangga

... ant	se-*mut* ...	semut ...
fire	*ah*-pee	api
biting	*gee*-git	gigit
butterfly	*koo*-poo-*koo*-poo/	kupu-kupu/
	rah-muh-*rah*-muh	rama-rama
centipede	*lee*-pahn	lipan
cockroach	*lee*-pahs	lipas
fly	*lah*-laht	lalat
leech (large, in rivers)	*lin*-tah(h)	lintah
(small, in grass)	*pah*-chaht	pacat

mosquito	nyah-mu(k)	*nyamuk*
spider	*lah*-bah(h)-*lah*-bah(h)	*labah-labah*
termite	*ah*-nai-*ah*-nai	*anai-anai*

flora & agriculture

dunia tumbuh-tumbuhan & pertanian

agriculture	per-*tah*-nee-ahn	*pertanian*
coconut palm	po-ko(k) ke-*lah*-puh	*pokok kelapa*
coconut	ke-*lah*-puh	*kelapa*
corn	*jah*-gung	*jagung*
flower	*boo*-nguh	*bunga*
fruit tree	po-ko(k) *boo*-ah(h)	*pokok buah*
to harvest	me-me-*ti(k)*	*memetik*
irrigation	*sah*-li-rahn	*saliran*
leaf	down	*daun*
oil palm	ke-*lah*-puh *sah*-wit	*kelapa sawit*
orchard	*doo*-sun	*dusun*
plantation	eh-*steht*/lah-*dahng*	*estet/ladang*

pull your sock up!

When camping, be aware that South-East Asia has a tremendous number of venomous snakes and some enormous pythons. One was caught during the '90s with a grisly mouthful: the head and shoulders of a man. It had presumably dropped on him in an overgrown area near his house, and squeezed him into submission.

to plant	me-*nah*-nahm	*menanam*
rice field	*sah*-wah(h)	*sawah*
rice terrace	*peh*-tah(k) *sah*-wah(h)	*petak sawah*
rubber	*geh*-tah(h)	*getah*
sugar cane	*teh*-boo	*tebu*
tobacco	tem-*bah*-kow	*tembakau*

The fabulous array of Malaysian food will impress you from the moment you arrive. You'll probably eat a lot of your meals in *kedai kopi*, ke-*dai ko*-pee, coffee shops or *gerai*, ge-*rai*, hawker stalls that serve tasty dishes, snacks and cooling drinks. Cooked up on the spot or served buffet-style, these are clean and delicious. Of course there are also restaurants in bigger cities, and fast food outlets are spreading around the country like fat on a hot grill. But for authentic tastes, try the hawkers' stalls and smaller restaurants, teeming with people from early in the morning till late at night.

During fasting month in the Malay areas, only Chinese or non-Muslim Indian shops will be open during daylight hours. Fast food chains usually remain open for non-Muslim clientele. However, in northern states and some rural areas, you should keep a low profile while eating and drinking in public out of respect for those who are fasting.

breakfast	*mah*-kahn *pah*-gee; *sah*-rah-pahn	*makan pagi; sarapan*
lunch	*mah*-kahn te-ngah-*hah*-ree	*makan tengahari*
dinner	*mah*-kahn *mah*-lahm	*makan malam*

breakfast

makan pagi

Having breakfast out is a national pastime. Some roadside stalls and *mamak*, *mah*-mah(k), (Muslim Indian) restaurants open before sunrise. A mid-morning snack or meal is also called breakfast, and many of these foods are available all day. Sweet *teh tarik*, teh *tah*-rik, is a must for a true Malaysian-style breakfast. Of course, for the unadventurous, hotels and fast

common malaysian breakfasts

nasi lemak   *nah*-see le-*mah*(k)
rice cooked with coconut milk and pandan leaves, served
with a very spicy anchovy sauce, peanuts, a hardboiled egg,
tomato and cucumber, and sometimes chicken. Utterly,
utterly delicious. Don't leave Malaysia without trying it.

roti canai   *ro*-tee *chah*-nai
flat bread fried in ghee and served with curried lentils or
some other spicy sauce. A little milder than nasi lemak.

tosai   *to*-sai
similar to roti canai, but lighter and roasted rather than fried.

kueh   *koo*-eh(h)
include the savoury curry puff, as well as small sweet cakes.
Bite-sized, to add to your breakfast.

nasi dagang   *nah*-see *dah*-gahng
an east coast specialty, this super-rich coconut rice – served
with some form of curry or meat dish – will fill you up immediately.

food chains serve Western style breakfasts, and the big cities
have patisseries and bakeries.

vegetarian & special meals

makanan sayuran & makanan khas

If you're a vegetarian, you can specify *tanpa daging*, *tahn*-pah
dah-ging, 'without meat', or *sayur saja*, *sai*-yur *sah*-juh, 'vegetables only'. To some Malays *daging*, 'meat', means beef only, so
you may need to elaborate: *tanpa daging, ayam dan lain-lain*,
tahn-pah *dah*-ging, *ai*-yahm dahn lain-lain, 'without meat/
beef, chicken and other things.'

I'm vegetarian.

sai-yuh *mah*-kahn *sai*-yur Saya makan sayur
sah-juh/*sai*-yuh tah(k) saja/saya tak
mah-kahn *dah*-ging makan daging.

I don't/	*sai*-yuh tah(k) *soo*-kuh/	Saya tak suka/
can't eat ...	bo-*leh(h)* *mah*-kahn ...	boleh makan ...
chicken	*ai*-yahm	ayam
beef	*dah*-ging *lehm*-boo	daging lembu
eggs	te-*lur*	telur
fish	*ee*-kahn	ikan
ham	*dah*-ging *bah*-bee;	daging babi;
	hahm	ham
meat	*dah*-ging	daging
milk and cheese	*soo*-soo dahn *keh*-joo	susu dan keju
prawns	*oo*-dahng	udang

I'm allergic to ...	*sai*-yuh ah-*ler*-jik	Saya alergik
	kah-low *mah*-kahn ...	kalau makan ...
dairy products	*soo*-soo	susu
peanuts	*kah*-chahng	kacang

Do you have any vegetarian dishes?

ah-duh *mah*-kah-nahn Ada makanan
sai-yu-rahn *sah*-juh? sayuran saja?

Does this dish have meat/chicken?

ah-duh *dah*-ging/ Ada daging/
ai-yahm tah(k) dah-*lahm* ayam tak dalam
mah-sah-kahn *ee*-nee? masakan ini?

Can I get this without meat/chicken?

bo-*leh(h)* tah(k) *mah*-sah(k) Boleh tak masak
tahn-puh *dah*-ging/*ai*-yahm? tanpa daging/ayam?

Does it contain eggs?

mah-kah-nahn *ee*-nee Makanan ini
ah-duh te-*lur* tah(k)? ada telur tak?

Kosher restaurants are unknown in Malaysia, however *halal*, *hah*-lahl, restaurants do not use pork products.

food

157

Is there a halal restaurant here?

ah-duh *reh*-sto-rahn   *Ada restoran*
hah-lahl dee see-nee?   *halal di sini?*

Is this halal?

ee-nee hah-lahl-kah(h)?   *Ini halalkah?*

eating out

		makan di luar
Where can I find a ... ?	... dee *mah*-nuh?	*... di mana?*
food stall	ge-*rai*	*Gerai*
night market	*pah*-sahr *mah*-lahm	*Pasar malam*
restaurant	*reh*-sto-rahn	*Restoran*
Where's a ... restaurant?	*reh*-sto-rahn ... dee *mah*-nuh?	*Restoran ... di mana?*
cheap	moo-*rah*(h)	*murah*
fish head curry	*kah*-ree ke-*pah*-luh ee-kahn	*kari kepala ikan*

We'd like a table for (five), please.

to-long *bah*-gee *meh*-juh   *Tolong bagi meja*
oon-tu(k) (*lee*-muh) o-rahng   *untuk (lima) orang.*

I want to eat ...

sai-yuh nah(k) *mah*-kahn ...   *Saya nak makan ...*

What dish is that?

mah-sah-kahn *ah*-puh ee-too?   *Masakan apa itu?*

What's in that dish?

ah-duh *ah*-puh dah-*lahm*   *Ada apa dalam*
mah-sah-kahn ee-too?   *masakan itu?*

Is it spicy?

pe-*dahs* tah(k)?   *Pedas tak?*

they may say ...	
mah-kahn *ah*-puh?	**What would you like to drink?**
mah-kahn *ah*-puh?	**What would you like to drink?**

FOOD

158

There's a certain finesse that needs to be developed when eating food with your hands. Always use your right hand only. Hold a piece of *roti canai*, *ro-tee chah-nai*, or meat between your thumb and two smallest fingers and then use your pointer and index fingers to separate a bite-sized chunk. If you're eating rice, use your fingers like a scoop and shovel the food into your mouth with your thumb. Tastes even better!

How much does one portion cost?

ber-*rah*-puh *hahr*-guh *oon*-tu(k)   Berapa harga untuk
sah-too bah-*hah*-gee-ahn?   satu bahagian?

**We're in a hurry. Please
bring our food quickly.**

kah-mee nah(k) che-*paht* nee.   Kami nak cepat ni.
to-long *bah*-wuh *mah*-kah-nahn   Tolong bawa makanan
che-*paht* see-*kit*   cepat sikit.

**Do I get it myself or
do they bring it to us?**

lai-yahn *di*-ree ah-*tow*   Layan diri atau
me-*reh*-kuh yahng *bah*-wuh?   mereka yang bawa?

Please bring a/an/the ...	*to*-long *bah*-wuh ...	Tolong bawa ...
ashtray	be-*kahs* ah-*boo* ro-ko(k)	bekas abu rokok
bill	bil	bil
cup	*chah*-wahn	cawan
fork	*gahr*-foo	garfu
glass	ge-*lahs*	gelas
glass of water (with/ without ice)	se-ge-*lahs* air *ko*-song (de-*ngahn*/ *tahn*-puh ais)	segelas air kosong (dengan/ tanpa ais)
knife	*pee*-sow	pisau
menu	*meh*-noo	menu
plate	*ping*-gahn	pinggan

spoon	*soo*-doo	*sudu*
toothpick	pen-*choo*-li(k) *gee*-gee	*penculik gigi*

This isn't cooked properly.
tah(k) *choo*-kup *mah*-sah(k) nee   *Tak cukup masak ni.*

Not too spicy please.
jah-*ngahn* ter-*lah*-loo pe-dahs   *Jangan terlalu pedas.*

No MSG please.
to-long jah-*ngahn*   *Tolong jangan*
pah-kai *ah*-jee-no-*mo*-to   *pakai ajinomoto.*

No ice, please.
tahn-puh ais   *Tanpa ais.*

Less oily please.
koo-*rahng* min-yah(k)   *Kurang minyak.*

This is (too) ...	*mah*-kah-nahn	*Makanan*
	ee-nee (ter-*lah*-loo) ...	*ini (terlalu) ...*
bitter	pah-*hit*	*pahit*
cold	se-*joo*(k)	*sejuk*
delicious	se-*dahp*/*eh*-nah(k)	*sedap/enak*
fresh	se-*gahr*	*segar*
hot	pah-*nahs*	*panas*
salty	*mah*-sin	*masin*
sour	*mah*-sahm	*masam*
spicy	pe-*dahs*	*pedas*
spoiled	*bah*-see	*basi*
stale	*mah*-su(k) *ah*-ngin	*masuk angin*

sweet	*mah*-nis	*manis*
unripe	be-*lum mah*-sah(k)	*belum masak*
uncooked	*men*-tah(h)	*mentah*

typical dishes

makanan biasa

Many small restaurants, stalls and coffee shops don't have menus – what's available is usually advertised on the wall, the stall tarpaulin or the side of the *kaki-lima*, kah-*kee lee*-muh, 'footpath'.

The names of many dishes specify how they're prepared, such as *ayam bakar*, *ai*-yahm *bah*-kahr, 'grilled chicken'.

menu decoder

main course

arnab	*ahr*-nahb	rabbit
ayam ...	*ai*-yahm ...	... chicken
bakar	*bah*-kahr	grilled
goreng	*go*-rehng	fried
babi	*bah*-bee	pig
bakso/ba'so	*bah*(k)-so/*bah*-so	meatball soup
bubur nasi	*boo*-bur *nah*-see	rice porridge with anchovies, vegetables, and chicken
bubur kacang	*boo*-bur	mung bean

makanan utama

hijau	*kah*-chahng *hee*-jow	porridge (sweet)
capati	chah-*pah*-tee	Indian flat flour pancake
daging lembu	*dah*-ging *lehm*-boo	beef
daging biri-biri	*dah*-ging *bi*-ree-*bi*-ree	lamb/mutton
gado-gado	*gah*-do-*gah*-do	boiled vegetables and peanut sauce
hati	*hah*-tee	(chicken) liver
ikan	*ee*-kahn	fish
air tawar	air *tah*-wahr	freshwater
air masin	air *mah*-sin	saltwater
ikan bilis	*ee*-kahn *bi*-lis	dried anchovies, usually made into a spicy sauce
ikan keli	*ee*-kahn ke-*lee*	catfish
itik	*ee*-tik	duck
jagung bakar	*jah*-gung *bah*-kahr	roasted corn
kambing	*kahm*-bing	goat
kangkung	*kahng*-kung	water spinach
kari	kah-ree	curry
kentang	ken-*tahng*	potatoes
kepah	ke-*pah(h)*	mussels
ketam	ke-*tahm*	crab
ketupat	ke-*too*-paht	boiled pressed rice
kicap	*kee*-chahp	soy sauce
kuay teow	koo-*ay tee*-ow	flat, wide rice noodles
laksa Kelantan	*lah(k)*-suh ke-lahn-*tahn*	spicy rice noodle soup with coconut milk

---

that's not a knife!

When you eat in stalls or small restaurants, you'll usually receive a large spoon and a fork (in Chinese restaurants, of course, you'll get chopsticks). No knife is provided. Malaysians, if they're eating with their hands, have a technique of pinning down the meat with their thumb and tearing it with the other fingers (the left hand is not involved at all, since it is considered dirty). If you want a knife, you'll have to ask for one!

FOOD

162

laksa Penang	*lah(k)*-suh pe-*nahng*	rice noodle soup in fish sauce
mee	mee	wheat noodles
mee ...	mee ...	
goreng	*go*-rehng	fried noodles with meat and vegetables
kuah/sup	koo-*ah(h)*/ soop	noodle soup with meat and vegetables
rebus	*ree*-bus	noodle soup with starchy, spicy sauce, fried tofu and vegetables
murtabak	moor-*tah*-bah(k)	pancakes stuffed with beef or chicken filling with onions and spices
nan	nahn	Indian grilled bread
nasi	*nah*-see	cooked rice
nasi ...	*nah*-see ...	
campur	*chahm*-pur	cooked rice with a selection of meat and vegetable dishes on one plate
goreng	*go*-rehng	fried rice
goreng istimewa	*go*-rehng is-tee-*meh*-wuh	special fried rice
ayam	*ai*-yahm	chicken rice
beriyani	be-ree-*yah*-nee	Indian rice with spicy chicken, beef, or lamb curry
dagang	*dah*-gahng	special rice cooked with coconut milk eaten with fish shrimp, or eggs (Peninsular East Coast specialty)
impit	*im*-pit	cubes of pressed rice, often served with peanut sauce

food

163

kerabu	ke-*rah*-boo	rice with cut up vegetables and a roasted grated coconut (Peninsular East Coast specialty)
lemak	le-*mah(k)*	rice cooked in coconut milk with spicy sauce and anchovies, with or without meat
minyak	*min*-yah(k)	ghee rice with curries
patprik	*paht*-pri(k)	rice with beef in a special Thai sauce
otak	*o*-tah(k)	brains
perut	pe-*rut*	tripe
petai	pe-*tai*	large, tasty bean
pulut	*pu*-lut	glutinous rice
rendang	*rehn*-dahng	meat cooked slowly in spices and coconut
rojak	*ro*-jah(k)	fruit and vegetables cut up with a sweet and spicy peanut sauce
roti	*ro*-tee	bread
roti ...	*ro*-tee ...	
bakar	*bah*-kahr	toast with jam
canai	*chah*-nai	Indian breakfast bread shaped like a pancake served with curry or lentils
jala	*jah*-luh	thin, yellow netted bread eaten with curry
sambal	*sahm*-bahl	spicy sauce to eat with rice
sate ...	*sah*-teh ...	... satay
ayam	*ai*-yahm	chicken
daging	*dah*-ging	beef
kambing	*kahm*-bing	goat
soto	*so*-to	chicken soup with rice cubes

sotong	so-tong	squid
tahu	*tah*-hoo	tofu
telur ...	te-*lur* ...	... egg
goreng	*go*-rehng	fried
rebus	*ree*-bus	boiled
masak	*mah*-sah(k)	soft-boiled
separuh	se-*pahr*-u(h)	
telur dadar	te-*lur* dah-*dahr*	omelette
tempeh	*tehm*-peh(h)	tempeh (fermented soybean cakes)
tempeh	*tehm*-peh(h)	fried tempeh
goreng	*go*-rehng	
tiram	*ti*-rahm	oysters
ubi	*oo*-bee	potatoes
udang	*oo*-dahng	shrimp
udang	*oo*-dahng	lobster
karang	*kah*-rahng	

snacks & sweets

makanan ringan & makanan manis

agar-agar	ah-*gahr*-ah-*gahr*	gelatine (made with seaweed)
ais krim	ais krim	ice cream
dodol	*do*-dol	chewy, toffee-like sweet pudding, also in durian flavour

karipap	*kah*-ree-pahp	curry puff
keropok	ke-*ro*-po(k)	prawn or rice crackers
kueh	*koo*-eh(h)	sweet or savoury snack (various kinds)
kueh (lapis)	koo-eh(h) *lah*-pis	(layer) cake
manisan	*mah*-nee-sahn	sweets
onde-onde;	on-*deh*-on-*deh*;	glutinous rice
buah	*boo*-uh(h)	ball stuffed with
melaka	me-*lah*-kuh	palm sugar
pau	pow	steamed rice flour buns with a variety of fillings
pisang	*pee*-sahng	fried banana
goreng	*go*-rehng	
rojak	*ro*-jah(k)	fruit salad in a sweet, spicy peanut sauce
tahu	*tah*-hoo	tofu

self-catering

masakan sendiri

Can I please have ...?	*to*-long *bah*-gee ... ?	*Tolong bagi ...?*
an orange	o-rehn se-*bee*-jee	*oren sebiji*
a kilo of oranges	o-rehn se-*kee*-lo	*oren sekilo*
two kilos of oranges	*doo*-uh *kee*-lo o-rehn	*dua kilo oren*
half a kilo of oranges	se-te-*ngah*(h) *kee*-lo o-rehn	*setengah kilo oren*
seven mangoes	too-*juh bee*-jee *mahng*-guh	*tujuh biji mangga*

at the market

di pasar

Delicious fresh fruit, exotic vegetables and spices, fresh fish and meats abound in the Malaysian *pasar*, *pah*-sahr. Whether you want to cook a meal yourself or try to find a taste of home,

In Malaysia you'll find a variety of Chinese cuisines, including Cantonese, Hokkien, Szechuan, Teochew, Hakka, Shanghai, and Beijing styles of cooking.

Among the Indian restaurants, stalls and *kedai kopi*, ke-*dai ko*-pee, you'll get to try South Indian, Muslim Indian, mamat, *mah*-maht, and North Indian and Pakistani dishes. Of course Malay food is widely available, as is Indonesian – the two are very similar. *Nyonya* is a unique blend of Chinese and Malay styles of cooking, and *Baba-Nyonya* or *Peranakan* is the style of early Chinese immigrants who adopted some of the cooking of the Malays. Thai cuisine is also widely available in Malaysia.

this should be your first stop – the nucleus of any Malaysian town. A multitude of other goods are on offer: rice and grains, packaged goods, kitchenware, tobacco and so on. Your nose will tell you when you've hit the meat section.

How much is this?
be-*rah*-puh
hahr-guh-nyuh ee-nee?

Berapa harganya ini?

How much is a kilogram of ...?
be-*rah*-puh
hahr-guh se-*kee*-lo ... ?

Berapa harga sekilo ...?

Can I taste it?
bo-*leh(h)* choo-buh?

Boleh cuba?

I don't want that one.
tah(k) nah(k) yahng ee-too

Tak nak yang itu.

Please give me another one.
to-long *bah*-gee yahng lain

Tolong bagi yang lain.

bread	*ro*-tee	roti
noodles	mee	mee
rice (cooked)	*nah*-see	nasi
rice (uncooked)	be-*rahs*	beras

meat   daging

beef	*dah*-ging *lehm*-boo	*daging lembu*
brains	*o*-tahk	*otak*
chicken	*ai*-yahm	*ayam*
duck	*ee*-tik	*itik*
goat	*kahm*-bing	*kambing*
lamb	*ah*-nah(k) *bi*-ree-*bi*-ree	*anak biri-biri*
liver	*hah*-tee	*hati*
mutton	*bi*-ree-*bi*-ree	*biri-biri*
pig	*bah*-bee	*babi*
rabbit	*ahr*-nahb	*arnab*

seafood   makanan laut

catfish	*ee*-kahn ke-*lee*	*ikan keli*
cockles	ke-*rahng*	*kerang*
crab	ke-*tahm*	*ketam*
freshwater fish	ee-kahn air *tah*-wahr	*ikan air tawar*
lobster	*oo*-dahng *kah*-rahng	*udang karang*
mussels	ke-*pah(h)*	*kepah*
oysters	*ti*-rahm	*tiram*
saltwater fish	ee-kahn air *mah*-sin	*ikan air masin*
salted dried fish	*ee*-kahn ke-*ring*	*ikan kering*
shrimp	*oo*-dahng	*udang*
squid	*so*-tong	*sotong*

vegetables   sayur-sayuran

beans	*kah*-chahng	*kacang*
cabbage	*ku*-bis	*kubis*
carrot	*lo*-ba(k)	*lobak*
cauliflower	*ku*-bis boo-*nguh*	*kubis bunga*
corn	*jah*-gung	*jagung*
cucumber	*tee*-mun	*timun*
eggplant	te-*rung*	*terung*
mushrooms	*chen*-dah-wahn/*koo*-laht	*cendawan/kulat*
onion	*bah*-wahng	*bawang*
potato	*ken*-tahng	*kentang*
pumpkin	*lah*-boo	*labu*
tomato	to-*mah*-to	*tomato*

fruit   buah-buahan

Malaysia is the land of heavenly fruit. Whether you shop at
roadside stalls, in the markets or in supermarkets, you'll find a
devastatingly delicious variety of tropical and temperate fruits.
Some fruits are only found here, like the *ciku*, *chee*-koo, which
resembles a fuzzy potato with a hint of vanilla flavour.

apple	*eh*-pahl	*epal*
avocado	ah-vo-*kah*-do	*avokado*

feast on fruit

guava   *jahm*-boo   *jambu*
a hard, pear-shaped fruit. The small black seeds should not
be eaten. Jambu air, *jahm*-boo air, is a small, pink, smooth,
strawberry shaped variety with a fragrant taste.

jackfruit   *nahng*-kah   *nangka*
sellers often break the fruit up into segments, which are then
packed, ready to eat. The flesh is rubbery, sweet and strongly
flavoured. Jackfruit trees are everywhere and can be recognised by their huge pendulous fruit, often wrapped in plastic
bags for protection while they ripen on the tree.

mangosteen   *mang*-gis   *manggis*
easily recognised by its thick, purple-brown, fibrous skin,
which protects mouth-watering, sweet-sour, white flesh.

rambutan   *rahm*-boo-tahn   *rambutan*
bright red fruit covered in soft, hairy spines, and con-tain-
ing a delicious, lychee-like, sweet white flesh.

salak   *sah*-lak   *salak*
brown snake-skin fruit of the Zalacca palm, the flesh of which
is crunchy and nutty. An Indonesian fruit, occasionally sold in
Malaysian markets.

starfruit   be-*lim*-bing   *belimbing*
A watery, thirst-quenching fruit shaped like a star, end on.
It's one of the few fruits eaten without being peeled.

An encounter with *durian*, *doo-ree-ahn*, the 'king of fruits', is a memorable experience for the fruit lover. Durians announce themselves in any market by exuding an incredibly pungent stench. If you can hold your breath long enough to approach, and swallow the rich, creamy flesh, you may get to crave the unique flavour.

banana	*pee*-sahng	*pisang*
cempedak	*chem*-pe-dah(k)	*cempedak*
coconut	ke-*lah*-puh	*kelapa*

Look for *kelapa muda*, (ke-*lah*-puh *moo*-duh), 'young coconut', which makes a refreshing drink.

lemon	*leh*-mon	*lemon*
lime	*lee*-mow	*limau*
mango	*mang*-guh	*mangga*
orange	*o*-rehn	*oren*
papaya	*beh*-ti(k)	*betik*
peanuts	*kah*-chang	*kacang*
pineapple	*neh*-nahs	*nenas*
strawberry	*strah*-beh-ree	*strawberi*
soursop	doo-*ree*-ahn be-*lahn*-duh	*durian belanda*
watermelon	tem-*bee*-kai	*tembikai*

spices & condiments
rempah-rempahan

chilli	*chi*-lee	*cili*
chilli shrimp paste	*sam*-bahl be-*lah*-chahn	*sambal belacan*
chilli sauce	*sam*-bahl; sos *chi*-lee	*sambal*; sos cili
cinnamon	*kai*-yoo *mah*-nis	*kayu manis*
cloves	*cheng*-ki(h)	*cengkih*
curry	*kah*-ree	*kari*
garlic	*bah*-wahng *poo*-ti(h)	*bawang putih*
ginger	*hah*-lee-uh	*halia*
mortar and pestle	*bah*-too *toom*-bu(k)	*batu tumbuk*

cili (the smaller, the hotter)	*chi*-lee	**chilli**
pedas	pe-*dahs*	**spicy**
sambal	*sahm*-bahl	**chilli sauce/paste**

MSG	*ah*-jee-no-*mo*-to	*ajinomoto*
oil	*min*-yah(k)	*minyak*
black pepper	*lah*-duh *hee*-tahm	*lada hitam*
salt	*gah*-rahm	*garam*
soy sauce (salty)	*kee*-chahp (*mah*-sin)	*kicap (masin)*
sugar	*goo*-luh	*gula*
sweet soy sauce	*kee*-chahp *mah*-nis	*kicap manis*
tomato sauce	sos to-*mah*-to	*sos tomato*
turmeric	*koon*-yit	*kunyit*
vinegar	*choo*-kuh	*cuka*

cooking methods   cara masakan

baked	bah-*kahr dah*-lahm o-vehn/ke-*too*-hahr	*bakar dalam oven/ketuhar*
boiled	*ree*-bus	*rebus*
cooked in coconut milk	*mah*-sah(k) le-*mah(k)*; *goo*-lai	*masak lemak; gulai*
fried	*go*-rehng	*goreng*
grilled	*bah*-kahr	*bakar*
smoked	*ah*-sahp	*asap*
spit-roasted	*pahng*-gang	*panggang*
steamed	*koo*-koos	*kukus*

drinks

I want to drink ...
sai-yuh nah(k) *mee*-num ...   Saya nak minum ...

Do you have ...?
ah-duh …?   Ada ...?

hot/warm drinks

minuman
panas/suam

Except in upmarket restaurants and hotels, tea and coffee are nearly always served sweet and milky. If you want black coffee or plain tea, ask for *teh/kopi kosong*, 'empty tea/coffee'.

coffee ...	*ko*-pee ...	kopi ...
without sugar	*tahn*-puh *goo*-luh	tanpa gula
without milk	o	o
without milk and sugar	o *ko*-song	o kosong
coffee with milk	*ko*-pee *soo*-soo	kopi susu
tea without sugar	teh *tahn*-puh *goo*-luh	teh tanpa gula
tea without milk	teh o	teh o
tea with milk	teh *soo*-soo	teh susu
frothed tea	teh *tah*-rik	teh tarik

too much is barely enough

Most Malaysians can't imagine drinking tea or coffee or any other drink without a lot of sweeteners in it. Coffee and tea, as well as iced tea, will be served with sweetened condensed milk unless you specify *kopi o* or *teh o* which will then be sweetened with sugar before it is brought to you! In traditional restaurants and stalls, the milk used in drinks is usually sweetened condensed milk. Drinks like 'ABC', air batu campur, 'mixed ice', are more of a dessert than a drink, and are often served in a bowl. Drinks served in Malaysian homes are almost always sweetened, too.

cold drinks		*minuman sejuk*
cincau	*chin*-chow	black agar, 'seaweed' jelly with fruit syrup and ice
air limau	air *lee*-mow	citrus juice
air kelapa muda	air ke-*lah*-puh moo-duh	coconut milk
cendol	*chehn*-dol	coconut milk with rice jelly and ice
air batu campur	air *bah*-too *chahm*-pur	ABC or coconut milk with fruit, jelly, nuts, sweet milk and shaved ice
pekatan	pe-*kah*-tahn	cordial
kopi ais	*ko*-pee ais	iced coffee with milk
kopi o ais	*ko*-pee o ais	iced coffee without milk
teh ais	teh ais	iced tea with milk
teh o ais	teh o ais	iced tea without milk
the o ais kosong	teh o ais *ko*-song	iced tea without milk or sugar
teh o ais limau	teh o ais *lee*-mow	iced tea with lime
Horlicks ais	*hor*-liks ais	iced milky malt drink
Milo ais	*mi*-lo ais	iced chocolate milk
susu	*soo*-soo	milk
air	air	water
... *botol*	... *bo*-tol	bottled ...

boiled water	air *mah*-sah(k)	*air masak*
warm water	air swahm	*air suam*
ginger tea	teh *hah*-lee-uh	*teh halia*

alcohol

minuman keras

beer	bir	bir
grape wine	wain	wain
palm tree spirits	*to*-dee	todi
rice wine	*too*-ah(k)	tuak

Ambulance and paramedic services in Malaysia are slow at best. It's often better to get yourself to the nearest hospital if you need medical services.

Help!	*to*-long!	Tolong!
Stop!	ber-*hehn*-tee!	Berhenti!
Go away!	*per*-gee/be-*lah(h)*)!	Pergi/Belah!
Watch out!	*ah*-wahs/	Awas/
	ber-*hah*-ti-*hah*-ti!	Berhati-hati!
Thief!	pen-*choo*-ree!	Pencuri!
Pickpocket!	pe-nye-*luk sah*-koo!	Penyeluk saku!
Fire!	ke-*bah*-kah-rahn!	Kebakaran!
It's an emergency!	ke-che-*mah*-sahn!	Kecemasan!

There's been an accident.
ah-duh ke-*mah*-lah-ngah! — Ada kemalangan!

Help me please!
min-tuh *to*-long! — Minta tolong!

Could I use the telephone?
bo-*leh(h) goo*-nai teh-*leh*-fon? — Boleh gunai telefon?

I'm lost.
sai-yuh ter-*seh*-saht — Saya tersesat.

Where are the toilets?
tahn-duhs dee *mah*-nuh? — Tandas di mana?

Call the police!
pahng-gil *po*-lis! — Panggil polis!

I'll get the police!
sai-yuh ah-*kahn pahng*-gil *po*-lis! — Saya akan panggil polis!

Where's the police station?
bah-lai *po*-lis dee *mah*-nuh? — Balai polis di mana?

emergencies

I've been robbed!
sai-yuh te-*lah(h)* dee-*rom*-pah(k)!   *Saya telah dirompak!*

I speak English.
sai-yuh *tah*-hoo ber-*chah*-kahp   *Saya tahu bercakap*
bah-*hah*-suh *ing*-ge-ris   *bahasa Inggeris.*

I've lost my ...	... *sai*-yuh *hee*-lahng	... *saya hilang.*
My ... was/were stolen.	... *sai*-yuh dee-*choo*-ree	... *saya dicuri.*
backpack	behg *sahn*-dahr	*beg sandar*
bags	behg	*beg*
handbag	behg *tah*-ngahn	*beg tangan*
money	*doo*-it/wahng	*duit/wang*
papers	*do*-koo-mehn/ *ker*-tahs	*dokumen/ kertas*
passport	*pahs*-port	*pasport*
travellers cheques	chehk kem-*bah*-ruh	*cek kembara*
wallet	*dom*-peht	*dompet*

dealing with the police

Good manners go a long way in Malaysia. As a foreign visitor you are considered a guest, and guests are on best behaviour! At least be patient and try to keep your voice low.

My possessions are insured.
sai-yuh *ah*-duh in-*soo*-rahns   *Saya ada insurans*
oon-tu(k) *bah*-rahng-   *untuk barang-*
bah-rahng *sai*-yuh   *barang saya.*

What am I accused of?
sai-yuh dee-*too*-du(h) *ah*-puh?   *Saya dituduh apa?*

I (don't) understand.
sai-yuh (tah(k)) *fah*-hahm   *Saya (tak) faham.*

I didn't realise I was doing anything wrong.
sai-yuh tah(k) se-*dahr sai*-yuh   *Saya tak sedar saya*
ber-sah-*lah(h)*   *bersalah.*

I didn't do it.
sai-yuh *tee*-dah(k) me-lah-*koo*-kahn ee-too

Saya tidak melakukan itu.

I'm sorry; I apologise.
sai-yuh me-nye-*sahl*; *sai*-yuh *min*-tuh mah-*ahf*

Saya menyesal; Saya minta maaf.

We're innocent.
kah-mee *tee*-dah(k) ber-sah-*lah(h)*

Kami tidak bersalah.

We're foreigners.
kah-mee *o*-rahng *ah*-sing

Kami orang asing.

Can I call someone?
bo-*leh(h)*-kah(h) *sai*-yuh me-neh-*leh*-fon se-se-*o*-rahng?

Bolehkah saya menelefon seseorang?

Can I see a lawyer who speaks English?
bo-*leh(h)*-kah(h) *sai*-yuh ber-*jum*-puh de-*ngahn* pe-*gwahm* yahng ber-bah-*hah*-suh *ing*-ge-ris?

Bolehkah saya berjumpa dengan peguam yang berbahasa Inggeris?

Is there a fine we can pay to clear this?
bo-*leh(h)*-kah(h) *kah*-mee mem-*bai*-yahr *den*-duh *oon*-tu(k) me-nye-le-*sai*-kahn mah-*sah*-luh(h) ee-nee?

Bolehkah kami membayar denda untuk menyelesaikan masalah ini?

Can we pay an on-the-spot fine?
bo-*leh(h)* bai-yahr *den*-duh se-*kah*-rahng?

Boleh bayar denda sekarang?

I know my rights.
sai-yuh *tah*-hoo hahk *sai*-yuh

Saya tahu hak saya.

I want to contact my embassy/consulate.
sai-yuh nah(k) meng-hoo-*boo*-ngee ke-*doo*-tah-ahn/*kon*-soo-laht *sai*-yuh

Saya nak menghubungi kedutaan/konsulat saya.

the police may say ...

ahn-duh dee-too-duh me-lah-koo-kahn ...	Anda dituduh melakukan ...	You'll be charged with ...
dee-uh dee-too-duh me-lah-koo-kahn ...	Dia dituduh melakukan ...	She'll/He'll be charged with ...
be-ker-juh tahn-puh ee-zin	bekerja tanpa izin	working without a permit
ke-gee-ah-tahn sub-ver-sif	kegiatan subversif	anti-government activity
mah-su(k) tahn-puh ee-zin mah-su(k) tahn-puh vee-suh	masuk tanpa izin masuk tanpa visa	illegal entry entry without a visa
meng-gahng-goo ke-ah-mah-nahn	mengganggu keamanan	disturbing the peace
me-mee-li-kee bah-rah-ngahn hah-rahm	memiliki barangan haram	possession of illegal substances
pe-lahng-gah-rahn pe-rah-tu-rahn lah-loo-lin-tahs	pelanggaran peraturan lalulintas	traffic violation
pem-boo-noo-hahn	pembunuhan	murder
pen-choo-ree-ahn	pencurian	theft
pen-choo-ree-ahn dee ke-dai	pencurian di kedai	shoplifting
pe-rom-pah-kahn	perompakan	robbery
pe-ro-go-lahn	perogolan	rape
se-rahng-ahn	serangan	assault
me-le-bee-hee tehm-po(h) sah(h) vee-suh	melebihi tempoh sah visa	overstaying your visa

the bill

It's best to address the police as 'sir' or 'ma'am'.

Sir	twahn/en-*chi(k)*	*tuan/encik*
Ma'am	pwahn/*chi(k)*	*puan/cik*

arrested	dee-*tahng*-kahp	*ditangkap*
cell	sehl	*sel*
consulate	*kon*-soo-laht	*konsulat*
court	*mah(h)*-khah-mah(h)	*mahkamah*
embassy	ke-*doo*-tah-ahn	*kedutaan*
fine	*dehn*-duh	*denda*
(not) guilty	(*tee*-dah(k))	*(tidak) bersalah*
	ber-sah-*lah(h)*	
lawyer	pe-*gwahm*	*peguam*
police officer	pe-*gah*-wai *po*-lis	*pegawai polis*
police station	*bah*-lai *po*-lis	*balai polis*
prison	pen-*jah*-ruh	*penjara*
trial	pe-*ngah*-di-lahn	*pengadilan*

health

kesihatan

For common ailments head to a walk-in clinic; go to a private hospital if you're really ill.

I'm ill.
sai-yuh *sah*-kit   *Saya sakit.*

My friend is ill.
kah-wahn *sai*-yuh *sah*-kit   *Kawan saya sakit.*

Call an ambulance!
to-long *pang*-gil *ahm*-boo-lahns!   *Tolong panggil ambulans!*

Call a doctor!
pang-gil *dok*-tor!   *Panggil doktor!*

Please take me/us to a hospital.
to-long *hahn*-tahr-kahn
sai-yuh/*kah*-mee ke *hos*-pi-tahl

Tolong hantarkan saya/kami ke hospital.

**My blood group is
(A, B, O, AB) positive/negative.**
koom-poo-lahn *dah*-ruh *sai*-yuh
ee-*ah*-lah(h) (ay, bee, oh, ay bee)
po-si-tif/*neh*-gah-tif

Kumpulan darah saya ialah (A, B, O, AB) positif/negatif.

My contact number is ...
nom-bor teh-*leh*-fon *sai*-yuh ...

Nombor telefon saya ...

The number of my next of kin is ...
nom-bor teh-*leh*-fon *oon*-tu(k)
ke-loo-*ahr*-guh *sai*-yuh
ee-*ah*-lah(h) ...

Nombor telefon untuk keluarga saya ialah ...

I have medical insurance.
sai-yuh *ah*-duh in-*soo*-rahns
ke-see-*hah*-tahn

Saya ada insurans kesihatan.

Please get medicine from the chemist for me.
to-long be-*lee* oo-baht *oon*-tu(k)
sai-yuh dee *fahr*-mah-see

Tolong beli ubat untuk saya di farmasi.

Health
Kesihatan

Public health is generally excellent and you're unlikely to get seriously ill during your travels in Malaysia. If you do need to talk about illness, the all-purpose word is *sakit*, *sah*-kit, which means 'to feel sick' or 'to hurt'. Government clinics and hospitals can accommodate foreigners, although there is usually a long wait. Private clinics and hospitals are fast, do not generally require appointments and are reasonably priced.

at the doctor

di klinik

Almost all doctors and most nurses speak English, even in rural areas. Most doctors dispense medicine and prescriptions as you need them, so there is seldom the need make an extra trip to a pharmacy. Malaysia enjoys a good standard of health, so as long as you observe the general guidelines for health in the tropics, you should be fine.

Where's a ...	... dee *mah*-nuh?	... *di mana?*
chemist	*fahr*-mah-see	*farmasi*
dentist	*dok*-tor *gee*-gee	*doktor gigi*
doctor	*dok*-tor	*doktor*
hospital	hos-*pi*-tahl	*hospital*
clinic	*kli*-nik	*klinik*

I'm sick.
sai-yuh *sah*-kit   *Saya sakit.*

My friend is sick.
kah-wahn *sai*-yuh *sah*-kit   *Kawan saya sakit.*

Is there a doctor here who speaks English?
  ah-duh *dok*-tor yahng
  ber-*bah*-hah-suh *ing*-ge-ris?

Ada doktor yang berbahasa Inggeris?

Could the doctor come to the hotel?
  bo-*leh(h)*-kah(h)
  dok-tor *dah*-tahng ke *ho*-tehl?

Bolehkah doktor datang ke hotel?

I've had a blood test.
  dah-rah(h) *sai*-yuh *soo*-dah(h)
  dee-per-*eek*-suh

Darah saya sudah diperiksa.

I need a blood test.
  sai-yuh me-mer-*loo*-kahn
  pe-mer-*eek*-sah-ahn *dah*-rah(h)

Saya memerlukan pemeriksaan darah.

Is that a new syringe?
  jah-*rum* soon-*ti(k)*
  ee-too bah-*roo*-kah(h)?

Jarum suntik itu barukah?

Please use this syringe.
  to-long *pah*-kai jah-*rum*
  soon-*ti(k)* ee-nee

Tolong pakai jarum suntik ini.

What are you doing?
  ahn-duh *boo*-aht *ah*-puh?

Anda buat apa?

What do you want to do?
  ahn-duh *boo*-aht nah(k) *ah*-puh?

Anda buat nak apa?

I feel better/worse.
  sai-yuh be-*rah*-suh le-*bi(h)*
  bai(k)/te-*ru(k)*

Saya berasa lebih baik/teruk.

This is my usual medicine.
  ee-nee *oo*-baht
  bee-*ah*-suh *sai*-yuh

Ini ubat biasa saya.

I've been vaccinated.
  sai-yuh *soo*-dah(h)
  dee-i-moo-ni-*sah*-see

Saya sudah diimunisasi.

I don't want a blood transfusion.
  sai-yuh tah(k) nah(k)
  pe-nahm-*bah*-hahn *dah*-rah(h)

Saya tak nak penambahan darah.

What's the matter?
sah-kit *ah*-puh?   *Sakit apa?*

Where does it hurt?
ahn-duh ber-*rah*-suh   *Anda berasa*
sah-kit dee *mah*-nuh?   *sakit di mana?*

Are you allergic to anything?
ahn-duh ah-duh *ah*-lah-hahn?   *Anda ada alahan?*

Do you ...?   *ahn*-duh … ?   *Anda ...?*
   smoke   me-*ro*-ko(k)   *merokok*
   drink   *mee*-num   *minum*
            mee-nu-mahn   *minuman*
            ke-*rahs*   *keras*
   take drugs   men-*goo*-nah-kahn   *mengunakan*
            dah-dah(h)   *dadah*

Do you have a temperature?
ahn-duh de-*mahm pah*-nahs?   *Anda demam panas?*

Are you menstruating?
ah-duh-kah(h) *ahn*-duh   *Adakah anda*
se-*dahng dah*-tahng haid?   *sedang datang haid?*

Are you pregnant?
ahn-duh me-*ngahn*-dung/   *Anda mengandung/*
hah-mil?   *hamil?*

Do you feel any pain?
ahn-duh te-*rah*-suh *sah*-kit?   *Anda terasa sakit?*

Have you had this before?
per-nah(h) ke-*nuh*   *Pernah kena*
pe-*nyah*-kit ee-nee tah(k)?   *penyakit ini tak?*

Are you on medication?
ahn-duh se-*dahng*   *Anda sedang*
mah-kahn oo-baht?   *makan ubat?*

How long have you been like this?
soo-dah(h) be-*rah*-puh   *Sudah berapa*
lah-muh *ahn*-duh   *lama anda*
be-*rah*-suh be-*gee*-nee?   *berasa begini?*

health

I need a receipt for my insurance.

sai-yuh per-*loo*-kahn *reh*-sit   *Saya perlukan resit*
oon-tu(k) in-*soo*-rans *sai*-yuh   *untuk insurans saya.*

ailments

I feel under the weather.

sai-yuh *koo*-rahng   *Saya kurang*
se-*dahp bah*-dahn   *sedap badan.*

I feel nauseous.

sai-yuh *moo*-ahl   *Saya mual.*

I've been vomiting.

sai-yuh *soo*-dah(h) *moon*-tah(h)   *Saya sudah muntah.*

I'm having a hard time sleeping.

sai-yuh *soo*-sah(h) *tee*-dur   *Saya susah tidur.*

I feel ...	*sai*-yuh ber-*rah*-suh ...	*Saya berasa ...*
dizzy	pe-*ning*	*pening*
shivery	meng-*gee*-gil	*menggigil*
weak	le-*mah(h)*	*lemah*

My leg is broken.

too-lahng *kah*-kee   *Tulang kaki saya patah.*
sai-yuh *pah*-tah(h)

My foot is sprained.

kah-kee *sai*-yuh   *Kaki saya tersiliuh.*
ter-see-*lee*-u(h)

I have low/high blood pressure.

sai-yuh *ah*-duh te-*kah*-nahn   *Saya ada tekanan*
dah-rah(h) *rehn*-dah(h)/*ting*-gee   *darah rendah/tinggi.*

My ... hurts

... *sai*-yuh *sah*-kit   *... saya sakit.*

I'm suffering   *sai*-yuh *sah*-kit ...   *Saya sakit ...*
from (a/an) ...

addiction	ke-*tah*-gee-hahn	*ketagihan*
allergy	*ah*-ler-gee/*ah*-lah-hahn	*alergi/alahan*
anaemia	ah-*nee*-mee-uh	*anemia*
asthma	*leh*-lah(h)	*lelah*
bite	*gee*-gee-tahn	*gigitan*
burns	ke-*nuh ah*-pee	*kena api*
cancer	*kan*-ser	*kanser*
cholera	*tah*-oon	*taun*
cold	sel-*seh*-muh	*selsema*
constipation	sem-be-*lit*	*sembelit*
cough	*bah*-tu(k)	*batuk*
cystitis	*sah*-kit *ken*-ching	*sakit kencing*
diarrhoea	*chir*-rit-*bir*-it	*cirit-birit*
dog bite	*gee*-gee-tahn *ahn*-jing	*gigitan anjing*
dysentery	*di*-sen-tree	*disentri*
fever	de-*mahm* pah-nahs	*demam panas*
food poisoning	ke-*rah*-choo-nahn	*keracunan*
	mah-kah-nahn;	*makanan;*
	sah-lah(h) mah-kahn	*salah makan*
gastroenteritis	*sah*-kit *gas*-trik	*sakit gastrik*
headache	*sah*-kit ke-*pah*-luh	*sakit kepala*
heart condition	mah-*sah*-ah-lah(h)	*masalah*
	jahn-tung	*jantung*
hepatitis	heh-*pah*-tai-tis	*hepatitis*
high blood	te-*kah*-nahn	*tekanan*
pressure	*dah*-rah(h) *ting*-gee	*darah tinggi*
indigestion	tah(k) *hah*-zahm	*tak hazam*
	mah-kah-nahn	*makanan*
infection	in-*fehk*-see	*infeksi*
influenza	sel-*seh*-muh/floo	*selsema/flu*
itch	*gah*-tahl	*gatal*
lice	*koo*-too	*kutu*
malaria	mah-*lah*-ree-uh	*malaria*
migraine	*sah*-kit ke-*pah*-luh	*sakit kepala*
	be-*raht*;	*berat;*
	mai-grehn	*migraine*
pain	*sah*-kit	*sakit*

rabies	*ray*-bees; pe-*nyah*-kit *ahn*-jing *gee*-luh	*rabies; penyakit anjing gila*
rheumatism	*sah*-kit *sen*-dee	*sakit sendi*
sore throat	*sah*-kit te-*kah(k)*	*sakit tekak*
sprain	ter-se-*lee*-oo(h)	*terseliuh*
stomachache	*sah*-kit pe-*root*	*sakit perut*
sunburn	ter-*bah*-kar mah-tuh-*hah*-ree	*terbakar matahari*
travel sickness	*mah*-buk per-*jah*-lah-nahn	*mabuk perjalanan*
typhoid	de-*mahm* ke-pee-*ah*-loo	*demam kepialu*
urinary tract infection	*sah*-kit *ken*-ching	*sakit kencing*
venereal disease	pe-*nyah*-kit ke-*lah*-meen	*penyakit kelamin*
worms	*chah*-ching	*cacing*

women's health

Private maternity clinics would have information on specific matters to do with women's health. Testing for STDs is available at most clinics and larger hospitals.

Is there a female doctor here?
ah-duh *dok*-tor
wah-*nee*-tuh dee *see*-nee?
Ada doktor wanita di sini?

Is there a doctor especially for women?
ah-duh *dok*-tor *khoo*-soos
oon-tu(k) wah-*nee*-tuh?
Ada doktor khusus untuk wanita?

I'd like to use contraception.
sai-yuh nah(k) *goo*-nuh *ah*-laht/
oo-*baht* pen-*ceh*-gah(h) *hah*-mil
Saya nak guna alat/ubat pencegah hamil.

I haven't menstruated for ... weeks.
sai-yuh be-*lum dah*-tahng
haid se-*lah*-muh ... *ming*-goo
Saya belum datang haid selama ... minggu.

These pills must be taken three times a day.
pill *ee*-nee *mes*-tee	*Pil ini mesti*
dee *ahm*-bil *tee*-guh	*di ambil tiga*
kah-lee se-*hah*-ree	*kali sehari.*

Shake the bottle before taking.
gon-chahng-kahn	*Goncangkan*
bo-tol *doo*-loo	*botol dulu*
se-be-*lum* *mee*-num	*sebelum minum.*

I'm on the Pill.
sai-yuh *mah*-kahn pil	*Saya makan pil*
men-*cheh*-gah(h) *hah*-mil	*mencegah hamil.*

(Maybe) I'm pregnant.
(moong-kin) *sai*-yuh	*(Mungkin) Saya*
me-*ngahn*-dung/*hah*-mil	*mengandung/hamil.*

abortion	peng-*goo*-goo-rahn	*pengguguran*
	ah-nah(k)	*anak*
cystitis	*sah*-kit *ken*-ching	*sakit kencing*
diaphragm	*dai*-ah-frahm	*diaphram*
IUD	ai oo deh	*IUD*
mammogram	*mah*-mo-gram	*mamogram*
menstruation	*dah*-tahng haid	*datang haid*
miscarriage	ke-*goo*-goo-rahn	*keguguran*
pap smear	smir	*smear*
period pain	se-*goo*-gup	*segugup*
the Pill	pil pen-*cheh*-gah(h)	*pil pencegah*
	hah-mil	*hamil*
premenstrual	ke-*teh*-gah-ngahn	*ketegangan*
tension	se-be-*lum*	*sebelum*
	dah-tahng haid	*datang haid*
thrush	*goo*-ahm	*guam*
ultrasound	*ul*-trah-sownd	*ultrasound*

special health needs

anaemia	ah-*nee*-mee-uh	*anaemia*
asthma	*leh*-lah(h)	*lelah*
diabetes	*ken*-ching *mah*-nis	*kencing manis*

I'm allergic to ...	sai-yuh ah-*ler*-jik	*Saya alergik*
	ke-pah-duh ...	*kepada ...*
antibiotics	an-tai-bai-*o*-tik	*antibiotik*
aspirin	*as*-pi-rin	*aspirin*
bees	*leh*-bah(h)	*lebah*
codeine	*ko*-deen	*kodein*
dairy products	*pro*-duk	*produk*
	ber-*soo*-soo	*bersusu*
penicillin	pe-ni-*si*-lin	*penisilin*
pollen	de-*boo*-nguh	*debunga*

I have a skin allergy.
sai-yuh *ah*-duh   *Saya ada alahan kulit.*
ah-lah-hahn *koo*-lit

I have my own syringe.
sai-yuh *ah*-duh *jah*-rum   *Saya ada jarum*
soon-*ti(k)* sen-*di*-ree   *suntik sendiri.*

I need a new pair of glasses.
sai-yuh per-*loo*-kahn   *Saya perlukan*
cher-*min mah*-tuh *bah*-roo *cermin mata baru.*

I'm on medication for ...
sai-yuh se-*dahng pah*-kai *Saya sedang pakai*
oo-baht *oon*-tu(k) ...   *ubat untuk ...*

alternative treatments

Although Western-style medical treatment is the norm, alternative treatments, including some that are unique to Malaysia, are widely practised.

aromatherapy	ah-ro-mah-*teh*-rah-pee	*aromaterapi*
acupuncture	ah-koo-*punk*-toor	*akupunktur*
faith healer	*bo*-mo(h)/doo-koon/	*bomoh/dukun/*
	pah-wahng	*pawang*
herbalist	*ah*-lee *jah*-moo	*ahli jamu*
massage	oo-*root*	*urut*
masseur/masseuse	*too*-kahng oo-*root*	*tukang urut*
meditation	per-*tah*-pah-ahn	*pertapaan*
physiotherapy	fi-see-o-*tehr*-ah-pee	*fisioterapi*
reflexology	ree-flek-*so*-lo-gee	*refleksologi*
yoga	*yo*-guh	*yoga*

parts of the body

bahagian tubuh

ankle	ke-*ting*	*keting*
anus	*doo*-bur	*dubur*
appendix	ah-*pehn*-dik	*apendik*
arm	*leh*-ngahn	*lengan*
back	be-*lah*-kahng	*belakang*
bladder	kahn-*du*-ngahn	*kandungan*
	ken-ching	*kencing*
blood	*dah*-rah(h)	*darah*
bone	*too*-lahng	*tulang*
breast	boo-ah(h) *dah*-duh	*buah dada*
buttocks	*pong*-gong	*ponggong*
chest	*dah*-duh	*dada*
chin	*dah*-goo	*dagu*
ear	te-*li*-nguh	*telinga*
eye	*mah*-tuh	*mata*
face	*moo*-kuh	*muka*
finger	*jah*-ree *tah*-ngahn	*jari tangan*
foot	*kah*-kee	*kaki*
hands	*tah*-ngahn	*tangan*
head	ke-*pah*-luh	*kepala*
heart	*jahn*-tung	*jantung*
hip	*ping*-gahn	*pinggan*

kidney	*boo*-ah(h) *ping*-gahng	buah pinggang
knee	*loo*-tut	lutut
leg	*kah*-kee	kaki
liver	*hah*-tee	hati
lung	*pah*-roo-*pah*-roo	paru-paru
mouth	*moo*-lut	mulut
muscle	*o*-tot	otot
neck	*leh*-hehr	leher
nose	*hee*-dung	hidung
penis	*zah*-kahr	zakar
ribs	*too*-lahng *roo*-su(k)	tulang rusuk
shoulder	*bah*-hoo	bahu
skin	*koo*-lit	kulit
stomach	pe-*root*	perut
testicles	*boo*-ah(h) *peh*-lir	buah pelir
throat	te-*kah(k)*	tekak
toes	*jah*-ree *kah*-kee	jari kaki
tooth	*gee*-gee	gigi
vagina	*fah*-rahj	faraj
vein	oo-*raht dah*-rah(h)	urat darah
	hah-loos	halus

at the chemist

di farmasi

Some internationally known painkillers are not sold off the shelf in Malaysian pharmacies. Although you do not need a prescription, you will have to ask the chemist to dispense them to you.

I need medicine for ...
sai-yuh per-*loo*-kahn
oo-baht *oon*-tu(k) ...

Saya perlukan
ubat untuk ...

How many times a day?
be-*rah*-puh *kah*-lee se-*hah*-ree?

Berapa kali sehari?

| antibiotics | an-tai-bai-*o*-tik | antibiotik |
| antiseptic | an-ti-*sehp*-tik | antiseptik |

aspirin	*as*-pi-rin	*aspirin*
Band-aids	*plas*-ter	*plaster*
bandage	*pem*-bah-loot	*pembalut*
condoms	*kon*-dom	*kondom*
contraceptives	*ah*-laht/*oo*-baht	*alat/ubat*
	pen-*ceh*-gah(h) *hah*-mil	*pencegah hamil*
cotton wool	*kah*-pahs	*kapas*
cough medicine	*oo*-baht *bah*-tu(k)	*ubat batuk*
gauze	kain *kah*-suh	*kain kasa*
gastrolyte	ga-*stroh*-leet	*gastrolyte*
headache tablets	*oo*-baht *sah*-kit	*ubat sakit*
	ke-*pah*-luh	*kepala*
laxatives	*joo*-lahp	*julap*
painkillers	*oo*-baht *tah*-hahn	*ubat tahan sakit*
	sah-kit	
penicillin	pe-ne-*si*-lin	*penisilin*
quinine	*kwee*-nin	*kuinin*
rubbing alcohol	*al*-ko-hol *go*-so(k)	*alkohol gosok*
sleeping pills	*oo*-baht *tee*-dur	*ubat tidur*
tablet	*tab*-leht	*tablet*
vitamins	vee-*tah*-min	*vitamin*

useful words

accident	ke-*mahl*-ah-ngahn	*kemalangan*
breath	*nah*-fahs	*nafas*
disease	pe-*nyah*-kit	*penyakit*
faeces	*tah*-hee	*tahi*
fast (n)	*pwah*-suh	*puasa*
to fast	ber-*pwah*-suh	*berpuasa*
health	ke-see-*hah*-tahn	*kesihatan*
injection	*soon*-tee-kahn	*suntikan*
injury	ke-che-de-*rah*-ahn	*kecederaan*
medicine	*oo*-baht	*ubat*
poisonous	be-*rah*-choon	*beracun*
urine	air *ken*-ching	*air kencing*
wound	*loo*-kuh	*luka*

at the dentist

I have a toothache.
sai-yuh *sah*-kit *gee*-gee — *Saya sakit gigi.*

I have a cavity.
ah-duh *gee*-gee ber-*loo*-bahng — *Ada gigi berlubang.*

My tooth is broken.
gee-gee *sai*-yuh *pah*-tah(h) — *Gigi saya patah.*

I've lost a filling.
tahm-pah-lahn — *Tampalan*
gee-gee *sai*-yuh *hee*-lang — *gigi saya hilang.*

My gums hurt.
goo-see *sai*-yuh *sah*-kit — *Gusi saya sakit.*

Don't extract it.
jah-*ngahn chah*-but — *Jangan cabut.*

Please give me an anaesthetic.
to-long *kah*-si(h) — *Tolong kasih*
oo-baht bee-*oos* — *ubat bius.*

Ouch!   ah-*doo(h)*!   *Aduh!*

SUSTAINABLE TRAVEL

As the climate change debate heats up, the matter of sustainability becomes an important part of the travel vernacular. In practical terms, this means assessing our impact on the environment and local cultures and economies – and acting to make that impact as positive as possible. Here are some basic phrases to get you on your way …

communication & cultural differences

I'd like to learn some of your local dialects.
sai-yuh *ee*-ngin mem-pe-*lah*-jah-ree
be-be-*rah*-puh *dee*-yuh-le(k)
tem-*pah*-tahn *ahn*-dah
Saya ingin mempelajari beberapa dialek tempatan anda.

Would you like me to teach you some English?
ah-duh-kah(h) *ahn*-dah mow
sai-yuh me-*ngah*-jahr *ahn*-dah
se-*dee*-kit bah-*hah*-suh *ing*-ge-ris?
Adakah anda mahu saya mengajar anda sedikit Bahasa Inggeris?

Is this a local or national custom?
ah-duh-kah(h) *ee*-nee *ah*-daht
tem-*pah*-tahn ah-*tow* ne-*gah*-ruh?
Adakah ini adat tempatan atau negara?

I respect your customs.
sai-yuh meng-hor-*mah*-ti
ah-daht *ahn*-dah
Saya menghormati adat anda.

community benefit & involvement

What sorts of issues is this community facing?
ah-puh-kah(h) je-nis ee-soo
yahng dee-hah-dah-pee
mah-shah-rah-kaht dee see-nee?

*Apakah jenis isu
yang dihadapi
masyarakat di sini?*

drug abuse	sah-lah(h) goo-nah dah-dah(h)	*salah guna dadah*
environmental cleanliness	keh-ber-si(h)-ahn ah-lahm se-kee-tahr	*kebersihan alam sekitar*
social issues among the youth	ge-jah-lah so-see-ahl dee kah-lah-ngahn re-mah-jah	*gejala sosial di kalangan remaja*

I'd like to volunteer my skills.
sai-yuh ee-ngin me-nah-wahr-kahn
ke-mah-hee-rahn sai-yuh
se-chah-rah soo-kuh-re-lah

*Saya ingin menawarkan
kemahiran saya
secara sukarela.*

Are there any volunteer programs available in the area?
ah-duh-kah(h) se-bah-rahng
pro-grahm soo-kuh-re-lah-wahn
yahng bo-leh(h) dee-dah-pah-tee
dee kah-wah-sahn ee-nee?

*Adakah sebarang
program sukarelawan
yang boleh didapati
di kawasan ini?*

environment

Where can I recycle this?
dee mah-nuh-kah(h) bo-leh(h)
sai-yuh me-ngee-tahr
se-moo-luh bah-rahng ee-nee?

*Di manakah boleh
saya mengitar
semula barang ini?*

transport

Can we get there by public transport?
bo-*leh(h)*-kah(h) *kah*-mee ke
sah-*nah* de-*ngan* me-*nai*-kee
peng-ang-*koo*-tan *ah*-wam?

*Bolehkah kami ke
sana dengan menaiki
pengangkutan awam?*

Can we get there by bike?
bo-*leh(h)*-kah(h) *kah*-mee ke
sah-*nuh* de-*ngahn*
me-*noong*-gahng bah-*see*-kahl?

*Bolehkah kami ke
sana dengan
menunggang basikal?*

I'd prefer to walk there.
sai-yuh le-*bih(h)* soo-kuh
ber-*jah*-lahn ke *sah*-nuh

*Saya lebih suka
berjalan ke sana.*

accommodation

I'd like to stay at a locally-run hotel.
sai-yuh ee-ngin meng-*hee*-nahp dee
ho-*tehl* yahng dee-ken-*dah*-lee-kuhn
o-*leh(h)* o-rahng tem-*pah*-tahn

*Saya ingin menghinap di
hotel yang dikendalikan
oleh orang tempatan.*

Are there any ecolodges here?
ah-*puh*-kah(h) ter-*dah*-paht
se-*bah*-rahng *roo*-mah(h)
toom-*pah*-ngahn dee *see*-nee?

*Apakah terdapat
sebarang rumah
tumpangan di sini?*

Can I turn the air conditioning off and open the window?
bo-*leh(h)*-kah(h) *sai*-yuh
me-mah-*tee*-kahn pe-*nyah*-mahn
oo-*dah*-ruh dan mem-*boo*-kuh
ting-kahp?

*Bolehkah saya
mematikan penyaman
udara dan membuka
tingkap?*

There's no need to change my sheets.
tee-dah(k) per-*loo* me-*nyah*-leen
chah-dahr *sai*-yuh

*Tidak perlu menyalin
cadar saya.*

shopping

Where can I buy locally produced goods/souvenirs?
dee *mah*-nuh-kah(h) bo-*leh(h)*
sai-yuh mem-be-*lee bah*-rahng-ahn/
chen-de-ruh-*hah*-ti
ke-loo-*ah*-ruhn tem-*pah*-tahn?

*Di manakah boleh
saya membeli barangan/
cenderahati
keluaran tempatan?*

**Is this made
from …?**

ah-duh-kah(h) *ee*-nee
dee-per-*boo*-aht

*Adakah ini
diperbuat*

n this dictionary, root words are given in square brackets after verbs. Root words are often used in place of active verbs by Malay speakers. Verbs are preceeded by 'to' to distinguish them from nouns of similar spelling.

    to look   me-*lee*-haht [*lee*-haht]   *melihat [lihat]*

Remember that nouns don't change their form according to whether they're singular or plural. When a word can be either a noun or an adjective, the adjective form is followed by the marking (adj).

Bullets separate more than one alternative word and slashes words that are interchangeable.

A

to be able (can)	bo-*leh(h)*	*boleh*

Can (may) I take your photo?
bo-*leh(h)* ahm-bil fo-to *ahn*-duh?   *Boleh ambil foto anda?*

Can you show me (on the map)?
to-long toon-*joo(k)*-kahn   *Tolong tunjukkan*
(dee pe-*tuh*)?   *(di peta)?*

aboard	dee ah-*tahs*	*di atas*
abortion	peng-goo-*goo*-rahn	*pengguguran*
above	dee ah-*tahs*	*di atas*
to accept	me-ne-*ree*-muh	*menerima*
	[te-ree-*muh*]	*[terima]*
accident	ke-mah-*lah*-ngahn	*kemalangan*
accommodation	pe-*ngee*-nah-pahn	*penginapan*
to accompany	me-ne-*mah*-nee	*menemani*
across	se-be-*rahng*	*seberang*
activist	*ahk*-ti-vis	*aktivis*
adaptor (electric)	a-*dap*-ter eh-*lehk*-trik	*adapter elektrik*
address (of house)	*ah*-lah-maht	*alamat*
admission (entry)	ke-mah-*su(k)*-kahn	*kemasukan*
adult	deh-*wah*-suh	*dewasa*
aeroplane	*kah*-pahl *ter*-bahng	*kapal terbang*
afraid	tah-*kut*	*takut*
after	se-le-*pahs* •	*selepas* •
	se-te-*lah(h)* •	*setelah* •
	se-soo-*dah(h)*	*sesudah*

afternoon	te-ngah-*hah*-ree • pe-*tahng*	tengahari • petang
in the afternoon	pah-*duh wahk*-too te-ngah-*hah*-ree/ pe-*tahng*	pada waktu tengahari/ petang
this afternoon	te-ngah-*hah*-ree/ pe-*tahng ee*-nee	tengahari/ petang ini
again	se-*moo*-luh	semula
against (opposed)	me-*nen*-tahng	menentang
age	*oo*-mur	umur
ago	le-*pahs*	lepas
(half an hour) ago	(se-te-*ngah(h)* jahm) le-*pahs*	(setengah jam) lepas
(three days) ago	(tee-*guh hah*-ree) le-*pahs*	(tiga hari) lepas
to agree	ber-se-*too*-joo [se-*too*-joo]	bersetuju [setuju]

I don't agree.
sai-yuh *tee*-dah(k) se-*too*-joo — Saya tidak setuju.

Agreed.
se-*too*-joo — Setuju.

ahead	dee de-*pahn*/ hah-dah-*pahn*	di depan/ hadapan
straight ahead	te-*rus* ke hah-dah-*pahn*	terus ke hadapan
AIDS	ehds	AIDS
air	oo-*dah*-ruh	udara
air-conditioner	pen-*dee*-ngin oo-*dah*-ruh	pendingin udara
airmail	mehl oo-*dah*-ruh	mel udara
airport	lah-*pah*-ngahn ter-*bahng*	lapangan terbang
airport tax	*choo*-kai pe-ner-*bah*-ngan	cukai penerbangan
alarm clock	jahm *lo*-chehng	jam loceng
alive	*hee*-dup	hidup
all	se-*moo*-uh	semua
allergy	*ah*-ler-jee • ah-lah-*hahn*	alergi • alahan
alley	lo-*rong*	lorong
to allow	mem-be-*nahr*-kahn • me-*ngee*-zin-kahn	membenarkan • mengizinkan

It's (not) allowed.
dee-*lah*-rahng — Dilarang.

almost	*hahm*-pir • *nyah*-ris-*nyah*-ris	hampir • nyaris-nyaris
alone	ber-*sen*-dee-ree-ahn	bersendirian
already	soo-dah(h) • te-*lah(h)* • per-*nah(h)*	sudah • telah • pernah
also	*joo*-guh • pun	juga • pun
altitude	ke-*teeng*-gee-ahn	ketinggian

always	se-*lah*-loo • *sen*-tee-ah-sah	selalu • sentiasa
ambassador	doo-*tah*	duta
among	dee *ahn*-tah-ruh/	di antara/
	kah-*lah*-ngahn	kalangan
anarchist	hoo-roo-hah-*ruh*	huru-hara
ancient	*pur*-buh • *koo*-no • *too*-uh	purba • kuno • tua
and	dahn	dan
angry	mah-*rah(h)*	marah
animal	bee-*nah*-tahng •	binatang •
	hai-wahn	haiwan
to annoy	meng-*gahng*-goo	mengganggu
	[*gahng*-goo]	[ganggu]
to answer	men-*jah*-wahb [*jah*-wahb]	**menjawab [jawab]**
ant	se-*mut*	semut
antibiotics	an-tai-bai-*o*-tik	antibiotik
antiques	*bah*-rahng *ahn*-tik	barang antik
antiseptic	pem-*bahs*-mee koo-*mahn*	pembasmi kuman
any	*ah*-puh pun •	apa pun •
	se-*bah*-rahng	sebarang
anything	*ah*-puh-*ah*-puh	apa-apa
anytime	*bee*-luh-*bee*-luh	bila-bila
anywhere	mah-*nuh*-mah-*nuh*	mana-mana
apple	*eh*-pahl	epal
appointment	te-moo-*jahn*-jee	temujanji
appropriate	se-soo-ai	sesuai
approximately	*kee*-ruh-*kee*-ruh	kira-kira
archaeological	kah-jee-*pur*-buh •	kajipurba •
	ahr-kee-o-lo-ji	arkeologi
architecture	se-nee-*bee*-nuh	senibina
to argue	mem-*bahn*-tah(h)	membanta
	[*bahn*-tah(h)]	[bantah]
arm (of body)	le-*ngahn*	lengan
to arrive	dah-tahng • *tee*-buh •	datang • tiba
	sahm-*pai*	• sampai
arrivals	ke-dah-*tah*-ngahn	kedatangan
	[*dah*-tahng] •	[datang] •
	ke-*tee*-buh-an [*tee*-buh]	ketibaan [tiba]
art	se-*nee*	seni
artist	se-*nee*-mahn/	seniman/
	se-*nee*-wah-tee **(m/f)**	seniwati
artwork	ka-ri-*ah* se-*nee*	karya seni
ashtray	be-*kahs* ah-boo ro-ko(k)	bekas abu rokok
to ask for something	me-*min*-tuh [*min*-tuh]	meminta [minta]
to ask a question	ber-*tah*-nyuh [*tah*-nyuh]	bertanya [tanya]
asleep	*tee*-dur	tidur

assault	se-*rah*-ngahn	serangan
assistance	per-*to*-lo-ngan • *bahn*-too-ahn	pertolongan • bantuan
asthma	*sah*-kit le-*lah(h)*	sakit lelah
at (location)	dee • de-*kaht*	di • dekat
at (time)	pah-*duh*	pada
ATM	ay tee ehm	ATM
atmosphere (of place)	*swah*-sah-nuh	suasana
atmosphere (of planet)	*aht*-mos-fe-rah	atmosfera
aunt	e-*mah(k)* sow-*dah*-ruh	emak saudara
autumn	*moo*-sim *loo*-ru(h)	musim luruh
avenue	*jah*-lahn	jalan
avocado	ah-vo-*kah*-do	avokado

B

baby	*bah*-yee	bayi
babysitter	pen-*jah*-guh *ah*-nah(k)	penjaga anak
back (of body)	*ping*-gahng	pinggang
at the back (behind)	dee be-*lah*-kahng	di belakang
backpack	behg *sahn*-dahr	beg sandar
bad	boo-*ru(k)*	buruk
bad (attitude)	see-*kahp*	sikap
bad (weather)	coo-*ah*-chuh	cuaca
bag	behg	beg
baggage	bah-*gah*-see • *bah*-rahng-*bah*-rahng	bagasi • barang-barang
baggage claim	*toon*-tu-tahn bah-*gah*-see	tuntutan bagasi
bakery	ke-*dai* ro-tee	kedai roti
ball (for sport)	*bo*-luh	bola
banana	*pee*-sahng	pisang
band (music)	*koom*-poo-lahn	kumpulan
bandage	kain *pem*-bah-lut	kain pembalut
bank	bank	bank
bank clerk	ke-*rah*-nee bank	kerani bank
bar (drinks)	bahr	bar
barber	peng-*gun*-ting *rahm*-but	penggunting rambu
to bargain	*tah*-wahr-me-*nah*-wahr [*tah*-wahr]	tawar-menawar [tawar]
basket	*bah*-kul	bakul
to bathe	*mahn*-dee	mandi
bathing suit	*bah*-joo re-*nahng*	baju renang
bathroom	*bee*-li(k) air	bilik air
battery	*bah*-te-ree	bateri
to be (see Grammar, page 29)		

beach	*pahn*-tai	*pantai*
bean	*kah*-chahng	*kacang*
beautiful (scenery)	*in*-dah(h)	*indah*
beautiful (woman or object)	chahn-*ti(k)*	*cantik*
because	se-*bahb* • ke-*rah*-nuh	*sebab* • *kerana*
bed	*kah*-til	*katil*
bedroom	*bee*-li(k) *tee*-dur	*bilik tidur*
beef	*dah*-ging *lem*-boo	*daging lembu*
beer	bir • ah-*ra(k)*	*bir* • *arak*
before	se-*be*-lum	*sebelum*
beggar	pe-*nge*-mis	*pengemis*
to begin	moo-*luh*-kahn	*mulakan*
behind	dee be-*lah*-kahng	*di belakang*
below	dee bah-*wah(h)*	*di bawah*
beside	dee te-*pee*/*sahm*-ping	*di tepi/samping*
best	*ter*-bai(k)	*terbaik*
bet	tah-*ru*-hahn	*taruhan*
better	le-*bi(h)* bai(k)	*lebih baik*
between	*ahn*-tah-ruh	*antara*
bicycle	bah-*see*-kahl	*basikal*
big	be-*sahr*	*besar*
bill (account)	bil	*bil*
binoculars	te-*ro*-pong	*teropong*
bird	boo-*rung*	*burung*
birth certificate	soo-*raht* be-rah-*nah(k)*	*surat beranak*
birthday (cake)	(kehk) *hah*-ree *jah*-dee/lah-*hir*	*(kek) hari jadi/lahir*
to bite	meng-*gee*-git [*gee*-git]	*menggigit [gigit]*
bite (dog,insect)	*gee*-gee-tahn	*gigitan*
black	*hee*-tahm	*hitam*
blanket	se-*lee*-mut	*selimut*
to bleed	ber-*dah*-rah(h) [*dah*-rah(h)]	*berdarah [darah]*
blood	*dah*-rah(h)	*darah*
blood group	*koom*-poo-lahn *dah*-rah(h)	*kumpulan darah*
blood pressure	te-*kah*-nahn *dah*-rah(h)	*tekanan darah*
blood test	*oo*-jee-ahn *dah*-rah(h)	*ujian darah*
blue	*bee*-roo	*biru*
to board (ship, etc)	nai(k)	*naik*
boarding pass	pahs nai(k)	*pas naik*
boat	bot • pe-*rah*-hoo • *sahm*-pahn	*bot* • *perahu* • *sampan*
body	*bah*-dahn	*badan*
boiled water	air *mah*-sah(k)	*air masak*
bone	*too*-lahng	*tulang*

book	*boo*-koo	buku
to make a booking	mem-*boo*-aht	membuat
	tem-pah-hahn	tempahan
bookshop	ke-*dai boo*-koo	kedai buku
boots	boot • *kah*-sut boot	but • kasut but
border	*sem*-pah-dahn	sempadan
bored	*bo*-sahn	bosan
to borrow	me-*min*-jahm [*pin*-jahm]	meminjam [pinjam]
both	ke-*doo*-uh-*doo*-uh	kedua-dua

Don't bother.
bee-*ahr*-lah(h)   *Biarlah.*

bottle	bo-*tol*	botol
bottle opener	pem-*boo*-kuh bo-*tol*	pembuka botol
(at the) bottom	(dee) bah-*hah*-gee-ahn	(di) bahagian
	bah-*wah*(h) • dee dah-*sahr*	bawah • di dasar
box (package)	ko-*tah*(k)	kotak
boy	*ah*-nah(k) le-*lah*-kee	anak lelaki
boyfriend	te-*mahn* le-*lah*-kee •	teman lelaki •
	pah(k)-we	pakwe (col)
brain	o-*tah*(k)	otak
bread	*ro*-tee	roti
break (fracture)	pe-*chah*	pecah
breakfast	sah-rah-*pahn pah*-gee	sarapan pagi
to bribe	me-rah-soo-*ah*(h)	merasuah
bridge	*jahm*-bah-tahn	jambatan
brilliant	bah-*gus*	bagus
to bring	mem-*bah*-wuh [*bah*-wuh]	membawa [bawa]
broken	pah-*tah*(h)	patah
older brother	ah-*bahng*	abang
brown	chok-*laht*	coklat
bruise	*tahn*-duh le-*bahm*	tanda lebam
bucket	*bahl*-dee	baldi
Buddhist	pe-*ngah*-nut *boo*-duh	penganut Buda
bug (insect)	se-*rahng*-guh	serangga
to build	mem-*bee*-nuh [*bee*-nuh]	membina [bina]
building	*bah*-ngoo-nahn	bangunan
burn	*bah*-kahr	bakar
... bus	bahs ...	bas ...
city	*bahn*-dahr	bandar
intercity	ahn-tah-ruh *bahn*-dahr	antara bandar
bus station	*steh*-sehn bahs	stesen bas
bus stop	per-*hen*-tee-ahn bahs	perhentian bas
business	per-nee-ah-*gah*-ahn	perniagaan

busker	peng-hi-bur jah-lah-nahn	penghibur jalanan
busy (place/party)	rah-mai	ramai
(time)	si-bu(k)	sibuk
but	te-tah-pee	tetapi
butter	men-teh-guh	mentega
butterfly	koo-poo-koo-poo	kupu-kupu
buttons	boo-tahng	butang
to buy	mem-be-lee [be-lee]	membeli [beli]

C

cabin	bee-li(k)	bilik
calm	te-nahng	tenang
camera (shop)	(ke-dai) ka-me-rah	(kedai) kamera
to camp	ber-keh-mah(h) [keh-mah(h)]	berkhema [khemah]
campsite	kah-wah-sahn	kawasan
	per-keh-mah-han	perkhemahan
can (able)	bo-leh(h) • dah-paht •	boleh • dapat •
	mahm-poo	mampu

Can we camp here?
bo-leh(h) ta(k) kah-mee
ber-keh-mah(h) dee see-nee?   *Boleh tak kami berkhemah di sini?*

to cancel	mem-bah-tahl-kah [bah-tahl]	membatalka [batal]
candle	lee-lin	lilin
can opener	pem-boo-kuh tin	pembuka tin
car (park)	tem-paht le-tah(k) ke-reh-tuh	(tempat letak) kereta
cards (playing)	down te-rup	daun terup
careful	ber-hah-tee-hah-tee	berhati-hati
to carry	mem-bah-wuh [bah-wuh]	membawa [bawa]
cash	wahng too-nai	wang tunai
cashier	joo-roo-wahng	juruwang
cassette	kah-seht	kaset
cat	koo-ching	kucing
cave	goo-uh	gua
CD	see dee	CD
to celebrate	me-rah-yuh-kahn [rah-yuh]	merayakan [raya]
chair	ke-roo-see	kerusi
chance	ke-mung-ki-nahn •	kemungkinan •
	pe-loo-ahng	peluang
to change	me-noo-kahr [too-kahr]	menukar [tukar]
changing rooms	bee-li(k) too-kahr	bilik tukar
	pah-kai-ahn	pakaian
to chat up	me-ngoo-ruht	mengurat

cheap	*moo*-rah(h)	*murah*

Cheat!
pe-nee-*poo*!   *Penipu!*

to check	me-me-*rik*-sah [pe-*rik*-sah]	*memeriksa [periksa]*
check-in (desk)	(*kown*-ter) pen-*dahf*-tah-rahn	*(kaunter) pendaftara*
cheese	*keh*-joo	*keju*
chemist (pharmacy)	*fahr*-mah-see	*farmasi*
cheque	chehk	*cek*
chess	*chah*-tur	*catur*
chewing gum	gahm koo-*nyah(h)*	*gam kunyah*
chicken	*ai*-yahm	*ayam*
child	*ah*-nah(k)-*ah*-nah(k) • boo-*dah(k)*	*anak-anak* • *budak*
childminding	pen-jah-*gah*-ahn *ah*-nah(k)	*penjagaan anak*
chilli	*chee*-lee	*cili*
chocolate	*chok*-laht	*coklat*
to choose	me-*mee*-li(h) [*pee*-li(h)]	*memilih [pilih]*
Christmas Day	*hah*-ree *kris*-muhs	*Hari Krismas*
Christmas Eve	*mah*-lahm *kris*-muhs	*Malam Krismas*
church	ge-*reh*-juh	*gereja*
cigarette (papers)	(ker-*tahs*) ro-ko(k)	*(kertas) rokok*
clove cigarettes	*kreh*-teh(k)	*kretek*
cinema	*pahng*-gung *wai*-yahng	*panggung wayang*
citizenship	ke-*wahr*-guh-ne-gah-rah-ahn	*kewarganegaraan*
city	*bahn*-dahr	*bandar*
civil rights	ha(k) ah-*sah*-see mah-*noo*-see-uh	*hak asasi manusia*
(1st) class	ke-*lahs* (per-*tah*-muh)	*kelas (pertama)*
(2nd) class	ke-*lahs* (ke-*doo*-uh)	*kelas (kedua)*
to clean	mem-ber-*si(h)*-kahn [ber-*si(h)*]	*membersihkan [bersih]*
cliff	te-*bing ting*-gee	*tebing tinggi*
clock	jahm	*jam*
to close	me-*noo*-tup [*too*-tup]	*menutup [tutup]*
clothing (store)	(ke-*dai*) pah-*kai*-ahn	*(kedai) pakaian*
cloudy	*men*-dung • be-*rah*-wahn	*mendung • berawan*
(night)club	ke-*lahb* (*mah*-lahm)	*kelab (malam)*
coast	*ping*-gir lowt	*pinggir laut*
cocaine	ko-*kehn*	*kokain*
coconut	ke-*lah*-puh	*kelapa*
coffee	*ko*-pee	*kopi*
coins	*shee*-ling	*syiling*

| cold | se-*ju(k)* | *sejuk* |
| (to have a) cold | *ah*-duh sel-*se*-muh | *ada selsema* |

It's cold here.
se-*ju(k)* dee *see*-nee | *Sejuk di sini.*

cold water	air se-*ju(k)*	*air sejuk*
college	ko-*lehj*	*kolej*
colour	*wahr*-nuh	*warna*
to come (arrive)	dah-*tahng* • *tee*-buh	*datang • tiba*
to come from (origin)	be-*rah*-sahl [*ah*-sahl]	*berasal [asal]*

Come on!
joom! | *Jum!*

comfortable	se-*leh*-suh	*selesa*
company (friends)	kah-*wahn*-kah-*wahn*	*kawan-kawan*
(business)	*sha*-ree-kaht	*syarikat*
compass	*kom*-pahs	*kompas*
to complain	me-*ngah*-doo [*ah*-doo]	*mengadu [adu]*
computer game	per-*mai*-nahn kom-*piu*-ter	*permainan komputer*
concert	*kon*-sert	*konsert*
condom	*kon*-dom	*kondom*
to confirm (a booking)	me-nge-*sah(h)*-kahn [*sah(h)*]	*mengesahkan [sah]*

Congratulations!
tah(h)-nee-ah(h)! | *Tahniah!*

constipation	*sem*-be-lit • *kons*-tee-pah-see	*sembelit • konstipasi*
contraceptive	kon-trah-*sehp*-see	*kontrasepsi*
to cook	*mah*-sah(k)	*masak*
cool (temperature)	dee-*ngin*	*dingin*

Cool!
bah-*gus*! | *Bagus!*

corner	soo-*dut* • *pen*-joo-roo	*sudut • penjuru*
corrupt (adj)	*soo*-kuh me-ne-*ree*-muh rah-soo-ah(h)	*suka menerima rasuah*
cost (of object/service)	*hahr*-guh • kos	*harga • kos*
cotton	*kah*-pahs	*kapas*
cough (n/v)	*bah*-tu(k)	*batuk*
to count	me-*ngee*-ruh [*kee*-ruh]	*mengira [kira]*
country	ne-*gah*-ruh	*negara*

countryside	kah-*wah*-sahn *loo*-ahr *bahn*-dahr	kawasan luar bandar
court (legal)	mah(h)-*kah*-mah(h)	mahkamah
(tennis)	*pah*-dahng teh-*nis*	padang tenis
cow	*lem*-boo	lembu
crab	ke-*tahm*	ketam
crazy	*gee*-luh	gila
credit card	kahd *kreh*-dit	kad kredit
crossroad	sim-*pahng jah*-lahn	simpang jalan
crowded	pe-*nuh(h)* se-*sa(k)*	penuh sesak
cucumber	*tee*-mun	timun
cup	chah-*wahn*	cawan
custom (tradition)	*ah*-daht	adat
customs (border)	*kahs*-tahm	kastam
to cut	me-*mo*-tong [*po*-tong]	memotong [potong]
cute (baby)	cho-*mehl*	comel

D

daily	hah-ree-*ahn*	harian
to dance	ber-*dahn*-sah [*dahn*-sah]	berdansa [dansa]
dangerous	bah-*hah*-yuh	bahaya
dark	ge-*lahp*	gelap
date (appointment)	te-*moo*-jahn-jee	temujanji
(time)	tah-*rikh*	tarikh
date of birth	tah-*rikh* lah-*hir*	tarikh lahir
daughter	*ah*-nah(k) pe-*rem*-pwahn	anak perempuan
dawn (sunrise)	fah-*jahr* (mah-tuh-*hah*-ree ter-*bit*)	fajar (matahari terbit)
day	hah-*ree*	hari
day after tomorrow	*loo*-suh	lusa
day before yesterday	kel-*mah*-rin • *doo*-uh hah-ree le-*pahs*	kelmarin • dua hari lepas
in (six) days	dah-*lahm* (e-*nahm*) hah-ree	dalam (enam) hari
dead (battery/animal)	*mah*-tee	mati
dead (person)	me-*ning*-gahl *doo*-ni-uh	meninggal dunia
deaf	pe-*kah(k)* • *too*-lee	pekak • tuli
death	ke-*mah*-tee-ahn	kematian
to decide	me-moo-*tus*-kahn [poo-*tus*]	memutuskan [putus]
deep	dah-*lahm*	dalam
deer	*roo*-suh	rusa
deforestation	pe-ne-*bah*-ngahn hoo-*tahn*	penebangan hutan
delay	ke-*leh*-wah-tahn • pe-*nahng*-gu-hahn	kelewatan • penangguhan
delicious	se-*dahp*	sedap

delirious	*gee*-luh	gila
democracy	deh-mo-*krah*-see	demokrasi
demonstration	toon-*ju(k)* pe-rah-*sah*-ahn	tunjuk perasaan
dentist	*dok*-tor *gee*-gee	doktor gigi
to deny	me-nah-*fee*-kahn [nah-*fee*]	menafikan [nafi]
deodorant	di-o-do-rahn	deodoran
depart	be-*rahng*-kaht [*ahng*-kaht]	berangkat [angkat]
department stores	poo-*saht*	pusat
	mem-be-*lee*-be-*lah(h)*	membeli-belah
departure	pe-le-*pah*-sahn	pelepasan
desert	*goo*-run •	gurun •
	pah-dahng *pah*-sir	padang pasir
destination	*dehs*-tee-nah-see	destinasi
develop (film)	men-*choo*-chee [*choo*-chee]	mencuci [cuci]
diabetes	*ken*-ching *mah*-nis	kencing manis
diarrhoea	*chi*-rit-*bi*-rit	cirit-birit
diary	*boo*-koo *chah*-tah-tahn	buku catatan
dictionary	*kah*-mus	kamus
to die (person)	me-*ning*-gahl [*ting*-gahl]	meninggal [tinggal]
different	ber-*beh*-zuh	berbeza
difficult	soo-*sah(h)* • soo-*kahr*	susah • sukar
dinner	*mah*-kahn *mah*-lahm	makan malam
director (of film)	pe-*ngah*-rah(h) *(fee*-lem)	pengarah (filem)
dirty	ko-*tor*	kotor
disabled	cha-*chat*	cacat
disco	*dis*-ko	disko
discount	*dis*-kown	diskaun
to discover	men-*joom*-pah-ee	menjumpai
	[*joom*-pah]	[jumpa]
disease	pe-*nyah*-kit	penyakit
distance (length)	jah-*rah(k)*	jarak
to dive	me-nye-*lahm* [se-*lahm*]	menyelam [selam]
diving equipment	*ah*-laht se-*lahm*	alat selam
dizzy	pe-*ning*	pening
to do	me-lah-*koo*-kahn [lah-*koo*] •	melakukan [laku] •
	mem-*boo*-aht [*boo*-aht]	membuat [buat]

What are you doing?	*Buat apa?*
boo-aht *ah*-puh?	
I didn't do it.	*Bukan saya.*
boo-*kahn sai*-yuh	

doctor	*dok*-tor	doktor
documentary	do-kiu-men-*tah*-ree	dokumentari
dog	*ahn*-jing	anjing

door	*peen*-too	*pintu*
dope (drugs)	dah-*dah(h)*	*dadah*
double bed	*kah*-til ke-*lah*-min	*katil kelamin*
drama (arts)	(se-*nee*) *drah*-mah	*(seni) drama*
to dream	ber-*mim*-pee	*bermimpi [mimpi]*
dress	*bah*-joo gown	*baju gaun*
drink	mee-nu-*mahn*	*minuman*
to drink	*mee*-num	*minum*
to drive	me-*mahn*-doo	*memandu [pandu]*
drivers licence	leh-*sehn* me-*mahn*-doo	*lesen memandu*
drug (prescription)	*oo*-baht	*ubat*
(illegal)	dah-*dah(h)*	*dadah*
drug dealer	pen-joo-*ahl* dah-*dah(h)*	*penjual dadah*
drums	drahm • gen-*dahng*	*dram • gendang*
to be drunk	mah-*bu(k)*	*mabuk*
to dry	me-nge-*ring*-kahn [ke-*ring*]	*mengeringkan [kering]*
duck	ee-*ti(k)*	*itik*
dysentery	pe-*nyah*-kit beh-*ra(k)* dah-rah(h)	*penyakit berak darah*

E

each	se-*tee*-ahp • *tee*-ahp-*tee*-ahp	*setiap • tiap-tiap*
ear	te-*lee*-nguh	*telinga*
early	*ah*-wahl	*awal*

It's early. *Masih awal*
mah-si(h) ah-*wahl*

to earn	men-*dah*-paht [*dah*-paht]	*mendapat [dapat]*
earrings	soo-*bahng* • *ahn*-ting-*ahn*-ting	*subang • anting-anting*
earth	boo-*mee*	*bumi*
east	*tee*-mur	*timur*
easy	se-*nahng* • moo-*dah(h)*	*senang • mudah*
eat	*mah*-kahn	*makan*
economy (class)	(ke-*lahs*) ee-ko-*no*-mee	*(kelas) ekonomi*
editor	pe-*nyun*-ting	*penyunting*
to educate	men-dee-*di(k)* [dee-*di(k)*]	*mendidik [didik]*
education	pen-dee-*di(k)*-kahn	*pendidikan*
egg	te-*lur*	*telur*
elections	pee-lee-*hahn*-rah-yuh	*pilihanraya*
electricity	eh-*lehk*-trik	*elektrik*
embarrassment	*mah*-loo	*malu*

embassy	ke-*doo*-tah-ahn	*kedutaan*
emergency	ke-che-*mah*-sahn • dah-*roo*-raht	*kecemasan* • *darurat*
employee	pe-*ker*-juh	*pekerja*
employer	mah-*ji(k)*-kahn	*majikan*
empty	*ko*-song	*kosong*
to end	me-ngah-*khi*-ree [*ah*-khir]	*mengakhiri [akhir]*
endangered species	bee-*nah*-tahng *hahm*-pir poo-*pus*	*binatang hampir pupus*
engine	*ehn*-jin	*enjin*
engineer	joo-*roo*-te-ruh	*jurutera*
English	*ing*-ge-ris	*Inggeris*
to enjoy (oneself)	me-*nik*-mah-tee [*nik*-maht]	*menikmati [nikmat]*

Enough!
dah(h) *choo*-kup!   *Dah cukup!*

to enter	mah-*su(k)*	*masuk*
entertaining	meng-hee-*bur*-kahn [hee-*bur*]	*menghiburkan [hibur]*
entrance	*jah*-lahn/ *peen*-too mah-*su(k)*	*jalan/ pintu masuk*
envelope	sahm-*pul* soo-*raht*	*sampul surat*
environment	soo-ah-*sah*-nuh	*suasana*
epilepsy	sah-*wahn* bah-bee • eh-*pee*-lehp-see	*sawan babi* • *epilepsi*
equal opportunity	hah(k) *sah*-muh tah-*rahf*	*hak sama taraf*
equipment	ke-*leng*-kah-pahn [*leng*-kahp]	*kelengkapan [lengkap]*
essential	pah-*ling pen*-ting	*paling penting*
European	o-rahng eh-ro-*pah(h)*	*orang Eropah*
evening	pe-*tahng* • *mah*-lahm	*petang* • *malam*
every	se-*tee*-ahp • *tee*-ahp-*tee*-ahp	*setiap* • *tiap-tiap*
everyone	se-*moo*-uh o-rahng	*semua orang*
every day	se-*tee*-ahp hah-ree	*setiap hari*
everything	se-moo-*uh*-nyuh	*semuanya*
example	chon-*to(h)* • mi-*sah*-lahn	*contoh* • *misalan*

For example ...
mi-*sahl*-nyuh .../chon-*to(h)*-nyuh ...   *Misalnya ... /Contohnya ...*

| excellent | sa-*ngaht* bai(k)/*oo*-lung | *sangat baik/ulung* |
| exchange (rate) | (kah-*dahr*) per-too-*kah*-rahn | *(kadar) pertukaran* |

english–malay

209

Excuse me.
mah-*ahf*-kahn *sai*-yuh   *Maafkan saya.*

exhibition	pah-*meh*-rahn	*pameran*
exit	ke-*loo*-ahr	*keluar*
expensive	mah-*hahl*	*mahal*
exploitation	ehks-*ploy*-tah-see	*eksploitasi*
to export	me-*ngehks*-port	*mengeksport*
	[*ehks*-port]	[*eksport*]
express mail	mehl *ehks*-prehs	*mel ekspres*
eye	*mah*-tuh	*mata*

F

face	*moo*-kuh	*muka*
factory	kee-*lahng*	*kilang*
to faint	*pehng*-sahn	*pengsan*
to fall	jah-*tuh*(h) • *goo*-gur	*jatuh • gugur*
family	ke-*loo*-ahr-guh	*keluarga*
famous	ter-ke-*nahl*	*terkenal*
fan (machine)	kee-*pahs*	*kipas*
(of a team)	pe-*nyo*-kong [*so*-kong]	*penyokong [sokong*

Fantastic!
bah-*gus*!   *Bagus!*

far	jow(h)	*jauh*

Is it far?
jow(h) tah(k)   *Jauh tak?*

farm	lah-*dahng* • ke-*bun*	*lading • kebun*
farmer	pe-*tah*-nee	*petani*
fart	*ken*-tut	*kentut*
fast (quick)	che-*paht*	*cepat*
fat	ge-*mu*(k)	*gemuk*
father	ah-*yah*(h) • bah-*puh*	*ayah • bapa*
fault (someone's)	sah-*lah*(h)	*salah*
fear	ke-tah-*ku*-tahn	*ketakutan*
feelings	pe-*rah*-sah-ahn [*rah*-suh]	*perasaan [rasa]*
female (human)	pe-*rem*-pwahn	*perempuan*
(animal)	be-*tee*-nuh	*betina*
festival	pe-rah-*yah*-ahn • *pehs*-tah	*perayaan • pesta*
fever	de-*mahm*	*demam*
few	be-be-*rah*-puh	*beberapa*
fiance(e)	too-*nah*-ngahn	*tunangan*
fiction	*fik*-shen	*fiksyen*

English	Pronunciation	Malay
fight	per-gah-*du(h)*-hahn	*pergaduhan*
to fight	ber-gah-*du(h)* [gah-*du(h)*]	*bergaduh [gaduh]*
to fill	me-*ngee*-see [*ee*-see]	*mengisi [isi]*
film (speed)	(ke-*lah*-joo-ahn) *fee*-lem	*(kelajuan) filem*
filtered	ber-*tah*-pis	*bertapis*
to find	men-*joom*-pah-ee [*joom*-pah]	*menjumpai [jumpa]*
finger	*jah*-ree	*jari*
finished	*hah*-bis	*habis*
fire	ah-*pee*	*api*
first	per-*tah*-muh	*pertama*
first-aid kit	ko-*tah(k)* per-to-*lo*-ngahn ke-che-*mah*-sahn	*kotak pertolongan kecemasan*
first name	*nah*-muh per-*tah*-muh	*nama pertama*
fish	ee-*kahn*	*ikan*
to fish	me-*mahn*-ching [*pahn*-ching]	*memancing [pancing]*
flag	ben-*deh*-ruh	*bendera*
flea	koo-*too*	*kutu*
flight	pe-ner-*bah*-ngahn	*penerbangan*
floor (of room)	*lahn*-tai	*lantai*
(storey)	*ting*-kaht	*tingkat*
flower (seller)	(pen-*joo*-ahl) *boo*-nguh	*(penjual) bunga*
fluent	*fah*-si(h)	*fasih*
fly	*lah*-laht	*lalat*
foggy	ber-*kah*-bus	*berkabus*
to follow (join in)	me-*ngee*-ku-tee [*ee*-kut]	*mengikuti [ikut]*
food	mah-*kah*-nahn	*makanan*
food stall	ge-*rai* • wah-*rung*	*gerai • warung*
foot	kah-*kee*	*kaki*
football (soccer)	bo-luh seh-*pah(k)*	*bola sepak*
footpath	*jah*-lahn pe-*jah*-lahn kah-*kee*	*jalan pejalan kaki*
for (purpose)	oon-*tu(k)* • boo-*aht*	*untuk • buat*
(length of time)	se-*lah*-muh	*selama*
foreigner	o-rahng *ah*-sing	*orang asing*
forest	hoo-*tahn*	*hutan*
forever	se-*lah*-muh-*lah*-muh-nyuh	*selama-lamanya*
to forget	*loo*-puh	*lupa*

I forget.
sai-yuh ter-*loo*-puh

Saya terlupa.

Forget about it!
tah(k) ah-puh!

Tak apa!

to forgive	me-mah-*ahf*-kahn [mah-*ahf*]	memaafkan [maaf]
fork	*gahr*-foo	garfu
fortune teller	too-*kahng* te-*nung*/tee-*li(k)*	tukang tenung/tilik
free (not bound)	beh-*bahs*	bebas
(of charge)	per-*choo*-muh	percuma
to freeze	mem-*be*-koo [*be*-koo]	membeku [beku]
fresh	se-*gahr*	segar
Friday	hah-ree joo-mah-aht	hari Jumaat
fried	go-*rehng*	goreng
friend	kah-*wahn* • te-*mahn*	kawan • teman
frog	*kah*-tah(k) • *ko*-do(k)	katak • kodok
from	dah-*ree* • dah-ree-*pah*-duh	dari • daripada
fruit	boo-*ah(h)*-boo-ah-hahn	buah-buahan
full	pe-*nu(h)*	penuh
full (of food)	ke-*nyahng*	kenyang
fun	se-*ro*-no(k)	seronok
to have fun	oon-*tu(k)* ber-se-*ro*-no(k)	untuk berseronok
to make fun of	me-*ngeh*-jeh(k)	mengejek
funeral	pe-mah-*kah*-mahn	pemakaman
funny	lah-*wah(k)* • ke-*lah*-kahr • *loo*-choo	lawak • kelakar • lucu
future	mah-*suh* de-*pahn*	masa depan

G

game (boardgame)	per-*mai*-nahn	permainan
(sport)	per-*mai*-nahn	permainan
game show	kuiz	kuiz
garage	gah-*rahj*	garaj
garden	ke-*bun*	kebun
gardens (botanical)	ke-*bun* bo-*tah*-nee	kebun botani
garlic	*bah*-wahng *poo*-ti(h)	bawang putih
gay	geh	gay
general	*oo*-mum • ahm	umum • am
generous	*moo*-rah(h) hah-*tee*	murah hati
gentle	*lem*-but	lembut
geography	ji-o-grah-fee	geografi
gift	pem-be-*ree*-ahn [be-*ree*]	pemberian [beri]
girl	boo-*dah(k)*/*ah*-nah(k) pe-*rem*-pwahn	budak/anak perempuan
girlfriend	te-*mahn* wah-*nee*-tah • *mah(k)*-we	teman wanita • makwe
give	mem-be-*ree* [be-*ree*]	memberi [beri]

Could you give me ...?
to-long bah-*gee* ...?   *Tolong bagi ...?*

glass	*kah*-chuh	*kaca*
glasses (eye)	cher-*min mah*-tuh	*cermin mata*
glue	gahm	*gam*
to go	*per*-gee	*pergi*

Let's go.
joom *per*-gee   *Jum pergi.*

We'd like to go to ...
kah-mee nah(k) *per*-gee ke ...   *Kami nak pergi ke ...*

Go straight ahead.
per-gee te-*rus*   *Pergi terus.*

to go home	poo-*lahng*	*pulang*
to go out with	ke-*loo*-ahr ber-*sah*-muh	*keluar bersama*
goal	gol	*gol*
goalkeeper	pen-jah-*guh* gol	*penjaga gol*
goat	*kahm*-bing	*kambing*
God (Muslim)	too-*hahn* • ahl-*luh(h)*	*Tuhan* • *Allah*
gold	e-*mahs*	*emas*
good	bai(k)	*baik*

Good afternoon.
se-*lah*-maht te-ngah-*hah*-ree/   *Selamat tengahari/*
pe-*tahng*   *petang*

Goodbye. (speaker leaving)
se-*lah*-maht *ting*-gahl   *Selamat tinggal.*

Goodbye. (speaker staying)
se-*lah*-maht *jah*-lahn   *Selamat jalan.*

Goodbye. (inf)
bai   *Bye.*

Good evening.
se-*lah*-maht pe-*tahng*   *Selamat petang.*

Good morning.
se-*lah*-maht *pah*-gee   *Selamat pagi.*

Good night.
se-*lah*-maht *mah*-lahm   *Selamat malam.*

government	ke-rah-*jah*-ahn	*kerajaan*
gram	grahm	*gram*

grammar	tah-tah-bah-*hah*-suh	tatabahasa
grandchild	choo-*choo*	cucu
grandfather	dah-*tu(k)* • ah-*tu(k)*	datuk • atuk
grandmother	neh-*neh(k)*	nenek
grape	*ahng*-gur	anggur
grass	*room*-put	rumput
grave	koo-*bur*	kubur

Great!
bah-*gus!*   *Bagus!*

green	*hee*-jow	hijau
grey	ke-*lah*-boo	kelabu
ground	tah-*na(h)*	tanah
group	*koom*-poo-lahn •	kumpulan •
	ke-*lom*-po(k)	kelompok
to guess	me-ne-*kuh* [te-*kuh*]	meneka [teka]
guest	te-*tah*-moo	tetamu
guide (person or audio)	pe-*mahn*-doo	pemandu
guidebook	*boo*-koo pahn-dwahn	buku panduan
guide dog	*ahn*-jing pe-*mahn*-doo	anjing pemandu
guided trek	trehk ber-*pahn*-doo	trek perbandu
guitar	gee-*tahr*	gitar

H

habit	ke-bee-ah-*sah*-ahn	kebiasaan
hair	*rahm*-but	rambut
hairbrush	be-*rus rahm*-but	berus rambut
half	se-te-*ngah(h)*	setengah
half a litre	se-te-*ngah(h) lee*-ter	setengah liter
to hallucinate	ber-*khah*-yahl [*khah*-yahl]	berkhayal [khayal]
ham	*dah*-ging bah-*bee*	daging babi
hammock	boo-*ai*-ahn	buaian
hand	tah-*ngahn*	tangan
handbag	behg tah-*ngahn*	beg tangan
handicrafts	*krahf*-tah-ngahn	kraftangan
handmade	boo-*ah*-tahn tah-*ngahn*	buatan tangan
handsome (male)	*hehnd*-sem • kah-*chah(k)*	hendsem • kacak
happy	gem-*bee*-ruh	gembira

Happy birthday!
se-*lah*-maht *hah*-ree *jah*-dee!   *Selamat hari jadi!*

harbour	pe-lah-*bu*-hahn	pelabuhan
hard (not soft)	ke-*rahs*	keras
(difficult)	soo-*sah(h)* • soo-*kahr*	susah • sukar

harassment	*gahng*-goo-ahn	gangguan
hashish	*gahn*-jah • *hah*-sis	ganja • hasis
hat	*to*-pee	topi
to have	ah-*duh* • mem-*poo*-nyah-ee [*poo*-nyah]	ada • mempunyai [punya]

Do you have ...?
ahn-dah ah-*duh* ... tah(k)

Anda ada ... tak?

I have ...
sai-yuh mem-*poo*-nyah-ee ...

Saya mempunyai ...

he	*dee*-uh	dia
head	ke-*pah*-luh	kepala
headache	*sah*-kit ke-*pah*-luh	sakit kepala
healthy	si-*haht*	sihat
to hear	men-de-*ngahr* [de-*ngahr*]	mendengar [dengar]
heart	*jahn*-tung	jantung
heat	hah-*buh* • *pah*-nahs	haba • panas
heavy	be-*raht*	berat

Hello.
heh-lo

Helo.

| helmet | *to*-pee ke-leh-*dahr* | topi keledar |
| to help | me-*no*-long [*to*-long] • mem-*bahn*-too [*bahn*-too] | menolong [tolong] • membantu [bantu] |

Help!
to-long!

Tolong!

herbs	*her*-bah	herba
herbalist (person)	*sin*-seh(h)	sinseh
herbalist shop	ke-*dai* oo-*baht* chee-nuh	kedai ubat Cina
here	dee *see*-nee	di sini
heroin (addict)	(pe-*nah*-gi(h)) *heh*-ro-in	(penagih) heroin
high	*teeng*-gee	tinggi
high school	se-ko-*lah*(h) me-ne-*ngah*(h)	sekolah menengah (SM)
to hike	ber-*jah*-lahn kah-*kee*	berjalan kaki
hiking boots	boot *jah*-lahn	but jalan
hill	boo-*kit*	bukit
Hindu	*hin*-doo	Hindu
to hire (rent)	me-*nyeh*-wuh [*seh*-wuh]	menyewa [sewa]
historical ruins	run-*tu*-hahn ber-se-*jah*-rah(h)	runtuhan bersejarah
history	se-*jah*-rah(h)	sejarah

to hitchhike	me-*noom*-pahng	menumpang
HIV positive	ehch ai vee *po*-si-tif	HIV positif
holiday	coo-*tee*	cuti
homeless	pe-*ngahng*-gur	penganggur
homosexual	ho-mo-*sehk*-soo-ahl	homoseksual
honest	*joo*-jur	jujur
honeymoon	*boo*-lahn mah-*doo*	bulan madu
horny	gah-*tahl*	gatal
horrible	*dah(h)*-shaht • me-nge-*ree*-kahn	dahsyat • mengerikan
horse (riding)	(pe-*nung*-gah-ngahn) *koo*-duh	(penunggangan) kuda
hospital	hos-*pee*-tahl	hospital
hospitality	ke-rah-*mah(h)*-tah-*mah(h)*-hahn	keramah-tamahan
hot (temperature)	*pah*-nahs	panas
(spicy)	pe-*dahs*	pedas

It's hot here.
pah-nahs dee *see*-nee   *Panas di sini.*

to be hot	ke-*pah*-nahs-sahn [*pah*-nahs]	kepanasan [panas]
hotel	ho-*tehl*	hotel
hour	jahm	jam
house	*roo*-mah(h)	rumah
how	mah-*chahm mah*-nuh • bah-*gai*-mah-nuh	macam mana • bagaimana

How can I get to ...?
mah-chahm *mah*-nuh *sai*-yuh bo-*leh(h)* per-gee ke ...?   *Macam mana saya boleh pergi ke ...?*

How do you say ... in Malay?
mah-chahm *mah*-nuh chah-*kahp* ... dah-*lahm* bah-hah-suh me-*lah*-yoo?   *Macam mana cakap ... dalam bahasa Melayu?*

How many? (animals)
be-*rah*-puh *eh*-kor?   *Berapa ekor?*

How many? (goods)
be-*rah*-puh *bah*-nya(k)?   *Berapa banyak?*

How much?
be-*rah*-puh?   *Berapa?*

hug	pe-*lu(k)*	peluk
human rights	*ha(k)* ah-sah-*see* mah-*noo*-si-uh	hak asasi manusia

humid	*lem*-bahb	*lembab*
a hundred	se-*rah*-tus	*seratus*
hungry	*lah*-pahr	*lapar*
to hunt	ber-*boo*-roo [*boo*-roo]	*berburu [buru]*
husband	soo-*ah*-mee	*suami*

I

| I | *sai*-yuh • *ah*-koo | *saya • aku* |

I'm (Chris).
sai-yuh (kris)   *Saya (Chris).*

ice	ais	*ais*
ice cream	ais krim	*ais krim*
idea	*ai*-deh-ah	*idea*
identification	pe-*nge*-nah-lahn	*pengenalan*
ID	kahd pe-*nge*-nah-lahn	*kad pengenalan*
idiot	bo-*do(h)*	*bodoh*
if	kah-*low*	*kalau*
imagine	mem-bah-*yahng*-kahn	*membayangkan*
immediately	de-*ngahn* ser-*tah*-mer-*tah*	*dengan serta-merta*
immigration	ee-mee-*greh*-sen	*imigresen*
important	*pen*-ting	*penting*

It's (not) important.
(tah(k)) *pen*-ting   *(Tak) penting.*

in	dah-*lahm*	*dalam*
in a hurry	ter-boo-*roo*-boo-*roo*	*terburu-buru*
in front of	dee de-*pahn*	*di depan*
included	ter-*mah*-su(k)	*termasuk*
income tax	*choo*-kai pen-dah-*pah*-tahn	*cukai pendapatan*
indigenous	*ahs*-lee	*asli*
indigestion	*sah*-kit pe-*rut*	*sakit perut*
infection	*jahng*-ki-tahn	*jangkitan*
information	*mahk*-loo-maht •	*maklumat •*
	in-for-*mah*-see	*informasi*
to inject	me-nyun-*ti(k)*-kahn	*menyuntikkan*
		[suntik]
injection	sun-*ti(k)*-kahn	*suntika [suntik]*
injury	ke-che-de-*rah*-ahn	*kecederaan*
	[che-de-*rah*]	*[cedera]*
insect	se-*rahng*-guh	*serangga*
inside	dee dah-*lahm*	*di dalam*
instructor	joo-roo-*lah*-ti(h) • goo-roo	*jurulatih • guru*

insurance	in-soo-*rahns*	*insurans*
intense	*sah*-ngaht • men-*dah*-lahm	*sangat* • *mendalam*
interesting	me-*nah*-ri(k)	*menarik*
international	ahn-tah-rah-*bahng*-suh	*antarabangsa*
intersection	per-*sim*-pah-ngahn	*persimpangan*
interview	wah-wahn-*chah*-ruh	*wawancara*
island	poo-*low*	*pulau*
itch	gah-*tahl*	*gatal*
itinerary	jah-*doo*-ahl	*jadual*
	per-jah-*lah*-nahn	*perjalanan*
ivory	gah-*ding*	*gading*

J

jacket	ja-*keht*	*jaket*
jail	pen-*jah*-ruh	*penjara*
jar	*bo*-tol	*botol*
jeans	jeen	*jean*
jeep	jeep	*jip*
jewellery	*bah*-rahng ke-*mahs*	*barang kemas*
job	pe-ker-*jah*-ahn	*pekerjaan*
joke	lah-*wah(k)* • ke-lah-*kahr*	*lawak* • *kelakar*
to joke	ber-lah-*wah(k)* [lah-*wah(k)*]	*berlawak [lawak]*
journalist	wahr-*tah*-wahn	*wartawan*
journey	per-jah-*lah*-nahn	*perjalanan*
judge (court)	hah-*kim*	*hakim*
juice	joos	*jus*
jump (across)	lom-*paht*	*lompat*
(high)	lon-*chaht*	*loncat*
jumper (sweater)	*bah*-joo se-*ju(k)*	*baju sejuk*
just one	sah-*too sah*-juh	*satu saja*
justice	ke-ah-*di*-lahn	*keadilan*

K

key	*koon*-chee	*kunci*
keyboard	pah-*pahn* ke-*koon*-chee	*papan kekunci*
kick	*ten*-dah-ngahn [*ten*-dahng]	*tendangan [tendang]*
kick off	me-moo-*lah*-ee [moo-*luh*]	*memulai [mula]*
to kill	mem-boo-*nuh(h)*	*membunuh*
	[boo-*nuh(h)*]	*[bunuh]*
kilogram	kee-lo-*grahm*	*kilogram*
kilometre	*ki*-lo-*mee*-ter	*kilometer*
kind (adj)	bai(k) hah-*tee*	*baik hati*
kindergarten	tah-*dee*-kah	*tadika*
kiss	*chee*-um	*cium*

English	Pronunciation	Malay
to kiss	men-*chee*-um [*chee*-um]	*mencium [cium]*
kitchen	dah-*pur*	*dapur*
knee	loo-*tut*	*lutut*
knife	*pee*-sow	*pisau*
to know (someone)	ke-*nahl*	*kenal*
(something)	*tah*-hoo	*tahu*

I (don't) know.
sai-yuh (*tee*-dah(k)) *tah*-hoo   *Saya (tidak) tahu.*

L

English	Pronunciation	Malay
lake	tah-*si(k)*	*tasik*
lamb	*ah*-nah(k) bee-*ree*-bee-*ree*	*anak biri-biri*
land (ground)	tah-*nah(h)*	*tanah*
landscape	lahns-*kahp*	*lanskap*
language	bah-*hah*-suh	*bahasa*
large	loo-*ahs* • be-*sahr*	*luas • besar*
last (final)	te-rah-*khir*	*terakhir*
last month	*boo*-lahn le-*pahs*	*bulan lepas*
last night	*mah*-lahm se-*mah*-lahm	*malam semalam*
last week	ming-*goo* le-*pahs*	*minggu lepas*
last year	*tah*-hoon le-*pahs*	*tahun lepas*
late (not on time)	leh-*waht* • *lahm*-baht	*lewat • lambat*
later	ke-*moo*-dee-ahn • *nahn*-tee	*kemudian • nanti*
laugh	ge-*lah(k)* • ke-tah-*wuh*	*gelak • ketawa*
laundry (shop)	ke-*dai* do-*bee*	*kedai dobi*
law	oon-*dahng*-oon-*dahng*	*undang-undang*
lawyer	pe-*gwahm*	*peguam*
laxatives	oo-*baht* pen-*choo*-chee	*ubat pencuci*
	pe-*rut*	*perut*
lazy	mah-*lahs*	*malas*
leader	pe-*meem*-pin [*peem*-pin]	*pemimpin [pimpin]*
leak	bo-*chor*	*bocor*
to learn	be-*lah*-jahr [*ah*-jahr]	*belajar [ajar]*
leather	*koo*-lit	*kulit*
lecture	koo-lee-*ah(h)* •	*kuliah •*
	shah-rah-hahn	*syarahan*
lecturer	pen-shah-*rah(h)*	*pensyarah*
left (behind/over)	dee-*ting*-gahl-kahn	*ditinggalkan*
	[*ting*-gahl]	*[tinggal]*
left (not right)	*ki*-ree	*kiri*
left-handed	*ki*-dahl	*kidal*
left luggage	bah-*gah*-see yahng	*bagasi yang*
	dee-*ting*-*gahl*-kahn	*ditinggalkan*

left-wing	sah-*yahp ki*-ree	*sayap kiri*
leg (body)	*kah*-kee	*kaki*
(in race)	poo-*si*-ngahn	*pusingan*
lemon	*lee*-mow nee-pis	*limau nipis*
length	*pahn*-jahng	*panjang*
lens	kahn-*tuh* • lehn-*sah*	*kanta* • *lensa*
lesbian	lehs-*bee*-uhn	*lesbian*
less	koo-*rahng*	*kurang*
letter	soo-*raht*	*surat*
library	per-poos-*tah*-kah-ahn	*perpustakaan*
lice	*koo*-too	*kutu*
to lie	me-*nee*-poo [*tee*-poo]	*menipu* [*tipu*]
life	*hee*-dup	*hidup*
lift (elevator)	lif	*lif*
light (electric)	*lahm*-poo	*lampu*
(not dark)	te-*rahng*	*terang*
(not heavy)	ri-*ngahn*	*ringan*
light bulb	*mehn*-tul	*mentul*
lighter	pe-me-*ti(k)* ah-*pee*	*pemetik api*
to like	*soo*-kuh • *ge*-mahr	*suka* • *gemar*
lips	*bee*-bir	*bibir*
lipstick	*gin*-choo	*gincu*
to listen	men-*de*-ngahr [*de*-ngahr]	*mendengar* [*dengar*]
little (small)	ke-*chil*	*kecil*
(amount)	se-*dee*-kit	*sedikit*
to live (life)	*hee*-dup	*hidup*
(somewhere)	*ting*-gahl	*tinggal*
liver	*hah*-tee	*hati*
local	tem-*pah*-tahn	*tempatan*
local (city) bus	bahs (*bahn*-dahr) tem-*pah*-tahn	*bas (bandar) tempatan*
location	tem-*paht*	*tempat*
to lock	me-*ngun*-chee [*koon*-chee]	*mengunci* [*kunci*]
long (measurement)	*pahn*-jahng	*panjang*
(time)	*lah*-muh	*lama*
long distance	jah-*rah(k) pahn*-jahng	*jarak panjang*
long-distance bus	bahs jah-*rah(k)* jow(h)	*bas jarak jauh*
to look	me-*lee*-haht [*lee*-haht]	*melihat* [*lihat*]
to look after	men-*jah*-guh [*jah*-guh]	*menjaga* [*jaga*]
to look for	men-*chah*-ree [*chah*-ree]	*mencari* [*cari*]
loose	*long*-gahr	*longgar*
to lose (something)	meng-hee-*lahng*-kahn [*hee*-*lahng*]	*menghilangkan* [*hilang*]
loss	ke-kah-*lah*-hahn [*kah*-*lah(h)*]	*kekalahan* [*kalah*]

220

lost	ter-*se*-saht [*se*-saht]	*tersesat [sesat]*

a lot (quantity)	*bah*-nya(k)	*banyak*
loud	*bee*-sing	*bising*
lounge (room)	roo-*ahng tah*-moo	*ruang tamu*
love	*kah*-si(h) • *chin*-tuh •	*kasih • cinta •*
	sah-yahng	*sayang*

I love you.
sai-yuh me-nyin-tah-*ee* moo   *Saya menyintai mu.*

lover	ke-*kah*-si(h)	*kekasih*
low	ren-*dah(h)*	*rendah*
loyal	se-*tee*-uh	*setia*
luck	nah-*sib*	*nasib*
lucky	be-*roon*-tung	*beruntung*
luggage	bah-*gah*-see	*bagasi*
luggage lockers	ahl-*mah*-ree bah-*gah*-see	*almari bagasi*
lunch	*mah*-kahn te-ngah-*hah*-ree	*makan tengahari*
lunchtime	*wak*-too *mah*-kahn	*waktu makan*
	te-ngah-*hah*-ree	*tengahari*
luxury	ke-meh-*wah*-hahn	*kemewahan*

M

machine	me-*sin*	*mesin*
mad (angry)	*mah*-rah(h)	*marah*
made (of)	dee-per-*boo*-aht	*diperbuat*
	(dah-ree-*pah*-duh)	*(daripada)*
magazine	mah-jah-*lah(h)*	*majalah*
mail	mehl	*mel*
main ...	... oo-*tah*-muh	*... utama*
road	*jah*-lahn	*jalan*
square	dah-*tah*-rahn	*dataran*
majority	mah-*jo*-ree-tee	*majoriti*
to make	mem-*boo*-aht [*boo*-aht]	*membuat [buat]*
make-up	*ah*-laht so-*leh(k)*-kahn	*alat solekan*
malaria	mah-lah-*ree*-ah	*malaria*
Malay	bah-*hah*-suh me-*lah*-yoo	*Bahasa Melayu*

I (don't) speak Malay.
sai-yuh *(tee-dah(k)) tah*-hoo *chah*-kahp   *Saya (tidak) tahu cakap*
bah-*hah*-suh me-*lah*-yoo   *bahasa Melayu*

Malaysia	mah-*lay*-see-ah	*Malaysia*
male (person)	le-*lah*-kee	*lelaki*
(animal)	*jahn*-tahn	*jantan*
man	le-*lah*-kee	*lelaki*
manager	pe-*ngoo*-rus	*pengurus*
mango	*mang*-guh	*mangga*
many	*bah*-nya(k)	*banyak*
map	pe-*tuh*	*peta*

Can you show me ... on the map?
to-long toon-*joo(k)*-kahn ... dee pe-*tuh*?   *Tolong tunjukkan ... di peta?*

market (night)	pah-*sahr (mah*-lahm)	*pasar (malam)*
marriage	per-*kah(h)*-wi-nahn	*perkahwinan*
to marry	ber-*kah(h)*-win •	*berkahwin* •
	ber-*nee*-kah(h)	*bernikah*
mask (face)	to-*pehng*	*topeng*
massage	oo-ru-tahn	*urutan*
to massage	me-*ngoo*-rut [*oo*-rut]	*mengurut [urut]*
mat	*tee*-kahr	*tikar*
matches	*mahn*-chis	*mancis*
material (for clothing)	kain	*kain*

It doesn't matter.
ta(k) *ah*-puh   *Tak apa.*

What's the matter?
ke-*nah*-puh be-*gee*-nee?   *Kenapa begini?*

mattress	tee-*lahm*	*tilam*
may (can)	bo-*leh(h)*	*boleh*
maybe	*moong*-kin	*mungkin*
meaning	*mahk*-nuh • *er*-tee	*makna • erti*
meat	*dah*-ging	*daging*
mechanic	me-*ka*-nik	*mekanik*
medicine	oo-*baht*	*ubat*
meditation	tah-*fah*-kur	*tafakur*
to meet	ber-*te*-moo [*te*-moo]	*bertemu [temu]*
meeting	per-te-*moo*-ahn •	*pertemuan* •
	me-*shoo*-ah-raht	*mesyuarat*
menthol (cigarettes)	(*ro*-ko(k)) *mehn*-tol	*(rokok) mentol*
menu	*meh*-noo	*menu*
message	pe-*sah*-nahn	*pesanan*
metal	lo-*gahm*	*logam*
metre	*mee*-ter	*meter*
midnight	te-*ngah(h) mah*-lahm	*tengah malam*

migraine	*mai*-grehn	migraine
milk	soo-soo	susu
millimetre	mi-lee-*mee*-ter	milimeter
million	joo-*tuh*	juta
mineral water	air mi-*ne*-rahl	air mineral
(with/without gas)	(ber-*kar*-bo-naht/	(berkarbonat/
	bee-*ah*-suh)	biasa)
minibus	bahs mee-*nee*	bas mini
minute	mi-nit	minit

Just a minute.
se-ke-*jahp*   Sekejap.

in (five) minutes
dah-*lahm (lee-*muh) *mi*-nit lah-*gee*   dalam (lima) minit lagi

mirror	*cher*-min	cermin
to miss (feel absence)	me-*rin*-doo-ee [*rin*-doo]	merindui [rindu]
Miss	chi(k)	Cik
mistake	ke-see-lah-*pahn* •	kesilapan •
	ke-sah-*lah*-hahn	kesalahan
misunderstanding	sah-*lah(h)* fah-*hahm*	salah faham
to mix	men-cham-*pur*-kahn	mencampurkan
	[chahm-*pur*]	[campur]
mobile phone	teh-*leh*-fon *bim*-bit	telefon bimbit
modem	mo-*dem*	modem
moisturising cream	krim pe-*lem*-bahb	krim pelembab
monastery	bee-*ah*-ruh	biara
Monday	*hah*-ree ees-nin	hari Isnin
money	*doo*-it • wahng	duit • wang
monk	bee-*ah*-rah-wahn	biarawan
monkey	mo-*nyeht* • ke-*ruh*	monyet • kera
month (this)	*boo*-lahn (*ee*-nee)	bulan (ini)
moon	*boo*-lahn	bulan
more	le-*bi(h)*	lebih
morning	*pah*-gee	pagi
Moslem	o-rahng ees-lahm	orang Islam
mosque	*mahs*-jid	masjid
mosquito (net)	nyah-mu(k) (ke-*lahm*-boo)	nyamuk (kelambu)
most (the)	(yahng) *pah*-ling	(yang) paling
mother	e-*mah(k)* • *ee*-boo	emak/ibu
mother-in-law	*ee*-boo mer-*too*-uh	ibu mertua
motorboat	bot ber-*mo*-tor	bot bermotor
motorcycle	mo-to-*see*-kahl	motosikal
motorway (tollway)	*jah*-lahn ber-tol	jalan bertol
mountain	*goo*-nung	gunung

mountain bike	bah-*see*-kahl *goo*-nung	basikal gunung
mountaineering	men-*dah*-kee *goo*-nung	mendaki gunung
mountain hut	pon-*do(k)*	pondok
mountain path	*jah*-lahn *goo*-nung	jalan gunung
mountain range	per-goo-*nu*-ngahn	pergunungan
mouth	*moo*-lut	mulut
movie	*fee*-lem	filem
Mr	en-*chi(k)* • *too*-ahn	Encik • Tuan
Mrs	pwahn	Puan
much	*bah*-nya(k)	banyak
mud	*loom*-pur	lumpur
muscle	o-*tot*	otot
museum	moo-*zee*-um	muzium
music	*moo*-zik	muzik
musician	pe-*main moo*-zik	pemain muzik
Muslim	o-*rahng ees*-lahm	orang Islam
must	*mes*-tee • hah-*rus*	mesti • harus

N

| name | *nah*-muh | nama |

What's your name?
see-*ah*-puh *nah*-muh *ahn*-dah   *Siapa nama anda?*

nappy	kain *lahm*-pin	kain lampin
nappy rash	roo-*ahm bah*-yee	ruam bayi
nationality	*bahng*-suh	bangsa
national park	tah-*mahn* ne-*gah*-ruh	taman negara
nature	ah-*lahm*	alam
	se-moo-luh-*jah*-dee	semulajadi
nausea	*moo*-ahl	mual
near	de-*kaht*	dekat

Is it near here?
de-*kaht*-kuh dah-*ree see*-nee?   *Dekatkah dari sini?*

necessary	*per*-loo	perlu
necklace	*rahn*-tai	rantai
need	*per*-loo	perlu
needle	*jah*-rum	jarum
(sewing, syringe)		
neighbour	*jee*-rahn	jiran
nervous	che-*mahs* • coo-*ah(k)*	cemas • cuak
never	*tee*-dah(k) per-*nah(h)*	tidak pernah
never mind	ta(k) *ah*-puh	tak apa

new	bah-*roo*	*baru*
news	be-*ree*-tuh	*berita*
newspaper	soo-*raht kah*-bahr	*surat khabar*
next	yahng be-ree-*kut*-nyah •	*yang berikutnya* •
	de-*pahn*	*depan*

Next time.
lain *kah*-lee   *Lain kali.*

next to	dee se-be-*lah(h)*	*di sebelah*
nickname	*nah*-muh *pang*-gi-lahn	*nama panggilan*
night	*mah*-lahm	*malam*
Saturday night	*sab*-too *mah*-lahm	*Sabtu malam*
no	*tee*-dah(k)	*tidak*
noise	*boo*-nyee	*bunyi*
noisy	*bee*-sing	*bising*
none	tee-*ah*-duh	*tiada*
noodles	mee	*mee*
noon	te-ngah-*hah*-ree	*tengahari*
north	oo-*tah*-ruh	*utara*
nose	*hee*-dung	*hidung*
not	boo-*kahn*	*bukan*
not yet	be-*lum* lah-*gee*	*belum lagi*
notebook	*boo*-koo *chah*-tah-tahn	*buku catatan*
nothing	*tee*-dah(k) *ah*-puh-*ah*-puh	*tidak apa-apa*
novel (book)	no-*vel*	*novel*
now	se-*kah*-rahng	*sekarang*
nuclear energy	te-*nah*-guh noo-*klee*-er	*tenaga nuklear*
nuclear testing	oo-*jee*-ahn noo-*klee*-er	*ujian nuklear*
nude	bo-*gehl* • te-*lahn*-jahng	*bogel • telanjang*
number	*nom*-bor	*nombor*
nun	bee-*ah*-rah-*wah*-tee	*biarawati*
nurse	joo-roo-*rah*-waht	*jururawat*
nut (food)	*kah*-chahng	*kacang*

O

occupation	pe-ker-*jah*-ahn	*pekerjaan*
ocean	*low*-tahn	*lautan*
offer	tah-*wah*-rahn	*tawaran*
office worker	pe-*ker*-juh pe-*jah*-baht	*pekerja pejabat*
offside	of-*said*	*offside*
often	se-*ring* • ke-*rahp*	*sering • kerap*
oil (cooking)	*min*-ya(k) mah-*sah(k)*	*minyak masak*

OK.
oh-kay/bai(k)   *OK./Baik.*

old (person)	*too*-uh	*tua*
(building)	*lah*-muh	*lama*
older sister	kah-*kah(k)*	*kakak*
older brother	ah-*bahng*	*abang*
Olympic Games	ke-*soo*-kah-nahn o-*lim*-pik	*Kesukanan Olimpik*
on (location)	dee	*di*
on time	te-*paht pah*-duh	*tepat pada*
	mah-*sah*-nyuh	*masanya*
once	se-*kah*-lee	*sekali*
once again	se-*kah*-lee lah-*gee*	*sekali lagi*
one-way (ticket)	(tee-*keht*) se-*hah*-luh	*(tiket) sehala*
onion	*bah*-wahng	*bawang*
only	hah-*nyuh*	*hanya*
open	*boo*-kuh	*buka*
to open	mem-*boo*-kuh [*boo*-kuh]	*membuka [buka]*
operation	o-pe-*rah*-see	*operasi*
(telephone) operator	o-pe-*ray*-tor (teh-*leh*-fon)	*operator (telefon)*
opinion	pen-*dah*-paht	*pendapat*
opposite	lah-*wahn*	*lawan*
or	ah-*tow*	*atau*
oral	lee-*sahn*	*lisan*
orange (colour)	o-*rehn* • *jeeng*-gah	*oren • jingga*
(food)	o-*rehn*	*oren*
orchestra	or-*kehs*-truh	*orkestra*
to order	me-*nehm*-pah(h)	*menempah*
	[*tehm*-pah(h)]	*[tempah]*
to organise	me-*ngah*-tur [*ah*-tur]	*mengatur [atur]*
orgasm	or-*gahs*-mah	*orgasma*
original	*ahs*-lee	*asli*
other	lain	*lain*
outgoing	rah-*mah(h)*-tah-*mah(h)*	*ramah-tamah*
outside	*loo*-ahr	*luar*
over (above)	dee ah-*tahs*	*di atas*
overdose	ter-*lah*-loo bah-*nya(k)*	*terlalu banyak*
	mah-kahn oo-baht	*makan ubat*
over here	dee *see*-nee	*di sini*
over there	dee *sah*-nuh	*di sana*
to we	ber-*hoo*-tahng	*berhutang*
owner	pe-*mee*-li(k)	*pemilik*
oxygen	ok-*see*-jen	*oksigen*

P

English	Pronunciation	Malay
package	*boong*-ku-sahn	bungkusan
padlock	me-*mahng*-guh • *mang*-guh	memangga • mangga (col)
pain	*sah*-kit	sakit
pain in the neck	me-nyoo-*sah(h)*-kahn	menyusahkan
painful	me-nyah-*kit*-kahn	menyakitkan
painkillers	oo-*baht* tah-*hahn sah*-kit	ubat tahan sakit
painter (artist)	pe-*loo*-kis • *ahr*-tis • se-*nee*-mahn	pelukis • artis • seniman
painting (activity)	me-*loo*-kis	melukis
(picture)	loo-*ki*-sahn	lukisan
pair (a couple)	se-*pah*-sahng	sepasang
palace	*ees*-tah-nuh	istana
pap smear	smir	smir
paper	ker-*tahs*	kertas
paraplegic	*loom*-pu(h) kah-*kee*	lumpuh kaki
parents	*ee*-boo bah-*puh* • o-rahng *too*-uh	ibu bapa • orang tua
parliament	*pahr*-lee-men	parlimen
part (n)	bah-*hah*-gee-ahn	bahagian
party (fiesta)	*pehs*-tuh	pesta
(political)	*pahr*-tee	parti
to pass (give)	mem-*be*-ree [*be*-ree]	memberi [beri]
passenger	pe-*noom*-pahng	penumpang
passport (number)	(*nom*-bor) *pahs*-port	(nombor) pasport
past (before)	dah-*hoo*-loo • yahng *lah*-loo	dahulu • yang lalu
path	*jah*-lahn ke-*chil* • lo-*rong*	jalan keci • lorong
patient (adj)	sah-*bahr*	sabar
to pay	mem-*bah*-yahr [*bah*-yahr]	membayar [bayar]
payment	bah-*yah*-rahn	bayaran
peace	ah-*mahn* • dah-*mai*	aman • damai
peak (of mountain)	*pun*-chah(k)	puncak
pedestrian	pe-*jah*-lahn *kah*-kee	pejalan kaki
pen	pehn	pen
penalty	hoo-*koo*-mahn	hukuman
penis	zah-*kahr*	zakar
penknife	*pee*-sow *lee*-paht	pisau lipat
pensioner	pe-*sah*-ruh	pesara
people	o-rahng	orang
perfect	sem-*pur*-nuh	sempurna
performance	per-toon-*ju(k)*-kahn	pertunjukan
perhaps	*moong*-kin	mungkin

period pain	*sah*-kit haid	*sakit haid*
permission	*ee*-zin	*izin*
permit	per-*mit*	*permit*
person	o-rahng	*orang*
personality	pe-ree-*bah*-dee	*peribadi*
to perspire	ber-pe-*lu(h)* [pe-*lu(h)*]	*berpeluh [peluh]*
petrol	*peh*-trol • *min*-yah(k)	*petrol • minyak*
pharmacy	fahr-*mah*-see	*farmasi*
phone book	*boo*-koo teh-*leh*-fon	*buku telefon*
phone box	teh-*leh*-fon ah-wahm	*telefon awam*
phonecard	kahd teh-*leh*-fon	*kad telefon*
photograph	*gahm*-bahr • *fo*-to	*gambar • foto*

May I take a photograph?
bo-*leh(h)* sai-yuh *ahm*-bil
gahm-bahr/fo-to?

Boleh saya ambil
gambar/foto?

photograph	*gahm*-bahr • *fo*-to	*gambar • foto*
photographer	joo-roo-*gahm*-bahr	*jurugambar*
photography	se-*nee* fo-to	*senifoto*
to pick up	me-*ngahm*-bil [*ahm*-bil]	*mengambil [ambil]*
pickpocket	pe-nye-*lu(k)* sah-koo	*penyeluk saku*
picture	*gahm*-bahr	*gambar*
piece	*po*-tong	*potong*
pig	*bah*-bee	*babi*
pill	pil	*pil*
the Pill	oo-*baht* pen-che-*gah(h)*	*ubat pencegah*
	hah-mil	*hamil*
pillow	*bahn*-tahl	*bantal*
pillowcase	sah-*rung bahn*-tahl	*sarung bantal*
pineapple	*nah*-nahs • *neh*-nahs	*nanas • nenas*
pink	*meh*-rah(h) *jahm*-boo	*merah jambu*
pipe (plumbing)	paip	*paip*
piss	ken-*ching*	*kencing*
to piss	boo-*ahng* air ke-*chil*	*buang air kecil*
place	tem-*paht*	*tempat*
place of birth	tem-*paht* ke-la-*hi*-rahn	*tempat kelahiran*
plain (adj)	se-*der*-hah-nuh	*sederhana*
plan	pe-*lahn*	*pelan*
planet	plah-*neht*	*planet*
plant	tah-*nah*-mahn	*tanaman*
plastic	*plahs*-tik	*plastik*
plate	*peeng*-gahn	*pinggan*
plateau	dah-*tah*-rahn *teeng*-gee	*dataran tinggi*
play (theatre)	*drah*-mah	*drama*

English	Pronunciation	Malay
to play (a game, music)	ber-*main* [main]	bermain [main]
(cards)	main kahd •	main kad •
	main down te-*rup*	main daun terup
player	pe-*main*	pemain
please	see-*lah*-kahn • *to*-long	silakan • tolong
plug (electricity)	pluhg	plug
plus	*tahm*-bah(h)	tambah
pocket	po-*keht* • sah-*koo* • ko-*cheh*(k)	poket • saku • kocek
poetry	sah-*jah*(k) • poo-ee-see	sajak • puisi
poisonous	be-*rah*-chun	beracun
poker (the game)	*po*-ker	poker
police	*po*-lis	polis
political speech	oo-*chah*-pahn •	ucapan/
	pee-*dah*-to po-*lee*-tik	pidato politik
politicians	*ah*-lee po-*lee*-tik	ahli politik
pollen	de-*boo*-nguh	debunga
pollution	pen-che-*mah*-rahn	pencemaran
pool (swimming)	ko-*lahm* re-*nahng*	kolam renang
(game)	per-*mai*-nahn bee-*lee*-uhrd	permainan biliard
poor	*mis*-kin	miskin
popular	po-*piu*-luhr	popular
pork	*dah*-ging bah-bee	daging babi
port (harbour)	pe-lah-*bu*-hahn	pelabuhan
portrait sketcher	pe-*loo*-kis po-*treht*	pelukis potret
possible	bo-*leh*(h)	boleh

It's not possible.
tee-dah(k) bo-*leh*(h)/dee-*lah*-rahng   *Tidak boleh./Dilarang.*

English	Pronunciation	Malay
postage	bah-*yah*-rahn pos	bayaran pos
postcard	pos-*kahd*	poskad
postcode	pos-*kod*	poskod
poster	*pos*-ter	poster
post office	pe-*jah*-baht pos	pejabat pos
pot (cooking)	pe-*ree*-u(k)	periuk
(dope)	*gahn*-jah	ganja
potato	ken-*tahng*	kentang
pottery	se-*nee* tem-*bee*-kahr	seni tembikar
poverty	ke-*mees*-ki-nahn	kemiskinan
power	koo-ah-*suh*	kuasa
prayer	do-*ah* • sem-*bah*-yahng	doa • sembahyang
prayer book	*boo*-koo do-*ah*	buku doa
to prefer	le-*bi*(h) soo-kuh	lebih suka
pregnant	hah-*mil* • me-*ngahn*-dung	hamil • mengandung
prehistoric art	se-*nee* prah-se-jah-*rah*(h)	seni prasejarah

premenstrual tension	pee em es	*PMS*
to prepare	me-nye-dee-*ah*-kahn [se-dee-*uh*]	*menyediakan [sedia]*
prescription	ah-rah-*hahn* dok-tor ber-*too*-lis	*arahan doktor bertulis*
present (time)	se-*kah*-rahng • *kee*-nee	*sekarang • kini*
(gift)	pem-be-*ree*-ahn [be-*ree*] • *hah*-dee-ah(h)	*pemberian [beri]• hadiah*
presentation	pe-*nyahm*-pai-ahn [*sahm*-pai]	*penyampaian [sampai*
presenter (TV, etc)	pe-*nyahm*-pai	*penyampai*
president	preh-*see*-den	*presiden*
pressure	te-*kah*-nahn	*tekanan*
pretty (adj)	chahn-*ti(k)* • een-*dah*(h) • lah-*wah*	*cantik • indah • lawa*
to prevent	men-che-*gah*(h)	*mencegah*
price		
(of goods or service)	*hahr*-guh	*harga*
pride	ke-*bahng*-gah-ahn [*bahng*-guh]	*kebanggaan [bangga]*
priest		
(Catholic, Protestant)	pah-de-*ree*	*paderi*
prime minister	per-dah-*nuh* men-te-ree	*perdana menteri*
print (artwork)	cheh-*ta(k)*-kahn (kar-*yah* se-*nee*)	*cetakan (karya seni)*
prison	pen-*jah*-ruh	*penjara*
prisoner	bahn-*doo*-ahn	*banduan*
private	per-sen-dee-*ree*-ahn • pe-*ree*-bah-dee	*persendirian • peribadi*
private hospital	hos-*pee*-tahl swahs-tah	*hospital swasta*
problem	mah-sah-ah-*lah*(h)	*masalah*
to produce	meng-*hah*-sil-kahn [*hah*-sil]	*menghasilkan [hasil]*
producer (film)	pe-*ner*-bit [ter-*bit*] (*fee*-lem)	*penerbit [terbit] (filem)*
profession	pe-ker-*jah*-ahn	*pekerjaan*
program (TV)	rahn-*chah*-ngahn	*rancangan*
projector	pro-*jehk*-tor	*projektor*
promise	*jahn*-jee	*janji*
proposal	chah-*dah*-ngahn • *ahn*-joo-rahn	*cadangan • anjuran*
prostitute	pe-*lah*-chur • soon-*dahl*	*pelacur • sundal*
to protect	me-*lin*-du-ngee [*lin*-dung]	*melindungi [lindung]*
protected forest	hoo-*tahn* sim-*pahn*	*hutan simpan*
protected species	hai-*wahn* ter-*leen*-dung	*haiwan terlindung*
to protest	mem-bahn-*tah*(h) [bahn-*tah*(h)]	*membantah [bantah]*

public toilet	tahn-*dahs* ah-*wahm*	*tandas awam*
to pull	me-*nah*-ri(k) [*tah*-ri(k)]	*menarik [tarik]*
pump	pahm	*pam*
puncture	ke-bo-*cho*-rahn	*kebocoran*
to punish	meng-*hoo*-kum [*hoo*-kum]	*menghukum [hukum]*
puppet (leather)	(*koo*-lit) bo-*neh*-kah	*(kulit) boneka*
(wooden)	*pah*-tung kah-*yoo*	*patung kayu*
puppy	ah-*nah*(k) *ahn*-jing	*anak anjing*
pure	*moor*-nee • soo-*chee* • too-*lehn*	*murni • suci • tulen*
purple	oo-*ngoo*	*ungu*
purse	*dom*-peht • puhrs	*dompet • purse*
to push	me-no-*lah*(k) [to-*lah*(k)]	*menolak [tolak]*
to put	me-le-*tah*(k)-kahn [le-*tah*(k)]	*meletakkan [letak]*

Q

qualifications	ke-lah-*yah*(k)-kahn	*kelayakan*
quality	moo-*too* • kwah-lee-*tee*	*mutu • kualiti*
quantity	joom-*lah*(h)	*jumlah*
quarantine	kwah-*rahn*-teen	*kuarantin*
quarter	soo-*koo*	*suku*
question	per-*tah*-nyuh-ahn • so-*ah*-lahn	*pertanyaan • soalan*
to question	ber-*tah*-nyuh [*tah*-nyuh]	*bertanya [tanya]*
queue	be-*rah*-tur	*beratur*
quick	che-*paht* • pahn-*tahs*	*cepat • pantas*
quickly	de-*ngahn* che-*paht*/pahn-*tahs*	*dengan cepat/pantas*
quiet	se-*nyahp* • soo-*nyee* • se-*pee*	*senyap • sunyi • sepi*
quinine	kui-*nin*	*kuinin*
to quit	ber-*hen*-tee [*hen*-tee]	*berhenti [henti]*

R

race (breed)	*bahng*-suh • kowm	*bangsa • kaum*
(sport)	per-*loom*-bah-ahn	*perlumbaan*
racism	rah-*sis*-mah	*rasisme*
racquet	rah-*keht*	*raket*
radiator	rah-*dee*-ah-tor	*radiator*
railroad	*jah*-lahn ke-reh-tah-*ah*-pee	*jalan keretapi*
railway station	*steh*-sehn ke-reh-tah-*ah*-pee	*stesen keretapi*
rain	*hoo*-jahn	*hujan*

It's raining heavily.
hoo-*jahn* le-*baht*   *Hujan lebat.*

english–malay

231

rally (demonstration)	per-*him*-pu-nahn	perhimpunan
rape	pe-ro-*go*-lahn [ro-*gohl*]	perogolan [rogol]
rare (uncommon)	jah-*rahng*	jarang
rash	roo-*ahm*	ruam
rat	*tee*-kus	tikus
rate of pay	kah-*dahr* pem-bah-*yah*-rahn	kadar pembayaran
raw (food)	men-*tah(h)*	mentah
razor	*pee*-sow choo-kur	pisau cukur
to read	mem-*bah*-chuh [*bah*-chuh]	membaca [baca]
ready	se-dee-*uh* • see-*ahp*	sedia • siap
to realise	me-nye-*dah*-ree [se-*dahr*]	menyedari [sedar]
reason	se-*bahb* • ah-*lah*-sahn	sebab • alasan
receipt	re-*sit*	resit
to receive	me-ne-*ree*-muh [te-ree-muh]	menerima [terima]
recent	bah-*roo* ber-*lah*-koo	baru berlaku
to recognise	ke-*nahl* • me-ngah-*koo*-ee [ah-*koo*-ee]	kenal • mengakui [akui]
to recommend	me-nge-*shor*-kahn [shor]	mengesyorkan [syor]
recording	rah-*kah*-mahn	rakaman
to recycle	meng-goo-*nah*-kahn kem-*bah*-lee	menggunakan kembali
red	*meh*-rah(h)	merah
referee	pe-*ngah*-dil	pengadil
reforestation	pe-nah-*nah*-mahn hoo-*tahn* se-*moo*-luh	penanaman hutan semula
refrigerator	pe-*tee* se-*ju(k)*	peti sejuk
refugee	pe-lah-*ree*-ahn	pelarian
to refund	pe-ngem-*bah*-lee-ahn wahng	pengembalian wang
to refuse	me-no-*la(k)* [to-*la(k)*] • *eng*-gahn	menolak [tolak] • enggan
region	kah-*wah*-sahn • dah-*eh*-rah(h)	kawasan • daerah
registered mail	soo-*raht* ber-*dahf*-tahr	surat berdaftar
to regret	me-nye-*sahl* [se-*sahl*]	menyesal [sesal]
relationship	hoo-*bu*-ngahn	hubungan
to relax	be-reh-*haht* [reh-*haht*]	berehat [rehat]
religion	ah-*gah*-muh	agama
religious	ke-ah-*gah*-mah-ahn • be-*ree*-mahn	keagamaan • beriman
to remember	ee-*ngaht*	ingat
remote	jow(h) • ter-pen-*chil*	jauh • terpencil
to rent	me-*nyeh*-wuh [*seh*-wuh]	menyewa [sewa]
to repair	mem-per-*bai*-kee	memperbaiki [baik]
repeat	me-ngoo-*lah*-ngee [oo-*lahng*]	mengulangi [ulang]

reply	jah-*wah*-pahn • bah-lah-*sahn*	*jawapan • balasan*
to reply	men-jah-*wahb* [jah-*wahb*]	*menjawab [jawab]*
to report	me-lah-*por*-kahn [lah-*por*]	*melaporkan [lapor]*
republic	ree-*puhb*-lik	*republik*
reservation	tem-*pah(h)*-hahn	*tempahan*
to reserve	me-nem-*pah(h)* [tem-*pah(h)*]	*menempah [tempah]*
respect	hor-*maht*	*hormat*
responsibility	tang-gung-*jah*-wahb	*tanggungjawab*
rest (relaxation)	reh-*haht*	*rehat*
(what's left)	*see*-suh	*sisa*
to rest	be-reh-*haht* [reh-*haht*]	*berehat [rehat]*
restaurant	rehs-*to*-rahn	*restoran*
result	*hah*-sil • ah-*kee*-baht	*hasil • akibat*
resumé	reh-siu-*meh* • see-vee	*resume • CV*
return	kem-*bah*-lee	*kembali*
return ticket	ti-*keht per*-gee bah-li(k)	*tiket pergi balik*
review	pe-me-*rik*-sah-ahn	*pemeriksaan*
	kem-*bah*-lee	*kembali*
rheumatism	pe-*nyah*-kit se-*ngahl*-se-ngahl	*penyakit sengal-sengal*
	too-*lahng*	*tulang*
rhythm	ren-*tah(k)*	*rentak*
rice (cooked)	nah-*see*	*nasi*
(uncooked)	be-*rahs*	*beras*
rich (food)	sah-*ngaht* le-*mah(k)*	*sangat lemak*
(wealthy)	kah-*yuh*	*kaya*
to ride (bike, horse)	me-*nai(k)*-kee [nai(k)]	*menaiki [naik]*
(bus, car,	me-*noong*-gahng	*menunggang*
plane, train)	[*toong*-gahng]	[*tunggang*]
right (not left)	*kah*-nahn	*kanan*
(correct)	be-*tul*	*betul*

You're right.
ahn-dah be-*tul*   *Anda betul.*

right now	se-*kah*-rahng *joo*-guh	*sekarang juga*
right-wing	sah-*yahp kah*-nahn	*sayap kanan*
ring (on finger)	*chin*-chin	*cincin*
(sound)	boo-*nyee*	*bunyi*

I'll give you a ring.
sai-yuh teh-*leh*-fon *ahn*-dah nahn-*tee*   *Saya telefon anda nanti.*

ripe	*mah*-sah(k)	*masak*
rip-off	ter-*lah*-loo mah-*hahl*	*terlalu mahal*
risk	ree-*see*-ko	*risiko*
river	soo-*ngai*	*sungai*

road	*jah*-lahn	*jalan*
road map	pe-*tuh jah*-lahn	*peta jalan*
roasted	*pahng*-gahng	*panggang*
to rob	me-rom-*pa(k)* [rom-*pa(k)*]	*merompak [rompak]*
rock	bah-*too*	*batu*
rock climbing	pen-dah-*kee*-ahn	*pendakian*
	te-*bing* bah-*too*	*tebing batu*
rock group	koom-*pu*-lahn rok	*kumpulan rock*
rolling	ber-goo-*ling*	*berguling*
romance	per-*chin*-tah-ahn	*percintaan*
roof	ah-*tahp* • *boom*-bung	*atap • bumbung*
room (number)	(*nom*-bor) bee-li(k)	*(nombor) bilik*
rope	tah-*lee*	*tali*
rotten	boo-*su(k)* • ro-*sah(k)*	*busuk • rosak*
round (shape)	boo-*laht*	*bulat*
(at the) roundabout	(dee) boo-*lah*-tahn	*(di) bulatan*
to row	men-*dah*-yung	*mendayung*
rubbish	sahm-*pah(h)*	*sampah*
rug	per-*mai*-dah-nee	*permaidani*
ruins	run-*tu*-hahn	*runtuhan*
rules	pe-*rah*-tu-rahn	*peraturan*
run	lah-*ree*	*lari*

S

sad	se-*di(h)*	*sedih*
safe (secure)	se-*lah*-maht	*selamat*
safe (vault)	pe-*tee* be-*see*	*peti besi*
safe sex	sehks se-*lah*-maht	*seks selamat*
sail	lah-*yahr*	*layar*
sailor	*ah*-nah(k) *kah*-pahl	*anak kapal*
saint	o-*rahng* soo-*chee*	*orang suci*
(on) sale	joo-*ah*-lahn moo-*ra(h)*	*jualan murah*
sales department	bah-*hah*-gee-ahn	*bahagian*
	pen-joo-*ah*-lahn	*penjualan*
salt	gah-*rahm*	*garam*
salty	*mah*-sin	*masin*
same	*sah*-muh	*sama*
sand	*pah*-sir	*pasir*
sandals	se-*lee*-pahr	*selipar*
sanitary napkins	too-*ah*-luh wah-*nee*-tah	*tuala wanita*
Saturday	*hah*-ree *sab*-too	*hari Sabtu*
to save	me-nye-*lah*-maht-kahn	*menyelamatkan*
	[se-*lah*-maht]	*[selamat]*
to say	ber-*kah*-tuh [*kah*-tuh]	*berkata [kata]*

scared	tah-*kut*	*takut*
scenery	pe-*mahn*-dah-ngahn	*pemandangan*
school	se-ko-*lah(h)*	*sekolah*
science	*sains*	*sains*
scientist	*sain*-tis	*saintis*
scissors	*goon*-ting	*gunting*
scoreboard	pah-*pahn mah*-tuh/	*papan mata/*
	mahr-*kah(h)*	*markah*
screen (film)	lah-*yahr* pe-*rah(k)*	*layar perak*
script	mah-*niu*-skrip • nahs-*kah(h)*	*manuskrip • naskhah*
sculpture	se-*nee* oo-kir	*seni ukir*
sea	lowt	*laut*
to search	men-*chah*-ree [*chah*-ree]	*mencari [cari]*
seasick	mah-*bu(k)* lowt	*mabuk laut*
seaside	te-*pee* lowt	*tepi laut*
season	*moo*-sim	*musim*
seat	tem-*paht doo*-du(k)	*tempat duduk*
seat belt	tah-*lee peeng*-gahng	*tali pinggang*
	ke-leh-*dahr*	*keledar*
second (unit of time)	sah-*aht*	*saat*
(in order)	ke-*doo*-uh	*kedua*
secretary	se-*tee*-uh-oo-suh-huh	*setiausaha*
to see	lee-*haht*	*lihat*

I see. (understand)
sai-yuh fah-*hahm*   Saya faham.

See you later.
joom-*puh* lah-*gee*   Jumpa lagi.

See you tomorrow.
joom-*puh* eh-so(k)   Jumpa esok.

self-employed	be-*ker*-juh sen-*dee*-ree	*bekerja sendiri*
selfish	me-mee-*kir*-kahn dee-*ree*	*memikirkan diri*
	sen-dee-*ree sah*-juh	*sendiri saja*
self-service	lah-*yahn* dee-*ree*	*layan diri*
to sell	men-joo-*ahl* [joo-*ahl*]	*menjual [jual]*
to send	meng-*hahn*-tahr [*hahn*-tahr]	*menghantar [hantar]*
sensible	ah-*rif* • moo-*nah*-sah-bah(h)	*arif • munasabah*
sentence (words)	ah-*yaht*	*ayat*
(prison)	hoo-*ku*-mahn	*hukuman*
to separate	me-mee-*sah(h)*-kahn	*memisahkan*
	[pee-*sah(h)*]	*[pisah]*
serious	see-*ree*-uhs	*serius*
servant	*o*-rahng gah-*jee*	*orang gaji*

to serve	me-lah-*yah*-nee [lah-*yahn*]	melayani [layan]
service (assistance)	*khid*-maht • *jah*-suh	khidmat • jasa
several	be-be-*rah*-puh	beberapa
to sew	jah-*hit*	jahit
sex	sehks	seks
sexism	sehk-*sis*-muh	seksisme
sexy	mem-be-*rah*-hee-kahn [be-*rah*-hee]	memberahikan [berahi]
shade	te-*du(h)*	teduh
to shampoo	men-shehm-*poo* [shem-*poo*]	mensyampu [syempu]
shape	ben-*tu(k)*	bentuk
to share (with)	ber-*kong*-see (de-*ngahn*)	berkongsi (dengan)
to share a dorm	ber-*kong*-see bee-li(k)/dorm	berkongsi bilik/dorm
to shave	*choo*-kur	cukur
she	*dee*-uh	dia
sheet (bed)	*chah*-dahr	cadar
(of paper)	he-*lai*	helai
shell (sea)	*koo*-lit	kulit
ship	*kah*-pahl	kapal
shirt	*bah*-joo • ke-*meh*-juh	baju • kemeja
shit	tai(k)	tahi
to shit	boo-*ahng* air be-*sahr*	buang air besar
shoelaces	tah-*lee kah*-sut	tali kasut
shoes	*kah*-sut	kasut
to shoot	me-*nehm*-ba(k) [*tehm*-ba(k)]	menembak [tembak]
shop	ke-*dai*	kedai
to go shopping	mem-be-*lee*-be-*lah(h)* [be-*lee*]	membeli-belah [beli]
short (length, height)	*pehn*-deh(k)	pendek
short film	*fee*-lem *pehn*-deh(k)	filem pendek
short story	cher-*pehn*	cerpen
shortage	ke-koo-*rah*-ngahn	kekurangan
shorts (clothes)	se-loo-*ahr* pehn-*de(k)*	seluar pendek
shoulders	*bah*-hoo	bahu
to shout	men-je-*rit* [je-*rit*]	menjerit [jerit]
show	per-toon-*joo(k)*-kahn [toon-*joo(k)*]	pertunjukan [tunjuk]
to show	me-noon-*joo(k)*-kahn [toon-*joo(k)*]	menunjukkan [tunjuk]

Please show me (on the map).
to-long toon-*joo(k)*-kahn (dee pe-*tuh*)   *Tolong tunjukkan (di peta).*

to shower	*mahn*-dee	mandi
shrimp	oo-*dahng*	udang
shrine	tem-*paht* soo-*chee*	tempat suci

shut	*too*-tup	tutup
shy	*mah*-loo • se-*gahn*	malu • segan
sick	*sah*-kit	sakit
sickness	pe-nyah-*kit*	penyakit
side (of a street)	te-*pee (jah*-lahn)	tepi (jalan)
sign	*tahn*-duh	tanda
to sign	me-nahn-duh-*tah*-ngah-nee [tahn-duh-*tah*-ngahn]	menandatangani [tandatangan]
signature	tahn-duh-*tah*-ngahn	tandatangan
silk	*soo*-te-ruh	sutera
silver	peh-*ra(k)*	perak
of silver	dah-ree-*pah*-duh peh-*ra(k)*	daripada perak
similar	se-*mah*-chahm • se-*roo*-puh	semacam • serupa
simple	se-der-*hah*-nuh	sederhana
sin	do-*suh*	dosa
since	se-*jah(k)*	sejak
to sing	me-*nyah*-nyee [*nyah*-nyee]	menyanyi [nyanyi]
singer	pe-*nyah*-nyee	penyanyi
single room	*bee*-li(k) se-o-rahng	bilik seorang
to sit	*doo*-du(k)	duduk
size	saiz	saiz
skin	*koo*-lit	kulit
skinny	*koo*-rus	kurus
sky	lah-*ngit*	langit
sleazy (person)	ko-*tor* • *tee*-dah(k) ke-*mahs*	kotor • tidak kemas
to sleep	*tee*-dur	tidur
sleeping bag	kahn-*tung tee*-dur	kantung tidur
sleeping pills	oo-*baht tee*-dur	ubat tidur
sleepy	me-*ngahn*-tu(k)	mengantuk
to slice	meng-*hee*-ris	menghiris [hiris]
slide (film)	ge-*lahn*-sahr fee-*lem*	gelansar filem
slow	per-*lah*-hahn	perlahan
small	ke-*chil*	kecil
smell	bow	bau
to smell	meng-*hee*-doo [*hee*-doo]	menghidu [hidu]
to smile	se-*nyum*	senyum
smoke	ah-*sahp*	asap
to smoke	me-*ro*-ko(k) [*ro*-ko(k)]	merokok [rokok]
snake	oo-*lahr*	ular
soap	sah-*bun*	sabun
soap opera	*drah*-mah sah-*bun*	drama sabun
soccer	bo-*luh seh*-pah(k)	bola sepak
social welfare	ke-bah-*ji(k)*-kahn so-see-*ahl*	kebajikan sosial
socialist	so-see-*ah*-lis	sosialis
society	mah-*shah*-rah-kaht	masyarakat

237

socks	*sto*-king	stoking
soft	*lem*-but	lembut
some	be-be-*rah*-puh	beberapa
someone	se-se-o-rahng	seseorang
something	se-soo-*ah*-too	sesuatu
sometimes	kah-*dahng*-kah-dahng	kadang-kadang
son	*ah*-nah(k) le-lah-*kee*	anak lelaki
song	lah-*goo*	lagu
soon	se-ke-*jahp* lah-*gee*	sekejap lagi
sorry	mah-*ahf*	maaf

I'm sorry.
mah-*ahf*   *Maaf.*

sound	boo-*nyee*	bunyi
sour	*mah*-sahm	masam
south	se-lah-*tahn*	selatan
souvenir	chen-de-ruh-*mah*-tuh	cenderamata
souvenir shop	ke-*dai* chen-de-ruh-*mah*-tuh	kedai cenderamata
soy sauce	kee-*chahp*	kicap
space (area)	roo-*ahng*	ruang
speak	chah-*kahp*	cakap
to speak (Malay)	ber-bah-*hah*-suh me-*lah*-yoo	berbahasa Melayu
special	ees-tee-*meh*-wuh • khahs	istimewa • khas
specialist	pah-*kahr*	pakar
speed (limit)	(hahd) lah-*joo*	(had) laju
spicy	pe-*dahs*	pedas
spoon	soo-*doo*	sudu
sport	soo-*kahn*	sukan
sportsplayer	pe-*main* soo-*kahn*	pemain sukan
sprain	ter-se-*lee*-uh(h)	terseliuh
spring (season)	*moo*-sim boo-nguh	musim bunga
(coil)	pe-*gahs* • spring	pegas • spring
square (shape)	se-gee-*em*-paht	segiempat
(plaza)	dah-*tah*-rahn	dataran
stadium	stah-*dee*-um	stadium
stage	pen-*tahs*	pentas
stairs	*tahng*-guh	tangga
stale	bah-*see*	basi
stamp	se-*tehm*	setem
standard (adj)	stahn-*dahrd* • tah-*rahf*	standard • taraf
standard of living	tah-*rahf* ke-hee-*du*-pahn	taraf kehidupan
starfruit	be-*lim*-bing	belimbing
stars (in the sky)	bin-*tahng*	bintang
to start	me-moo-*luh*-kahn [moo-*luh*]	memulakan [mula]

station	*steh*-sehn	stesen
stationmaster	pe-gah-*wai* pe-*ngah*-wahs	pegawai pengawas
	steh-sehn ke-reh-tah-*ah*-pee	stesen keretapi
statue	*pah*-tung	patung
to stay (remain)	*ting*-gahl	tinggal
(overnight)	ber-*mah*-lahm [*mah*-lahm]	bermalam [malam]
to steal	men-*choo*-ree [*choo*-ree]	mencuri [curi]
steam	wahp	wap
steep (hill)	choo-*rahm*	curam
step	lang-*kah(h)*	langkah
still (yet)	*mah*-si(h)	masih
stomach	pe-*rut*	perut
stomachache	*sah*-kit pe-*rut*	sakit perut
stone	bah-*too*	batu
stoned (drugged)	mah-*bu(k)*	mabuk
to stop	ber-*hen*-tee [*hen*-tee]	berhenti [henti]

Stop!
ber-*hen*-tee!   *Berhenti!*

storm	ree-*but*	ribut
story	che-*ree*-tuh	cerita
stove	*dah*-pur	dapur
straight (line)	(gah-*ri*-sahn) loo-*rus*	(garisan) lurus
strange	pe-*li(k)* • *gahn*-jil • ah-*neh(h)*	pelik • ganjil • aneh
stranger	o-rahng yahng *tee*-dah(k)	orang yang tidak
	dee-ke-*nah*-lee	dikenali
stream (small river)	soo-*ngai*	sungai
street	*jah*-lahn	jalan
strength	ke-koo-*ah*-tahn	kekuatan
(on) strike	mo-*go(k)*	mogok
string	tah-*lee*	tali
stroll	*jah*-lahn-*jah*-lahn •	jalan-jalan •
	see-*ahr*-see-*ahr*	siar-siar
strong	koo-*aht*	kuat
student (school)	pe-*lah*-jahr • moo-*rid*	pelajar • murid
student (university)	mah-*hah*-sis-wah •	mahasiswa •
	pe-*lah*-jahr	pelajar
studio	stoo-*dee*-o	studio
stupid	bo-*do(h)*	bodoh
style	*gah*-yuh	gaya
subtitles	tehks	teks
suburb	*ping*-gir bahn-*dahr*	pinggir bandar
suburbs of	*ping*-gir bahn-*dahr*	pinggir bandar
Kuala Lumpur	koo-*ah*-luh *loom*-pur	Kuala Lumpur

success	ke-jah-*yah*-ahn	*kejayaan*
to suffer	men-de-*ree*-tuh [de-*ree*-tuh]	*menderita [derita]*
sugar	*goo*-luh	*gula*
summer	*moo*-sim *pah*-nahs	*musim panas*
sun	mah-tuh-*hah*-ree	*matahari*
sunblock	krim pe-*leen*-dung	*krim pelindung*
	chah-*hah*-yuh	*cahaya*
	mah-tuh-*hah*-ree	*matahari*
sunburnt	*koo*-lit ter-bah-*kahr*	*kulit terbakar*
Sunday	*hah*-ree ah-*hahd*	*hari Ahad*
sunglasses	cher-*min mah*-tuh *hee*-tahm	*cermin mata hitam*
sunny	che-*rah(h)*	*cerah*
sunrise	mah-tuh-*hah*-ree ter-*bit*	*matahari terbit*
sunset	mah-tuh-*hah*-ree	*matahari*
	ter-be-*nahm*	*terbenam*
supermarket	pah-sah-*rah*-yuh	*pasaraya*

| **Sure.** | | |
| bo-*leh(h)* | | *Boleh.* |

surface mail	mehl bee-*ah*-suh	*mel biasa*
to surf	ber-se-*lahn*-chahr	*berselancar*
	[se-*lahn*-chahr]	*[selancar]*
surfboard	pah-*pahn* se-*lahn*-chahr	*papan selancar*
surname	*nah*-muh ke-loo-*ahr*-guh	*nama keluarga*
surprise	ke-joo-*tahn*	*kejutan*
to survive	hee-*dup*	*hidup*
to sweat	ber-*pe*-lu(h) [pe-*lu(h)*]	*berpeluh [peluh]*
sweet (adj)	mah-*nis*	*manis*
sweets	*goo*-luh-*goo*-luh	*gula-gula*
to swim	be-re-*nahng* [re-*nahng*]	*berenang [renang]*
swimming pool	ko-*lahm* re-*nahng*	*kolam renang*
swimsuit	*bah*-joo re-*nahng*	*baju renang*
sword	pe-*dahng*	*pedang*
sympathetic	ber-sim-*pah*-tee	*bersimpati*
synagogue	ge-*reh*-juh yah-*hoo*-dee	*gereja Yahudi*
synthetic	sin-*teh*-tik	*sintetik*
syringe	*jah*-rum soon-*ti(k)*	*jarum suntik*

T

table	*meh*-juh	*meja*
tablet	bee-*jee* oo-*baht*	*biji ubat*
table tennis	ping-*pong*	*ping-pong*
tail (of animal)	*eh*-kor	*ekor*
tailor	too-*kahng* jah-*hit*	*tukang jahit*

to take (away)	me-*ngahm*-bil [*ahm*-bil]	mengambil [ambil]
(train)	me-*nai(k)*-kee	menaiki [naik]
to take off (depart)	ber-le-*pahs* [le-*pahs*] • be-*rahng*-kaht [*ahng*-kaht]	berlepas [lepas] • berangkat [angkat]
to take photographs	me-*ngahm*-bil fo-to/ *gahm*-bahr	mengambil foto/ gambar
to talk (chat)	ber-*chah*-kahp [*chah*-kahp]	bercakap [cakap]
tall	*ting*-gee	tinggi
tampon	*tahm*-pon	tampon
taste	*rah*-suh	rasa
tasty	se-*dahp* • *eh*-nah(k)	sedap • enak
tax	*choo*-kai	cukai
taxi (stand)	(*steh*-sehn) *tehk*-see	(stesen) teksi
tea	teh(h)	teh
teacher	*goo*-roo • *chi(k)*-goo	guru • cikgu (col)
teaching	me-*ngah*-jahr	mengajar
team (sport)	pah-*su(k)*-kahn	pasukan
tear (crying)	air mah-*tuh*	air mata
teeth	*gee*-gee	gigi
telegram	teh-leh-*grahm*	telegram
telephone	teh-*leh*-fon	telefon
to telephone	me-neh-*leh*-fon [teh-*leh*-fon]	menelefon [telefon]
television	teh-leh-*vee*-shen	televisyen
to tell (inform)	mem-be-ree-*tah*-hoo [*tah*-hoo]	memberitahu [tahu]
teller	teh-ler	teler (col)
temperature (fever)	soo-*hoo* bah-*dahn*	suhu badan
(weather)	soo-*hoo* oo-*dah*-ruh	suhu udara
temple		
(Buddhist)	to-*kong* boo-*dah*	tokong Buda
(Chinese)	to-*kong* chee-nuh	tokong Cina
(Hindu)	*koo*-il	kuil
tennis (court)	(pah-*dahng*) teh-*nis*	(padang) tenis
tent	kheh-*mah(h)*	khemah
tent pegs	pah-*koo* kah-*yoo* • pahn-*chahng* kheh-*mah(h)*	paku kayu • pancang khemah
tenth	ke-se-*poo*-lu(h)	kesepuluh
terrible	me-nge-*ree*-kahn [nge-*ree*]	mengerikan [ngeri]
test (exam)	oo-*jee*-ahn (pe-pe-*rik*-sah-ahn)	ujian (peperiksaan)
to thank	ber-te-*ree*-muh *kah*-si(h)	berterima kasih

Thank you.
te-*ree*-muh *kah*-si(h)   *Terima kasih.*

that	*ee*-too	*itu*
theatre (play)	*pahng*-gung	*panggung*
	sahn-dee-*wah*-rah	*sandiwara*
there (distant)	dee *sah*-nuh	*di sana*
(nearby)	dee *see*-too	*di situ*

they	me-*reh*-kuh	*mereka*
thief	pen-choo-*ree*	*pencuri*
thin	*nee*-pis • *ti*-pis	*nipis • tipis*
to think	ber-*fee*-kir [*fee*-kir]	*berfikir [fikir]*
third	ke-*tee*-guh	*ketiga*
thirsty	hows • dah-*hah*-guh	*haus • dahaga*
this	*ee*-nee	*ini*
thought	fee-ki-*rahn*	*fikiran*
thread	be-*nahng*	*benang*
throat	te-*kah(k)* • ke-*rong*-kong	*tekak • kerongkong*
Thursday	*hah*-ree kah-*mis*	*hari Khamis*
ticket	tee-*keht*	*tiket*
ticket collector	pe-moo-*ngut* tee-*keht*	*pemungut tiket*
ticket office	pe-*jah*-baht tee-*keht*	*pejabat tiket*
tide (low/high)	air (*soo*-rut/pah-*sahng*)	*air (surut/pasang)*
tiger	hah-*ree*-mow	*harimau*
tight	ke-*taht* • sem-*pit*	*ketat • sempit*
time	mah-*suh*	*masa*

What time is it?
poo-kul be-*rah*-puh?   *Pukul berapa?*

timetable	jah-doo-*ahl* wak-too	*jadual waktu*
tin opener	pem-*boo*-kuh tin	*pembuka tin*
tired	pe-*naht*	*penat*
tissues	ti-*soo*	*tisu*
to	ke	*ke*
toad	*kah*-tah(k) • *ko*-do(k)	*katak • kodok*
toast (bread)	(ro-tee) *bah*-kahr	*(roti) bakar*
tobacco	tem-*bah*-kow	*tembakau*
today	*hah*-ree *ee*-nee	*hari ini*
together	ber-*sah*-muh	*bersama*
toilet paper	*tee*-soo	*tisu*
toilet	*tahn*-duhs	*tandas*
tomorrow	*eh*-so(k)	*esok*
tomorrow afternoon	te-*ngah*-*hah*-ree/	*tengahari/*

	pe-*tahng eh*-so(k)	*petang esok*
tomorrow morning	*eh*-so(k) *pah*-gee	*pagi esok*
tongue	lee-*dah(h)*	*lidah*
tonight	*mah*-lahm *ee*-nee	*malam ini*
too (excessive)	ter-*lah*-loo	*terlalu*
too (as well)	*joo*-guh • pun	*juga • pun*

Too expensive!
ter-*lah*-loo mah-*hahl!*   *Terlalu mahal!*

Too many/much!
ter-*lah*-loo *bah*-nya(k)!   *Terlalu banyak!*

tool	*ah*-laht	*alat*
tooth	*gee*-gee	*gigi*
tooth	*gee*-gee	*gigi*
(front/back)	(de-*pahn*/be-*lah*-kahng)	*(depan/belakang)*
toothache	*sah*-kit *gee*-gee	*sakit gigi*
toothbrush	be-*rus gee*-gee	*berus gigi*
toothpaste	oo-*baht gee*-gee	*ubat gigi*
torch (flashlight)	*lahm*-poo soo-*lu(h)*	*lampu suluh*
to touch	me-nyen-*tu(h)*[sen-*tu(h)*]	*menyentuh [sentuh]*
tour	ber-ke-*lee*-ling	*berkeliling*
tourist	pe-*lahn*-chong [*lahn*-chong]	*pelancong [lancong]*
tourist information	pe-*jah*-baht	*pejabat*
office	*mah(k)*-loo-maht	*maklumat*
	pe-*lahn*-chong	*pelancong*
toward	ke ah-*rah(h)*	*ke arah*
towel	too-*ah*-luh	*tuala*
tower	me-*nah*-ruh	*menara*
toxic waste	*see*-suh boo-ah-*ngahn*	*sisa buangan*
	tok-sik	*toksik*
track (footprints)	ke-*sahn* je-*ja(k)*	*kesan jejak*
(sports)	o-*lah(h)*-rah-guh	*olahraga*
(path)	*jah*-lahn ke-*chil* • lo-*rong*	*jalan kecil • lorong*
traffic	lah-loo-*lin*-tahs	*lalulintas*
traffic jam	ke-se-*sah*-tahn	*kesesatan*
	lah-loo-*lin*-tahs	*lalu lintas*
traffic lights	*lahm*-poo ee-*shah*-raht	*lampu isyarat*
trail (route)	*jah*-lahn	*jalan*
train	ke-reh-tuh-*ah*-pee	*keretapi*
train station	*steh*-sehn ke-reh-tuh-*ah*-pee	*stesen keretapi*
to translate	men-ter-je-*mah(h)*-kahn	*menterjemahkan*
	[ter-je-*mah(h)*]	*[terjemah]*
to travel	me-ngem-*bah*-ruh	*mengembara*

travel agency	eh-jen-*see* pe-*lahn*-cho-ngahn	*agensi pelancongan*
travel book	*boo*-koo kem-*bah*-ruh	*buku kembara*
travellers cheque	chehk kem-*bah*-ruh	*cek kembara*
travel sickness	mah-*bu(k)* jah-lahn	*mabuk jalan*
tree	*po*-ko(k) • *po*-hon	*pokok • pohon*
to trek	per-jah-*lah*-nahn [*jah*-lahn] • pe-ngem-*bah*-ruh-ahn [kem-*bah*-ruh]	*perjalanan [jalan] • pengembaraan [kembara]*
trip (journey)	per-jah-*lah*-nahn	*perjalanan*
trousers	se-loo-*ahr* pahn-*jahng*	*seluar panjang*
truck	lo-*ree*	*lori*
true	be-*nahr*	*benar*

It's true.
be-*nahr*   *Benar.*

to trust	per-*chah*-yuh	*percaya*
truth	ke-be-*nah*-rahn	*kebenaran*
to try (attempt)	men-*choo*-buh [*choo*-buh]	*mencuba [cuba]*
T-shirt	*bah*-joo tee	*baju T*
Tuesday	*hah*-ree se-*lah*-suh	*hari Selasa*
tune (song)	lah-*goo* • *nah*-duh	*lah-goo • nada*
turn	be-*lo(k)* • *poo*-sing	*belok • pusing*

Turn left/right.
beh-*lo(k) ki*-ree/*kah*-nahn   *Belok kiri/kanan.*

TV	teh-leh-*vee*-shen	*televisyen*
twice	*doo*-uh *kah*-lee	*dua kali*
twin beds	*kah*-til *kem*-bahr	*katil kembar*
twins	*kem*-bahr	*kembar*
type (of product)	je-*nis*	*jenis*
to type	me-*naip* (taip)	*menaip [taip]*
typhoid	tai-*foid*	*tifoid*
typical	bee-*ah*-suh	*biasa*
tyre	*tai*-yahr	*tayar*

U

umbrella	*pah*-yung	*payung*
under	*bah*-wah(h)	*bawah*
to understand	fah-*hahm*	*faham*

I (don't) understand.
sai-yuh (*tee*-dah(k)) fah-*hahm*   *Saya (tidak) faham.*

underwear	se-loo-*ahr* dah-*lahm*	*seluar dalam*
unemployed	pe-*ngahng*-gur	*penganggur*
unions	per-sah-*too*-ahn se-*ker*-juh	*persatuan sekerja*
universe	ah-*lahm* se-*mes*-tah	*alam semesta*
university	yoo-ni-*ver*-si-tee	*universiti*
unripe	be-*lum mah*-sah(k)	*belum masak*
unsafe	*tee*-dah(k) se-*lah*-maht	*tidak selamat*
until (June)	se-*hing*-guh (joon)	*sehingga (Jun)*
unusual	*loo*-ahr bee-*ah*-suh	*luar biasa*
up	ah-*tahs*	*atas*
uphill (road)	(*jah*-lahn) nai(k) boo-*kit*	*(jalan) naik bukit*
urgent	men-de-*sah(k)* • *pen*-ting	*mendesak* • *penting*
useful	ber-*goo*-nuh	*berguna*
usual	bee-*ah*-suh	*biasa*

V

vacant	*ko*-song	*kosong*
vacation	*choo*-tee	*cuti*
vaccination	pen-chah-*chah*-rahn	*pencacaran*
valley	*lem*-bah(h)	*lembah*
valuable	ber-*har*-guh	*berharga*
value (price)	nee-*lai*	*nilai*
van	vahn	*van*
vegetables	*sai*-yur-*sai*-yu-rahn	*sayur-sayuran*
vegetarian (food)	*sai*-yu-rahn *sah*-juh	*sayuran saja*
(person)	(*o*-rahng yahng)	*(orang yang)*
	mah-kahn *sai*-yur *sah*-juh	*makan sayur saja*

I'm vegetarian.
sai-yuh *mah*-kahn *sai*-yur sah-*hah*-juh   *Saya makan sayur sahaja.*

vegetation	toom-*bu(h)*- toom-*bu(h)*-hahn	*tumbuh- tumbuhan*
vein	oo-*raht* dah-rah(h)	*urat darah*
venereal disease	pe-*nyah*-kit ke-*lah*-min	*penyakit kelamin*
very	sah-*ngaht* • ah-*maht*	*sangat* • *amat*
video cassette	*kah*-seht *vi*-dee-o	*kaset video*
view	pe-*mahn*-dah-ngahn [*pahn*-dahng]	*pemandangan [pandang]*
village	*kahm*-pung • deh-*suh*	*kampung* • *desa*
virus	vi-*rus*	*virus*
visa	*vee*-sah	*visa*
to visit	me-lah-*waht* [lah-*waht*] • me-*ngoon*-ju-ngee [*koon*-jung]	*melawat [lawat]* • *mengunjungi [kunjung]*

vitamin	vi-*tah*-min	vitamin
voice	soo-*ah*-ruh	suara
volcano	*goo*-nung be-*rah*-pee	gunung berapi
volume (sound)	soo-*ah*-ruh	suara
vomit (n/v)	moon-*tah(h)*	muntah
to vote	me-*ngun*-dee [*un*-dee]	mengundi [undi]
vulgar	bee-*ah*-dahb • kah-*sahr*	biadab • kasar

W

wait	*toong*-goo	tunggu
waiter	pe-*lah*-yahn	pelayan
waiting room	*bee*-li(k) me-*noong*-goo	bilik menunggu
to wake up	bah-*ngun* • *bahng*-kit	bangun • bangkit
to walk	ber-*jah*-lahn kah-*kee*	berjalan kaki
wall (inside)	*deen*-ding	dinding
(outside)	tehm-*bo(k)*	tembok
to want	hen-*da(k)* • ee-ngin • mow	hendak • ingin • mah
war	pe-*rahng*	perang
wardrobe	*ahl*-mah-ree	almari
warm	soo-*ahm*	suam
to wash (yourself)	*mahn*-dee	mandi
(something)	men-*choo*-chee [*choo*-chee]	mencuci [cuci]
washing machine	me-*sin* bah-*su(h)*	mesin basuh
watch (for wrist)	jahm tah-*ngahn*	jam tangan
to watch	me-*non*-ton (*ton*-ton)	menonton [tonton]

Watch out!
ber-hah-*tee*-hah-*tee*!/ah-*wahs*!   *Berhati-hati!/Awas!*

water	air ...	air
boiled	... *mah*-sah(k)	masak
mineral	... ee-*ne*-ruhl	mineral
purified	... u-*lehn*	tulen
water bottle	bo-*tol* air	botol air
waterfall	air *ter*-jun	air terjun
watermelon	tem-*bee*-kai	tembikai
waves	om-*bah(k)*	ombak
way	*jah*-lahn	jalan

Please tell me the way to ...
to-long be-ree-*tah*-hoo *sai*-yuh   *Tolong beritahu saya*
jah-lahn ke ...?   *jalan ke ...?*

Which way?
jah-lahn *mah*-nuh?   *Jalan mana?*

we (incl)	*kee*-tuh	*kita*
(excl)	*kah*-mee	*kami*
weak	le-*mah(h)*	*lemah*
wealthy	kah-*yuh*	*kaya*
to wear	me-mah-*kai* [pah-*kai*]	*memakai [pakai]*
weather	choo-*ah*-chuh	*cuaca*
wedding	per-kah-*wi*-nahn •	*perkahwinan* •
	per-nee-*kah(h)*-hahn	*pernikahan*
wedding cake	kehk per-kah-*wi*-nahn	*kek perkahwinan*
wedding present	*hah*-dee-ah(h)	*hadiah*
	per-kah-*wi*-nahn	*perkahwinan*
Wednesday	*hah*-ree rah-*boo*	*hari Rabu*
(this) week	*ming*-goo (*ee*-nee)	*minggu ini*
weekend	hoo-*jung meeng*-goo	*hujung minggu*
to weigh	me-*nim*-bahng	*menimbang*
	[*tim*-bahng]	*[timbang]*
weight	be-*raht*	*berat*

Welcome.
se-lah-*maht* dah-*tahng*   *Selamat datang.*

You're welcome.
sah-*muh*-sah-*muh*   *Sama-sama.*

welfare	ke-bah-*ji(k)*-kahn •	*kebajikan* •
	ke-se-*jah(h)*-te-rah-ahn	*kesejahteraan*
well (healthy)	si-*haht*	*sihat*
west	bah-*raht*	*barat*
Westerner (col)	o-rahng bah-*raht*	*orang barat*
wet	bah-*sah(h)*	*basah*
what	*ah*-puh	*apa*

What?
ah-puh?   *Apa?*

What's he saying?
dee-*uh* chah-*kahp ah*-puh?   *Dia cakap apa?*

What is that?
ah-puh too?   *Apa tu?*

What's your name?
see-*ah*-puh *nah*-muh *ahn*-dah?   *Siapa nama anda?*

What time is it?
poo-kul be-*rah*-puh se-*kah*-rahng?   *Pukul berapa sekarang?*

wheel	ro-*duh*	roda
wheelchair	ke-*roo*-see be-*ro*-duh	kerusi beroda
when (past, future)	bee-luh	bila

When?
bee-luh?   Bila?

When does (the train) leave?
bee-luh (ke-reh-tah-*ah*-pee) ber-to-*la(k)*?   Bila (keretapi) bertolak?

Where?
mah-*nuh*?   Mana?

Where's the bank?
bank dee mah-*nuh*?   Bank di mana?

which	yahng	yang
while (currently)	*sahm*-bil	sambil
white	*poo*-ti (h)	putih
who	see-*ah*-puh	siapa

Who?
see-*ah*-puh?   Siapa?

Who's calling?
see-*ah*-puh yahng teh-*leh*-fon?   Siapa yang telefon?

Who is it?
see-*ah*-puh nee?   Siapa ni?

Who are they?
see-*ah*-puh me-*reh*-kuh?   Siapa mereka?

whole (all)	se-loo-*ru(h)*	seluruh
why	ke-*nah*-puh • me-*ngah*-puh	kenapa • mengapa

Why is the bank closed?
ke-*nah*-puh bank tu *too*-tup?   Kenapa bank tu tutup?

wide	leh-*bahr*	lebar
wife	*ees*-te-ree	isteri
wild animal	bee-*nah*-tahng lee-*yahr*/	binatang liar/
	boo-*ahs*	buas
to win	me-*nahng*	menang
wind	*ah*-ngin	angin
window	*ting*-kahp	tingkap
to go window-shopping	me-*lee*-haht-*lee*-haht	melihat-lihat saja
	sah-juh [*lee*-haht]	[lihat]

windscreen	*kah*-chuh de-*pahn*	*kaca depan*
wine	wain	*wain*
wings	sah-*yahp*	*sayap*
winner	joo-*ah*-ruh • *jo*-hahn • pe-me-*nahng*	*juara • johan • pemenang*
winter	*moo*-sim se-*joo(k)*	*musim sejuk*
wire	wah-*yahr*	*wayar*
wise	bee-ja(k)-*sah*-nuh • *ah*-rif	*bijaksana • arif*
to wish	hah-*jaht* • hahs-raht • ke-*ee*-ngi-nahn [*ee*-ngin]	*hajat • hasrat • keinginan [ingin]*
with	de-*ngahn* • ber-*sah*-muh	*dengan • bersama*
within	dee dah-*lahm*	*di dalam*
within an hour	dah-*lahm* se-*jahm*	*dalam sejam*
without	*tahn*-puh	*tanpa*
without filter	*tahn*-puh *fil*-ter	*tanpa filter*
woman	wah-*nee*-tah • o-rahng pe-*rem*-pwahn	*wanita • orang perempuan*
wonderful	bah-*gus* se-kah-*lee* • meng-kah-*gum*-kahn	*bagus sekali • mengkagumkan*
wood (timber)	kah-*yoo* (bah-*la(k)*)	*kayu (balak)*
woodcarving	oo-ki-*rahn* kah-*yoo*	*ukiran kayu*
wool	boo-*loo* bee-*ree*-bee-*ree*	*bulu biri-biri*
word	per-kah-*tah*-ahn	*perkataan*
work	*ker*-juh	*kerja*
to work	be-*ker*-juh [*ker*-juh]	*bekerja [kerja]*
workout (sport)	lah-*ti(h)*-hahn (soo-*kahn*)	*latihan (sukan)*
work permit	*per*-mit *ker*-juh	*permit kerja*
world	doo-nee-*uh*	*dunia*
World Cup	pee-*ah*-luh doo-ni-*uh*	*Piala Dunia*
worried	ree-*sow* • *beem*-bahng • khoo-*ah*-tir	*risau • bimbang • khuatir*
worship	pe-nyem-*bah(h)*-hahn	*penyembahan*
worth	nee-*lai* • hahr-guh	*nilai • harga*
wound (injury)	loo-*kuh* (ke-che-de-*rah*-ahn)	*luka (kecederaan)*
wristwatch	jahm tah-*ngahn*	*jam tangan*
to write	me-*noo*-lis [*too*-lis]	*menulis [tulis]*
writer	pe-*noo*-lis	*penulis*
writing paper	*ker*-tahs *too*-lis	*kertas tulis*
wrong	sah-*lah(h)*	*salah*

I'm wrong. (my fault)
sai-yuh sah-*lah(h)*   *Saya salah.*

Y

year (this)	*tah*-hoon (*ee*-nee)	tahun (ini)
yellow	*koo*-ning	kuning
yes	yah	ya
yesterday	se-*mah*-lahm	semalam
yesterday afternoon	te-ngah-*hah*-ree/pe-*tahng*	tengahari/petang
	se-*mah*-lahm	semalam
yesterday morning	*pah*-gee se-*mah*-lahm	pagi semalam
yet	be-*lum*	belum
not yet	be-*lum* lah-*gee*	belum lagi
you (inf)	kah-*moo* • *eng*-kow	kamu • engkau
(pol)	*ahn*-dah	anda
(pl)	kah-*lee*-ahn	kalian
young	*moo*-duh	muda
younger (sibling)	ah-*di(k)*	adik
youth (collective)	be-*lee*-uh	belia
youth hostel	ahs-*rah*-mah be-*lee*-uh	asrama belia

Z

zebra	*zeh*-brah	zebra
zodiac	*bin*-tahng ke-lah-*hi*-rahn	bintang kelahiran
zoo	zoo	zoo

A

ada	*ah-duh*	to have
abang	ah-*bahng*	older brother
ada selsema	*ah*-duh sel-*se*-muh	(to have a) cold
adapter elektrik	a-*dap*-ter eh-*lehk*-trik	adaptor (electric)
adat	*ah*-daht	custom (tradition)
adik	ah-*di(k)*	younger (sibling)
agama	ah-*gah*-muh	religion
agensi pelancongan	ah-jen-*see* pe-*lahn*-cho-ngahn	travel agency
ahli politik	*ah*-lee po-*lee*-tik	politicians
AIDS	ayds	AIDS
air	air	water
air (surut/pasang)	air (*soo*-rut/pah-*sahng*)	(low/high) tide
air masak	air *mah*-sah(k)	boiled water
air mata	air *mah*-tuh	tear (crying)
air mineral (berkarbonat/biasa)	air mi-*ne*-rahl (ber-*kar*-bo-naht/ bee-*ah*-suh)	mineral water (with/without gas)
air sejuk	air se-*ju(k)*	cold water
air terjun	air *ter*-jun	waterfall
air tulen	air tu-*lehn*	purified water
ais	ais	ice
ais krim	ais krim	ice cream
akibat	ah-*kee*-baht	result
aktivis	*ahk*-ti-vis	activist
aku	*ah*-koo	I
alahan	*ah*-lah-hahn	allergy
alam semesta	ah-*lahm* se-*mes*-tah	universe
alam semulajadi	ah-*lahm* se-moo-luh-*jah*-dee	nature
alamat	*ah*-lah-maht	address (of house)
alasan	*ah*-lah-sahn	reason
alat	*ah*-laht	tool
alat selam	*ah*-laht se-*lahm*	diving equipment
alat solekan	*ah*-laht so-*leh(k)*-kahn	make-up
alergi	*ah*-ler-jee	allergy
Allah	ahl-*luh(h)*	God (Muslim)

almari	ahl-*mah*-ree	wardrobe
almari bagasi	ahl-*mah*-ree bah-*gah*-see	luggage lockers
am	ahm	general
aman	ah-*mahn*	peace
amat	ah-*maht*	very
anak anjing	*ah*-nah(k) *ahn*-jing	puppy
anak biri-biri	*ah*-nah(k) bee-*ree*-bee-*ree*	lamb
anak kapal	*ah*-nah(k) *kah*-pahl	sailor
anak lelaki	*ah*-nah(k) le-*lah*-kee	boy • son
anak perempuan	*ah*-nah(k) pe-*rem*-pwahn	girl • daughter
anak-anak	*ah*-nah(k)-*ah*-nah(k)	child
anda	*ahn*-dah	you (pol)
aneh	ah-*neh(h)*	strange
anggur	*ahng*-gur	grape
angin	*ah*-ngin	wind
anjing	*ahn*-jing	dog
anjing pemandu	*ahn*-jing pe-*mahn*-doo	guide dog
anjuran	*ahn*-joo-rahn	proposal
antara	*ahn*-tah-ruh	between
antara bandar	*ahn*-tah-ruh *bahn*-dahr	intercity
antarabangsa	*ahn*-tah-rah-*bahng*-suh	international
antibiotik	an-tai-bai-*o*-tik	antibiotics
anting-anting	*ahn*-ting-*ahn*-ting	earrings
apa	*ah*-puh	what
apa-apa	*ah*-puh-*ah*-puh	anything
apa pun	*ah*-puh pun	any
api	ah-*pee*	fire
arahan doktor bertulis	ah-rah-*hahn* *dok*-tor ber-*too*-lis	prescription
arak	ah-*rah(k)*	beer
arif	ah-*rif*	sensible • wise
arkeologi	*ahr*-kee-o-lo-ji	archaeological
artis	*ahr*-tis	painter (artist)
asap	ah-*sahp*	smoke
asli	*ahs*-lee	indigenous • original
asrama belia	as-*rah*-mah be-*lee*-uh	youth hostel
atap	ah-*tahp*	roof
atas	ah-*tahs*	up
atau	ah-*tow*	or
ATM	ay tee ehm	ATM
atmosfera	*aht*-mos-fe-rah	atmosphere (of planet)
avokado	ah-vo-*kah*-do	avocado

awal	*ah*-wahl	early
ayah	ah-*yah(h)*	father
ayam	*ai*-yahm	chicken
ayat	ah-*yaht*	sentence (words)

B

babi	*bah*-bee	pig
badan	*bah*-dahn	body
bagaimana	bah-*gai*-mah-nuh	how
bagasi	bah-*gah*-see	luggage • baggage
bagasi yang ditinggalkan	bah-*gah*-see yahng dee-ting-*gahl*-kahn	left luggage
bagus	bah-*gus*	brilliant • cool • fantastic
bagus sekali	bah-*gus* se-kah-*lee*	wonderful
bahagian	bah-*hah*-gee-ahn	part
(di) bahagian bawah	(dee) bah-*hah*-gee-ahn bah-*wah(h)*	(at the) bottom
bahagian penjualan	bah-*hah*-gee-ahn pen-joo-*ah*-lahn	sales department
bahasa	bah-*hah*-suh	language
Bahasa Melayu	bah-*hah*-suh me-*lah*-yoo	Malay
bahaya	bah-*hah*-yuh	dangerous
bahu	bah-*hoo*	shoulders
baik	bai(k)	good • OK
baik hati	bai(k) *hah*-tee	kind (adj)
baju	*bah*-joo	shirt
baju gaun	*bah*-joo gown	dress
baju renang	*bah*-joo re-*nahng*	bathing suit • swimsuit
baju sejuk	*bah*-joo se-*ju(k)*	jumper (sweater)
baju T	*bah*-joo tee	T-shirt
bakar	*bah*-kahr	burn
bakul	*bah*-kul	basket
balasan	bah-lah-*sahn*	reply
baldi	*bahl*-dee	bucket
bandar	*bahn*-dahr	city
banduan	bahn-*doo*-ahn	prisoner
bangkit	*bahng*-kit	to wake up
bangsa	*bahng*-suh	nationality • race (breed)
bangun	bah-*ngun*	to wake up
bangunan	*bah*-ngoo-nahn	building
bank	bank	bank

bantal	*bahn*-tahl	pillow
bantuan	*bahn*-too-ahn	assistance
banyak	*bah*-nya(k)	many • much
bapa	bah-*puh*	father
bar	bahr	bar (drinks)
barang antik	*bah*-rahng *ahn*-tik	antiques
barang kemas	*bah*-rahng ke-*mahs*	jewellery
barang-barang	*bah*-rahng-*bah*-rahng	baggage
barat	bah-*raht*	west
baru	bah-*roo*	new
baru berlaku	bah-*roo* ber-*lah*-koo	recent
bas	bahs	bus
bas jarak jauh	bahs jah-*rah(k)* jow(h)	long-distance bus
bas mini	bahs mee-*nee*	minibus
bas (bandar) tempatan	bahs *(bahn*-dahr) tem-*pah*-tahn	local (city) bus
basah	bah-*sah(h)*	wet
basi	bah-*see*	stale
basikal	bah-*see*-kahl	bicycle
basikal gunung	bah-*see*-kahl *goo*-nung	mountain bike
bateri	*bah*-te-ree	battery
batu	bah-*too*	rock • stone
batuk	*bah*-tu(k)	cough • to cough
bau	bow	smell
bawah	*bah*-wah(h)	under
bawang	*bah*-wahng	onion
bawang putih	*bah*-wahng poo-*ti(h)*	garlic
bayaran	bah-*yah*-rahn	payment
bayaran pos	bah-*yah*-rahn pos	postage
bayi	*bah*-yee	baby
bebas	beh-*bahs*	free (not bound)
beberapa	be-be-*rah*-puh	few • several • some
beg	behg	bag
beg sandar	behg *sahn*-dahr	backpack
beg tangan	behg tah-*ngahn*	handbag
bekas abu rokok	be-*kahs* ah-boo ro-ko(k)	ashtray
bekerja [kerja]	be-*ker*-juh [*ker*-juh]	to work
bekerja sendiri	be-*ker*-juh sen-*dee*-ree	self-employed
Belahlah! be-*la(h)*-la(h)!	**Get lost!**	
belajar [ajar]	be-*lah*-jahr [*ah*-jahr]	to learn
belia	be-*lee*-uh	youth (collective)

belimbing	be-*lim*-bing	starfruit
belok	be-*lo(k)*	turn
belum	be-*lum*	yet
belum lagi	be-*lum lah*-gee	not yet
belum masak	be-*lum mah*-sah(k)	unripe
benang	be-*nahng*	thread
benar	be-*nahr*	true
bendera	ben-*deh*-ruh	flag
bentuk	ben-*tu(k)*	shape
beracun	be-*rah*-chun	poisonous
berangkat [angkat]	be-*rahng*-kaht [*ahng*-kaht]	depart

beras	be-*rahs*	rice (uncooked)
berasal [asal]	be-*rah*-sahl [*ah*-sahl]	to come from (origin)
berat	be-*raht*	weight • heavy
beratur	be-*rah*-tur	queue
berawan	be-*rah*-wahn	cloudy
berbahasa (Melayu)	ber-bah-*hah*-suh (me-*lah*-yoo)	to speak (Malay)
berangkat [angkat]	be-*rahng*-kaht [*ahng*-kaht]	to take off (depart)
berbeza	ber-*beh*-zuh	different
berburu [buru]	ber-*boo*-roo [*boo*-roo]	to hunt
bercakap [cakap]	ber-*chah*-kahp [*chah*-kahp]	to talk (chat)
berdansa [dansa]	ber-*dahn*-sah [*dahn*-sah]	to dance
berdarah [darah]	ber-*dah*-rah(h) [*dah*-rah(h)]	to bleed
berehat [rehat]	be-*reh*-haht [*reh*-haht]	to relax • to rest
berenang [renang]	be-re-*nahng* [re-*nahng*]	to swim
berfikir [fikir]	ber-*fee*-kir [*fee*-kir]	to think
bergaduh [gaduh]	ber-gah-*du(h)* [gah-*du(h)*]	to fight
berguling	ber-goo-*ling*	rolling
berguna	ber-*goo*-nuh	useful
berharga	ber-*har*-guh	valuable
berhati-hati	ber-*hah*-tee-*hah*-tee	careful
berhenti [henti]	ber-*hen*-tee [*hen*-tee]	to quit • to stop
berhutang	ber-*hoo*-tahng	to owe

malay–english

255

beriman	be-*ree*-mahn	religious
berita	be-*ree*-tuh	news
berjalan kaki	ber-*jah*-lahn kah-*kee*	to walk • to hike
berkabus	ber-*kah*-bus	foggy
berkahwin	ber-*kah(h)*-win	marry
berkata [kata]	ber-*kah*-tuh [*kah*-tuh]	to say
berkeliling	ber-ke-*lee*-ling	tour
berkhayal [khayal]	ber-*khah*-yahl [*khah*-yahl]	to hallucinate
berkhema [khemah]	ber-*keh*-mah(h) [*keh*-mah(h)]	to camp
berkongsi (dengan)	ber-*kong*-see (de-*ngahn*)	to share (with)
berkongsi bilik/dorm	ber-*kong*-see bee-li(k)/dorm	to share a dorm
berlawak [lawak]	ber-lah-*wah(k)* [lah-*wah(k)*]	to joke
berlepas [lepas]	ber-le-*pahs* [le-*pahs*]	to take off (depart)
bermain [main]	ber-*main* [main]	to play (a game, music)
bermalam [malam]	ber-*mah*-lahm [*mah*-lahm]	to stay (overnight)
bermimpi [mimpi]	ber-*mim*-pee [*mim*-pee]	to dream
bernikah	ber-nee-kah(h)	to marry
berpeluh [peluh]	ber-pe-*lu(h)* [pe-*lu(h)*]	to perspire
bersama	ber-*sah*-muh	together • with
berselancar [selancar]	ber-se-*lahn*-chahr [se-*lahn*-chahr]	to surf
bersendirian	ber-*sen*-dee-ree-ahn	alone
bersetuju [setuju]	ber-se-*too*-joo [se-*too*-joo]	to agree
bersimpati	ber-sim-*pah*-tee	sympathetic
bertanya [tanya]	ber-*tah*-nyuh [*tah*-nyuh]	to ask a question
bertapis	ber-*tah*-pis	filtered
bertemu [temu]	ber-*te*-moo [*te*-moo]	to meet
berterima kasih	ber-te-*ree*-muh kah-si(h)	to thank
beruntung	be-*roon*-tung	lucky
berus gigi	be-*rus gee*-gee	toothbrush
berus rambut	be-*rus rahm*-but	hairbrush
besar	be-*sahr*	big • large
betina	be-*tee*-nuh	female (animal)
betul	be-*tul*	right (correct)
biadab	bee-*ah*-dahb	vulgar
biara	bee-*ah*-ruh	monastery
biarawan	bee-*ah*-ruh-wahn	monk
biarawati	bee-ah-ruh-*wah*-tee	nun

Biarlah.
bee-*ahr*-lah(h) — Don't bother.

biasa	bee-*ah*-suh	usual • typical
bibir	*bee*-bir	lips
bijaksana	bee-ja(k)-*sah*-nuh	wise
biji ubat	bee-*jee* oo-*baht*	tablet
bil	bil	bill (account)
bila	*bee*-luh	when
bila-bila	*bee*-luh-*bee*-luh	anytime
bilik	*bee*-li(k)	cabin • room
bilik air	*bee*-li(k) air	bathroom
bilik menunggu	*bee*-li(k) me-*noong*-goo	waiting room
bilik seorang	*bee*-li(k) se-o-rahng	single room
bilik tidur	*bee*-li(k) *tee*-dur	bedroom
bilik tukar pakaian	*bee*-li(k) too-*kahr* pah-kai-*ahn*	changing rooms
bimbang	*beem*-bahng	worried
binatang	bee-*nah*-tahng	animal
binatang hampir pupus	bee-*nah*-tahng *hahm*-pir poo-*pus*	endangered species
binatang liar/buas	bee-*nah*-tahng lee-*yahr*/ boo-*ahs*	wild animal
bintang	bin-*tahng*	stars (in the sky)
bintang kelahiran	bin-*tahng* ke-lah-*hi*-rahn	zodiac
bir	bir	beer
biru	*bee*-roo	blue
bising	*bee*-sing	loud • noisy
bocor	bo-*chor*	leak
bodoh	bo-*do(h)*	idiot • stupid
bogel	bo-*gehl*	nude
bola	*bo*-luh	ball (for sport)
bola sepak	*bo*-luh *seh*-pah(k)	football (soccer)
boleh	bo-*leh(h)*	to be able (can)

Boleh.		Sure.
bo-*leh(h)*		

(kulit) boneka	(koo-*lit*) bo-neh-*kah*	puppet (leather)
bosan	*bo*-sahn	bored
bot bermotor	bot ber-*mo*-tor	motorboat
bot	bot	boat
botol	bo-*tol*	bottle • jar
botol air	bo-*tol* air	water bottle
buah-buahan	boo-*ah(h)*-boo-*ah*-hahn	fruit
buaian	boo-*ai*-ahn	hammock
buang air besar	boo-*ahng* air be-*sahr*	to shit
buang air kecil	boo-*ahng* air ke-*chil*	to piss

buat	boo-*aht*	for (purpose)
buatan tangan	boo-*ah*-tahn tah-*ngahn*	handmade
budak	boo-*dah(k)*	child
budak perempuan	boo-*dah(k)* pe-*rem*-pwahn	girl
buka	*boo*-kuh	open
bukan	boo-*kahn*	not
bukit	boo-*kit*	hill
buku	*boo*-koo	book
buku catatan	*boo*-koo *chah*-tah-tahn	diary • notebook
buku doa	*boo*-koo do-*ah*	prayer book
buku kembara	*boo*-koo kem-*bah*-ruh	travel book
buku panduan	*boo*-koo *pahn*-dwahn	guidebook
buku telefon	*boo*-koo teh-*leh*-fon	phone book
bulan	*boo*-lahn	moon
bulan (ini)	*boo*-lahn *(ee*-nee)	(this) month
bulan depan	*boo*-lahn de-*pahn*	next month
bulan lepas	*boo*-lahn le-*pahs*	last month
bulan madu	*boo*-lahn mah-*doo*	honeymoon
bulat	boo-*laht*	round (shape)
(di) bulatan	(dee) boo-*lah*-tahn	(at the) roundabout
bulu biri-biri	boo-*loo* bee-*ree*-bee-*ree*	wool
bumbung	*boom*-bung	roof
bumi	boo-*mee*	earth
bunga	*boo*-nguh	flower
bungkusan	*boong*-ku-sahn	package
bunyi	*boo*-nyee	noise • sound
buruk	boo-*ru(k)*	bad
burung	boo-*rung*	bird
busuk	boo-*su(k)*	rotten
but	boot	boots
but jalan	boot *jah*-lahn	hiking boots
butang	boo-*tahng*	buttons

Bye.		
bai		**Goodbye. (inf)**

C

cacat	chah-*chaht*	disabled
cadangan	chah-*dah*-ngahn	proposal
cadar	*chah*-dahr	sheet (bed)
cakap	chah-*kahp*	speak
cantik	chahn-*ti(k)*	beautiful • pretty
catur	*chah*-tur	chess

Malay	Pronunciation	English
cawan	chah-*wahn*	cup
CD	see dee	CD
cek	chehk	cheque
cek kembara	chehk kem-*bah*-ruh	travellers cheque
cemas	che-*mahs*	nervous
cenderamata	chen-de-ruh-*mah*-tuh	souvenir
cepat	che-*paht*	fast (quick)
cerah	che-*rah(h)*	sunny
cerita	che-*ree*-tuh	story
cermin	cher-*min*	mirror
cermin mata	cher-*min mah*-tuh	glasses (eye)
cermin mata hitam	cher-*min mah*-tuh *hee*-tahm	sunglasses
cerpen	cher-*pehn*	short story
cetakan (karya seni)	cheh-*ta(k)*-kahn (kar-*yah* se-*nee*)	print (artwork)
Cik	chi(k)	Miss
cikgu (col)	*chi(k)*-goo	teacher
cili	*chee*-lee	chilli
cincin	*chin*-chin	ring (on finger)
cinta	*chin*-tuh	love
cirit-birit	*chi*-rit-*bi*-rit	diarrhoea
cium	*chee*-um	kiss
coklat	*chok*-laht	chocolate • brown
comel	cho-*mehl*	cute (baby)
contoh	chon-*to(h)*	example
cuaca	choo-*ah*-chuh	weather
cuak	choo-*ah(k)*	nervous
cucu	choo-*choo*	grandchild
cukai	choo-*kai*	tax
cukai pendapatan	choo-*kai* pen-dah-*pah*-tahn	income tax
cukai penerbangan	choo-*kai* pe-ner-*bah*-ngahn	airport tax
cukur	choo-*kur*	to shave
curam	choo-*rahm*	steep (hill)
cuti	choo-*tee*	vacation • holiday
CV	see vee	resumé

D

Malay	Pronunciation	English
dadah	dah-*dah(h)*	drug (illegal)
daerah	dah-*eh*-rah(h)	region
daging	*dah*-ging	meat
daging babi	*dah*-ging bah-*bee*	pork • ham

daging lembu	*dah*-ging *lem*-boo	beef

Dah cukup! dah(h) *choo*-kup!		**Enough!**

dahaga	dah-*hah*-guh	thirsty
dahsyat	*dah(h)*-shaht	horrible
dahulu	dah-*hoo*-loo	past (before)
dalam	dah-*lahm*	deep • in
damai	dah-*mai*	peace
dan	dahn	and
dapat	*dah*-paht	can (able)
dapur	dah-*pur*	kitchen • stove
darah	dah-rah(h)	blood
dari	dah-*ree*	from
daripada	dah-ree-*pah*-duh	from
daripada perak	dah-ree-*pah*-duh peh-*ra(k)*	of silver
darurat	dah-*roo*-raht	emergency
(di) dasar	(dee) dah-*sahr*	(at the) bottom
datang	*dah*-tahng	to come (arrive)
dataran	dah-*tah*-rahn	square
dataran tinggi	dah-*tah*-rahn *teeng*-gee	plateau
datuk	dah-*tu(k)*	grandfather
daun terup	down te-*rup*	playing cards
debunga	de-*boo*-nguh	pollen
dekat	de-*kaht*	near • at
demam	de-*mahm*	fever
demokrasi	deh-mo-*krah*-see	democracy
dengan	de-*ngahn*	with
dengan cepat	de-*ngahn* che-*paht*	quickly
dengan serta-merta	de-*ngahn* ser-*tah*-mer-tah	immediately
deodoran	di-*o*-do-rahn	deodorant
desa	deh-*suh*	village
destinasi	*dehs*-tee-nah-see	destination
dewasa	deh-*wah*-suh	adult
di	dee	at • on (location)
di antara	dee *ahn*-tah-ruh	among
di atas	dee ah-*tahs*	aboard • above • over
di bawah	dee bah-*wah(h)*	below
di belakang	dee be-*lah*-kahng	at the back (behind
di dalam	dee dah-*lahm*	inside
di depan	dee de-*pahn*	in front of • ahead
di hadapan	dee hah-dah-*pahn*	ahead

di kalangan	dee kah-*lah*-ngahn	among
di samping	dee *sahm*-ping	beside
di sana	dee *sah*-nuh	over there
di sana ada ...	dee *sah*-nuh ah-duh ...	there is/are ...
di sebelah	dee se-be-*lah(h)*	next to
di seberang	dee se-be-*rahng*	over
di sini	dee *see*-nee	here
di situ	dee *see*-too	there (nearby)

Di situ ada ...
dee *see*-too *ah*-duh ...   **There is/are ...**

di tepi	dee te-*pee*	beside
dia	*dee*-uh	he • she
dinding	*deen*-ding	wall (inside)
dingin	dee-*ngin*	cool (temperature)
diperbuat (daripada)	dee-per-*boo*-aht (dah-ree-*pah*-duh)	made (of)
diskaun	*dis*-kown	discount
disko	*dis*-ko	disco
ditinggalkan [tinggal]	dee-*ting*-gahl-kahn [*ting*-gahl]	to be left (behind, over)
doa	do-*ah*	prayer
doktor	*dok*-tor	doctor
doktor gigi	*dok*-tor *gee*-gee	dentist
dokumentari	do-kiu-men-*tah*-ree	documentary
dompet	*dom*-peht	purse
dosa	do-*suh*	sin
dram	drahm	drums
drama	*drah*-mah	play (theatre)
(seni) drama	(se-*nee*) *drah*-mah	drama (arts)
drama sabun	*drah*-mah *sah*-bun	soap opera
dua hari lepas	*doo*-uh *hah*-ree le-*pahs*	day before yesterday
dua kali	*doo*-uh *kah*-lee	twice
duduk	*doo*-du(k)	to sit
duit	*doo*-it	money
dunia	doo-nee-*uh*	world
duta	doo-*tah*	ambassador

E

(kelas) ekonomi	(ke-*lahs*) ee-ko-*no*-mee	economy (class)
ekor	*eh*-kor	tail (of animal)
eksploitasi	ehks-*ploy*-tah-see	exploitation

elektrik	eh-*lehk*-trik	**electricity**
emak saudara	e-*mah(k)* sow-*dah*-ruh	**aunt**
emak	e-*mah(k)*	**mother**
emas	e-*mahs*	**gold**
enak	*eh*-nah(k)	**tasty**
Encik	en-*chi(k)*	**Mr**
enggan	*eng*-gahn	**to refuse**
engkau	*eng*-kow	**you (inf)**
enjin	*ehn*-jin	**engine**
e*pal*	eh-*puhl*	**apple**
epilepsi	eh-*pee*-lehp-see	**epilepsy**
erti	*er*-tee	**meaning**
esok	*eh*-so(k)	**tomorrow**
esok pagi	*eh*-so(k) *pah*-gee	**tomorrow morning**

F

faham	fah-*hahm*	**to understand**
fajar (matahari terbit)	fah-*jahr*	**dawn (sunrise)**
	(mah-tuh-*hah*-ree ter-*bit)*	
farmasi	*fahr*-mah-see	**chemist (pharmacy)**
fasih	fah-si(h)	**fluent**
fikiran	fee-ki-*rahn*	**thought**
fiksyen	*fik*-shen	**fiction**
filem	*fee*-lem	**movie • film (camera)**
filem pendek	*fee*-lem pehn-*deh(k)*	**short film**
foto	*fo*-to	**photograph**

G

gading	gah-*ding*	**ivory**
gam	gahm	**glue**
gam kunyah	gahm koo-*nyah(h)*	**chewing gum**
gambar	*gahm*-bahr	**picture • photograph**
gangguan	*gahng*-goo-ahn	**harassment**
ganja	*gahn*-jah	**marijuana**
ganjil	*gahn*-jil	**strange**
garaj	gah-*rahj*	**garage**
garam	gah-*rahm*	**salt**
garfu	*gahr*-foo	**fork**
gatal	gah-*tahl*	**itch • horny (col)**
gay	geh	**gay**
gaya	*gah*-yuh	**style**
gelak	ge-*lah(k)*	**laugh**
gelansar filem	ge-*lahn*-sahr *fee*-lem	**slide (film)**

gelap	ge-*lahp*	dark
gemar	ge-mahr	to like
gembira	gem-*bee*-ruh	happy
gemuk	ge-*mu(k)*	fat
gendang	gen-*dahng*	drums
geografi	ji-o-grah-fee	geography
gerai	ge-*rai*	food stall
gereja	ge-*reh*-juh	church
gereja Yahudi	ge-*reh*-juh yah-*hoo*-dee	synagogue
gigi	*gee*-gee	tooth • teeth
gigitan	*gee*-gee-tahn	bite (dog, insect)
gila	*gee*-luh	crazy • delirious
gincu	*gin*-choo	lipstick
gitar	gee-*tahr*	guitar
gol	gol	goal
goreng	go-*rehng*	fried
gram	grahm	gram
gua	*goo*-uh	cave
gugur	*goo*-gur	to fall
gula	*goo*-luh	sugar
gula-gula	*goo*-luh-*goo*-luh	sweets
gunting	*goon*-ting	scissors
gunung	*goo*-nung	mountain
gunung berapi	*goo*-nung be-*rah*-pee	volcano
guru	*goo*-roo	teacher
gurun pasir	*goo*-run *pah*-sir	desert

H

haba	hah-*buh*	heat
habis	*hah*-bis	finished
hadiah	*hah*-dee-ah(h)	present (gift)
hadiah perkahwinan	*hah*-dee-ah(h) per-kah-*wi*-nahn	wedding present
haiwan	*hai*-wahn	animal
haiwan terlindung	*hai*-wahn ter-*leen*-dung	protected species
hajat	hah-*jaht*	to wish
hak asasi manusia	ha(k) ah-*sah*-see mah-*noo*-see-uh	civil rights • human rights
hak sama taraf	hah(k) *sah*-muh tah-*rahf*	equal opportunity
hakim	hah-*kim*	judge (court)
hamil	hah-*mil*	pregnant
hanya	hah-*nyuh*	only
harga	*hahr*-guh	price • cost
hari	*hah*-ree	day

hari Ahad	hah-ree ah-hahd	Sunday
hari ini	hah-ree ee-nee	today
hari Isnin	hah-ree ees-nin	Monday
hari jadi/lahir	hah-ree jah-dee/lah-hir	birthday
hari Jumaat	hah-ree joo-mah-aht	Friday
hari Khamis	hah-ree kah-mis	Thursday
hari Krismas	hah-ree kris-muhs	Christmas Day
hari Rabu	hah-ree rah-boo	Wednesday
hari Sabtu	hah-ree sahb-too	Saturday
hari Selasa	hah-ree se-lah-suh	Tuesday
harian	hah-ree-ahn	daily
harimau	hah-ree-mow	tiger
harus	hah-rus	must
hasil	hah-sil	result
hasis	hah-sis	hashish
hasrat	hahs-raht	to wish
hati	hah-tee	liver
haus	hows	thirsty
helai	he-lai	sheet (of paper)
hendak	hen-da(k)	to want
hendsem	hehnd-sem	handsome (male)
herba	her-bah	herbs
(penagih) heroin	(pe-nah-gi(h)) heh-ro-in	heroin (addict)
hidung	hee-dung	nose
hidup	hee-dup	to live (life) • alive
hijau	hee-jow	green
Hindu	hin-doo	Hindu
hitam	hee-tahm	black
HIV positif	ehch ai vee po-si-tif	HIV positive
homoseksual	ho-mo-sehk-soo-ahl	homosexual
hormat	hor-maht	respect
hospital	hos-pee-tahl	hospital
hospital swasta	hos-pee-tahl swahs-tah	private hospital
hotel	ho-tehl	hotel
hubungan	hoo-bu-ngahn	relationship
hujan	hoo-jahn	rain
hujung minggu	hoo-jung meeng-goo	weekend
hukuman	hoo-ku-mahn	sentence (prison)
huru-hara	hoo-roo-hah-ruh	anarchist
hutan	hoo-tahn	forest
hutan simpan	hoo-tahn sim-pahn	protected forest

I

ibu	*ee*-boo	mother
ibu bapa	*ee*-boo *bah*	parents
ibu mertua	*ee*-boo mer-*too*-uh	mother-in-law
idea	*ai*-deh-ah	idea
ikan	ee-*kahn*	fish
imigresen	ee-mee-*greh*-sen	immigration
indah	*in*-dah(h)	beautiful (scenery) • pretty
informasi	in-for-*mah*-see	information
ingat	ee-*ngaht*	to remember
Inggeris	*ing*-ge-ris	English
ingin	*ee*-ngin	to want
ini	*ee*-nee	this
insurans	in-soo-*rahns*	insurance
istana	*ees*-tah-nuh	palace
isteri	*ees*-te-ree	wife
istimewa	*ees*-tee-*meh*-wuh	special
itik	ee-*ti(k)*	duck
itu	*ee*-too	that
izin	*ee*-zin	permission

J

jadual perjalanan	jah-*doo*-ahl per-jah-*lah*-nahn	itinerary
jadual waktu	jah-doo-*ahl wak*-too	timetable
jahit	jah-*hit*	to sew
jaket	ja-*keht*	jacket
jalan	*jah*-lahn	avenue • road • street • trail • way
jalan bertol	*jah*-lahn ber-tol	motorway (tollway)
jalan gunung	*jah*-lahn *goo*-nung	mountain path
jalan-jalan	*jah*-lahn-*jah*-lahn	stroll
jalan kecil	*jah*-lahn ke-*chil*	path • track
jalan keretapi	*jah*-lahn ke-reh-tah-*ah*-pee	railroad
jalan masuk	*jah*-lahn mah-*su(k)*	entrance
jalan pejalan kaki	*jah*-lahn pe-*jah*-lahn kah-*kee*	footpath
jalan utama	*jah*-lahn oo-*tah*-muh	road
jam	jahm	clock • hour • watch
jam loceng	jahm *lo*-chehng	alarm clock

jam tangan	jahm tah-*ngahn*	wristwatch
jambatan	*jahm*-bah-tahn	bridge
jangkitan	*jahng*-ki-tahn	infection
janji	*jahn*-jee	promise
jantan	*jahn*-tahn	male (animal)
jantung	*jahn*-tung	heart
jarak	jah-*rah(k)*	distance (length)
jarak panjang	jah-*rah(k) pahn*-jahng	long distance
jarang	jah-*rahng*	rare (uncommon)
jari	*jah*-ree	finger
jarum	*jah*-rum	needle (sewing, syringe)
jarum suntik	*jah*-rum soon-*ti(k)*	syringe
jasa	*jah*-suh	service (assistance)
jatuh	jah-*tuh(h)*	to fall
jauh	jah-*uh(h)*	far
jawapan	jah-*wah*-pahn	reply
jean	jeen	jeans
jenis	je-*nis*	type (of product)
jingga	*jeeng*-gah	orange (colour)
jip	jeep	jeep
jiran	*jee*-rahn	neighbour
johan	*jo*-hahn	winner
jualan murah	joo-*ah*-lahn moo-*ra(h)*	(on) sale
juara	joo-*ah*-ruh	winner
juga	*joo*-guh	also • too
jujur	*joo*-jur	honest

Jum!	joom!	Come on!

jumlah	joom-*lah(h)*	quantity
jurugambar	joo-roo-*gahm*-bahr	photographer
jurulatih	joo-roo-*lah*-ti(h)	instructor
jururawat	joo-roo-*rah*-waht	nurse
jurutera	joo-roo-te-ruh	engineer
juruwang	joo-roo-*wahng*	cashier
jus	joos	juice
juta	joo-*tuh*	million

K

kaca	*kah*-chuh	glass
kaca depan	*kah*-chuh de-*pahn*	windscreen
kacak	kah-*chah(k)*	handsome (male)

Malay	Pronunciation	English
kacang	*kah*-chahng	bean · nut (food)
kad kredit	kahd *kreh*-dit	credit card
kad pengenalan	kahd pe-*nge*-nah-lahn	ID
kad telefon	kahd teh-*leh*-fon	phonecard
kadang-kadang	kah-*dahng*-kah-*dahng*	sometimes
kadar pembayaran	kah-*dahr* pem-bah-*yah*-rahn	rate of pay
kain	kain	material (clothing)
kain lampin	kain *lahm*-pin	nappy
kain pembalut	kain *pem*-bah-lut	bandage
kajipurba	kah-jee-*pur*-buh	archaeological
kakak	kah-*kah(k)*	older sister
kaki	kah-*kee*	foot · leg
kalau	kah-*low*	if
kalian	kah-*lee*-ahn	you (pl)
kambing	*kahm*-bing	goat
(kedai) kamera	(ke-*dai*) ka-me-rah	camera (shop)
kami	*kah*-mee	we (excl)
kampung	*kahm*-pung	village
kamu	kah-*moo*	you (inf)
kamus	*kah*-mus	dictionary
kanan	*kah*-nahn	right (not left)
kanta	kahn-*tuh*	lens
kantung tidur	kahn-*tung tee*-dur	sleeping bag
kapal	*kah*-pahl	ship
kapal terbang	*kah*-pahl *ter*-bahng	aeroplane
kapas	*kah*-pahs	cotton
karya seni	ka-ri-*ah* se-*nee*	artwork
kasar	kah-*sahr*	vulgar
kaset	*kah*-seht	cassette
kaset video	*kah*-seht *vi*-dee-o	video cassette
kasih	*kah*-*si(h)*	love
kastam	*kahs*-tahm	customs (border)
kasut	*kah*-sut	shoes
kasut but	*kah*-sut boot	boots
katak	*kah*-tah(k)	frog · toad
katil	*kah*-til	bed
katil kelamin	*kah*-til ke-*lah*-min	double bed
katil kembar	*kah*-til *kem*-bahr	twin beds
kaum	kowm	race (breed)
kawan	kah-*wahn*	friend
kawan-kawan	kah-*wahn*-kah-*wahn*	company (friends)
kawasan	kah-*wah*-sahn	region
kawasan luar bandar	kah-*wah*-sahn *loo*-ahr *bahn*-dahr	countryside

kawasan perkhemahan	kah-*wah*-sahn per-*keh*-mah-han	campsite
kaya	kah-*yuh*	rich (wealthy)
kayu	kah-*yoo*	puppet (wooden) • wood
ke	ke	to
ke arah	ke ah-*rah(h)*	toward
keadilan	ke-ah-*di*-lahn	justice
keagamaan	ke-ah-*gah*-mah-ahn	religious
kebajikan	ke-bah-*ji(k)*-kahn	welfare
kebajikan sosial	ke-bah-*ji(k)*-kahn so-see-*ahl*	social welfare
kebanggaan [bangga]	ke-*bahng*-gah-ahn [*bahng*-guh]	pride
kebenaran	ke-be-*nah*-rahn	truth
kebiasaan	ke-bee-ah-*sah*-ahn	habit
kebocoran	ke-bo-*cho*-rahn	puncture
kebun	ke-*bun*	garden • farm
kebun botani	ke-*bun* bo-*tah*-nee	gardens (botanical)
kecederaan [cedera]	ke-che-de-*rah*-ahn [che-de-*rah*]	injury
kecemasan	ke-che-*mah*-sahn	emergency
kecil	ke-*chil*	little (small)
kedai	ke-*dai*	shop
kedai buku	ke-*dai* boo-koo	bookshop
kedai cenderamata	ke-*dai* chen-de-ruh-*mah*-tuh	souvenir shop
kedai dobi	ke-*dai* do-*bee*	laundry (shop)
kedai roti	ke-*dai* ro-tee	bakery
kedai ubat Cina	ke-*dai* oo-baht *chee*-nuh	herbalist shop
kedatangan [datang]	ke-dah-*tah*-ngahn [*dah*-tahng]	arrivals
kedua	ke-*doo*-uh	second (in order)
kedua-dua	ke-*doo*-uh-*doo*-uh	both
kedutaan	ke-*doo*-tah-ahn	embassy
keinginan [ingin]	ke-*ee*-ngi-nahn [*ee*-ngin]	to wish
kejayaan	ke-jah-*yah*-ahn	success
keju	*keh*-joo	cheese
kejutan	ke-joo-*tahn*	surprise
kek hari jadi	kehk *hah*-ree *jah*-dee	birthday cake
kek lahir	kehk lah-*hir*	birthday cake
kek perkahwinan	kehk per-kah-*wi*-nahn	wedding cake
kekalahan [kalah]	ke-kah-*lah*-hahn [kah-*lah(h)*]	loss
kekasih	ke-*kah*-si(h)	lover

kekuatan	ke-koo-*ah*-tahn	strength
kekurangan	ke-koo-*rah*-ngahn	shortage
kelab (malam)	ke-*lahb (mah*-lahm)	(night)club
kelabu	ke-*lah*-boo	grey
(kelajuan) filem	(ke-*lah*-joo-ahn) *fee*-lem	film (speed)
kelakar	ke-*lah*-kahr	joke • funny
kelapa	ke-*lah*-puh	coconut
kelas kedua	ke-*lahs* ke-*doo*-uh	2nd class
kelas pertama	ke-*lahs* per-*tah*-muh	1st class
kelayakan	ke-lah-*yah*(k)-kahn	qualifications
kelompok	ke-*lom*-po(k)	group
kelengkapan [lengkap]	ke-*leng*-kah-pahn [*leng*-kahp]	equipment
kelewatan	ke-*leh*-wah-tahn	delay
kelmarin lepas	kel-*mah*-rin le-*pahs*	day before yesterday
keluar	ke-*loo*-ahr	exit
keluar bersama	ke-*loo*-ahr ber-*sah*-muh	to go out with
keluarga	ke-*loo*-*ahr*-guh	family
kemalangan	ke-mah-*lah*-ngahn	accident
kemasukan	ke-mah-*su*(k)-kahn	admission (entry)
kematian	ke-*mah*-tee-ahn	death
kembali	kem-*bah*-lee	return
kembar	*kem*-bahr	twins
kemeja	ke-*meh*-juh	shirt
kemewahan	ke-*meh*-*wah*-hahn	luxury
kemiskinan	ke-*mees*-ki-nahn	poverty
kemudian	ke-*moo*-dee-ahn	later
kemungkinan	ke-*mung*-ki-nahn	chance
kenal	ke-*nahl*	to know (someone) • to recognise
kenapa	ke-*nah*-puh	why
kencing	*ken*-ching	piss
kencing manis	*ken*-ching *mah*-nis	diabetes
kentang	ken-*tahng*	potato
kentut	*ken*-tut	fart
kenyang	ke-*nyahng*	full (of food)
kepala	ke-*pah*-luh	head
kepanasan [panas]	ke-*pah*-nahs-sahn [*pah*-nahs]	to be hot
kera	ke-*ruh*	monkey
kerajaan	ke-rah-*jah*-ahn	government
keramah-tamahan	ke-rah-*mah(h)*-tah-*mah(h)*-hahn	hospitality
kerana	ke-*rah*-nuh	because

kerani bank	ke-*rah*-nee bank	bank clerk
kerap	ke-*rahp*	often
keras	ke-*rahs*	hard (not soft)
(tempat letak) kereta	(tem-*paht* le-*tah(k)*) ke-*reh*-tuh	car (park)
keretapi	ke-reh-tuh-*ah*-pee	train
kerja	*ker*-juh	work
kerongkong	ke-*rong*-kong	throat
kertas	ker-*tahs*	paper
kertas rokok	ker-*tahs* ro-*ko(k)*	cigarette papers
kertas tulis	ker-*tahs* too-lis	writing paper
kerusi	ke-*roo*-see	chair
kerusi beroda	ke-*roo*-see be-*ro*-duh	wheelchair
kesejahteraan	ke-se-*jah(h)*-te-rah-ahn	welfare
kesalahan	ke-sah-*lah*-hahn	mistake
kesan jejak	ke-*sahn* je-*ja(k)*	track (footprints)
kesepuluh	ke-se-*poo*-lu(h)	tenth
kesesatan lalu lintas	ke-se-*sah*-tahn lah-loo-*lin*-tahs	traffic jam
kesilapan	ke-see-lah-*pahn*	mistake
Kesukanan Olimpik	ke-*soo*-kah-nahn o-*lim*-pik	Olympic Games
ketakutan	ke-tah-*ku*-tahn	fear
ketam	ke-*tahm*	crab
ketat	ke-*taht*	tight
ketawa	ke-tah-*wuh*	laugh
ketibaan [tiba]	ke-*tee*-buh-an [*tee*-buh]	arrivals
ketiga	ke-*tee*-guh	third
ketinggian	ke-*teeng*-gee-ahn	altitude
kewarganegaraan	ke-*wahr*-guh-ne-gah-rah-ahn	citizenship
khas	khahs	special
khemah	keh-*mah(h)*	tent
khidmat	*khid*-maht	service (assistance)
khuatir	khoo-*ah*-tir	worried
kicap	kee-*chahp*	soy sauce
kidal	*ki*-dahl	left-handed
kilang	kee-*lahng*	factory
kilogram	*ki*-lo-grahm	kilogram
kilometer	*ki*-lo-*mee*-ter	kilometre
kini	kee-nee	present (time)
kipas	kee-*pahs*	fan (machine)
kira-kira	kee-ruh-*kee*-ruh	approximately
kiri	*ki*-ree	left (not right)
kita	kee-tuh	we (incl)
kocek	ko-*cheh(k)*	pocket

Malay	Pronunciation	English
kodok	ko-do(k)	frog · toad
kokain	ko-kehn	cocaine
kolam renang	ko-lahm re-nahng	swimming pool
kolej	ko-lehj	college
komik	ko-mik	comics
kompas	kom-pahs	compass
kondom	kon-dom	condom
konsert	kon-sert	concert
konstipasi	kons-tee-pah-see	constipation
kontrasepsi	kon-trah-sehp-see	contraceptive
kopi	ko-pee	coffee
kos	kos	cost
kosong	ko-song	empty · vacant
kotak	ko-tah(k)	box (package)
kotak pertolongan	ko-tah(k) per-to-lo-ngahn	first-aid kit
kotor	ko-tor	dirty
kotor kemas	ko-tor ke-mahs	sleazy (person)
kraftangan	krahf-tah-ngahn	handicrafts
kretek	kreh-teh(k)	clove cigarettes
krim pelembab	krim pe-lem-bahb	moisturising cream
krim pelindung cahaya matahari	krim pe-leen-dung chah-hah-yuh mah-tah-hah-ree	sunblock
kualiti	kwah-lee-tee	quality
kuarantin	kwah-rahn-teen	quarantine
kuasa	koo-ah-suh	power
kuat	koo-aht	strong
kubur	koo-bur	grave
kucing	koo-ching	cat
(penunggangan) kuda	(pe-nung-gah-ngahn) koo-duh	horse (riding)
kuil	koo-il	temple (Hindu)
kuinin	kui-nin	quinine
kuiz	kuiz	game show
kuliah	koo-lee-ah(h)	lecture
kulit	koo-lit	skin · leather
kulit terbakar	koo-lit ter-bah-kahr	sunburnt
kumpulan	koom-poo-lahn	group (music) · band (music)
kumpulan darah	koom-poo-lahn dah-rah(h)	blood group
kumpulan rock	koom-poo-lahn rok	rock group
kuno	koo-no	ancient
kunci	koon-chee	key
kuning	koo-ning	yellow

kupu-kupu	*koo*-poo-*koo*-poo	**butterfly**
kurang	koo-*rahng*	**less**
kurus	*koo*-rus	**skinny**
kutu	*koo*-too	**flea ·**
lice		

L

ladang	lah-*dahng*	**farm**
lagu	lah-*goo*	**song · tune**
lain	lain	**other**

Lain kali.
lain *kah*-lee   **Next time**

(had) laju	(hahd) lah-*joo*	**speed (limit)**
lalat	*lah*-laht	**fly**
lalulintas	lah-loo-*lin*-tahs	**traffic**
lama	lah-*muh*	**long (time) · old**
lambat	*lahm*-baht	**late (not on time)**
lampu	*lahm*-poo	**light (electric)**
lampu isyarat	*lahm*-poo ee-*shah*-raht	**traffic lights**
lampu suluh	*lahm*-poo soo-*lu(h)*	**torch (flashlight)**
langit	lah-*ngit*	**sky**
langkah	lang-*kah(h)*	**step**
lanskap	lahns-*kahp*	**landscape**
lantai	*lahn*-tai	**floor (of room)**
lapangan terbang	lah-*pah*-ngahn *ter*-bahng	**airport**
lapar	*lah*-pahr	**hungry**
lari	lah-*ree*	**run**
latihan (sukan)	lah-*ti(h)*-hahn (soo-*kahn*)	**workout (sport)**
laut	lowt	**sea**
lautan	*low*-tahn	**ocean**
lawa	lah-*wah*	**pretty (adj)**
lawak	lah-*wah(k)*	**joke · funny**
lawan	lah-*wahn*	**opposite**
layan diri	lah-*yahn* dee-*ree*	**self-service**
layar	lah-*yahr*	**sail**
layar perak	lah-*yahr* pe-*rah(k)*	**screen (film)**
lebar	*leh*-bahr	**wide**
lebih	le-*bi(h)*	**more**
lebih baik	le-*bi(h)* bai(k)	**better**
lebih suka	le-*bi(h)* soo-kuh	**to prefer**
lelaki	le-*lah*-kee	**male · man**
lemah	le-*mah(h)*	**weak**

lembab	*lem*-bahb	humid
lembah	*lem*-bah(h)	valley
lembu	*lem*-boo	cow
lembut	*lem*-but	gentle • soft
lengan	le-*ngahn*	arm (of body)
lensa	lehn-*sah*	lens
lepas	le-*pahs*	ago
lesbian	lehs-*bee*-uhn	lesbian
lesen memandu	leh-*sehn* me-*mahn*-doo	drivers licence
lewat	leh-*waht*	late (not on time)
lidah	lee-*dah*(h)	tongue
lif	lif	lift (elevator)
lihat	lee-*haht*	to see
lilin	*lee*-lin	candle
limau nipis	*lee*-mow *nee*-pis	lemon
lisan	lee-*sahn*	oral
logam	lo-*gahm*	metal
lompat	lom-*paht*	jump (across)
loncat	lon-*chaht*	jump (high)
longgar	*long*-gahr	loose
lori	lo-*ree*	truck
lorong	lo-*rong*	alley • path
luar	loo-*ahr*	outside
luar biasa	*loo*-ahr bee-*ah*-suh	unusual
luas	loo-*ahs*	large
luka (kecederaan)	loo-*kuh* (ke-che-de-*rah*-ahn)	wound (injury)
lukisan	loo-*ki*-sahn	painting (picture)
lucu	*loo*-choo	joke • funny
lumpuh kaki	*loom*-pu(h) kah-*kee*	paraplegic
lumpur	*loom*-pur	mud
lupa	*loo*-puh	to forget
(garisan) lurus	(gah-*ri*-sahn) loo-*rus*	straight (line)
lusa	*loo*-suh	day after tomorrow
lutut	loo-*tut*	knee

M

maaf	mah-*ahf*	sorry

Maafkan saya. mah-*ahf*-kahn *sai*-yuh		**Excuse me.**

mabuk	mah-*bu(k)*	to be drunk

mabuk jalan	mah-*bu(k) jah*-lahn	travel sickness
mabuk laut	mah-*bu(k)* lowt	seasick
macam mana	*mah*-chahm *mah*-nuh	how
mahal	mah-*hahl*	expensive
mahasiswa	mah-*hah*-sis-wah	student (university)
mahkamah	*mah(h)*-kah-mah(h)	court (legal)
mahu	mow	to want
main daun terup	main down te-*rup*	to play cards
main kad	main kahd	to play cards
majalah	mah-jah-*lah(h)*	magazine
majikan	mah-*ji(k)*-kahn	employer
majoriti	mah-*jo*-ree-tee	majority
makan	*mah*-kahn	eat
makan malam	*mah*-kahn *mah*-lahm	dinner
makan sayur saja	*mah*-kahn sah-*yur sah*-juh	vegetarian
makan tengahari	*mah*-kahn te-ngah-*hah*-ree	lunch
makanan	mah-*kah*-nahn	food
maklumat	*mahk*-loo-maht	information
makna	*mahk*-nuh	meaning
maksud	*mahk*-sud	wish
malam	*mah*-lahm	night · evening
malam ini	*mah*-lahm ee-nee	tonight
Malam Krismas	*mah*-lahm *kris*-muhs	Christmas Eve
malam semalam	*mah*-lahm se-*mah*-lahm	last night
malaria	mah-lah-*ree*-ah	malaria
malas	mah-*lahs*	lazy
Malaysia	mah-*lay*-see-ah	Malaysia
malu	*mah*-loo	embarrassment · shy
mampu	*mahm*-poo	can (able)

mana-mana	mah-*nuh*-mah-*nuh*	anywhere
mancis	*mahn*-chis	matches
mandi	*mahn*-dee	to bathe/shower · to wash (yourself)
mangga	*mang*-guh	mango · padlock (col
manis	mah-*nis*	sweet (adj)
manuskrip	mah-*niu*-skrip	script
marah	mah-*rah(h)*	angry
masa	mah-*suh*	time
masa depan	mah-*suh* de-*pahn*	future

masak	mah-sah(k)	to cook • ripe
masalah	mah-sah-ah-lah(h)	problem
masam	mah-sahm	sour
masih	mah-si(h)	still (yet)
masin	mah-sin	salty
masjid	mahs-jid	mosque
masuk	mah-su(k)	to enter
masyarakat	mah-shah-rah-kaht	society
mata	mah-tuh	eye
matahari	mah-tuh-hah-ree	sun
matahari terbenam	mah-tuh-hah-ree ter-be-nahm	sunset
matahari terbit	mah-tuh-hah-ree ter-bit	sunrise
mati	mah-tee	dead (battery, animal)
mee	mee	noodles
meja	meh-juh	table
mekanik	me-ka-nik	mechanic
mel	mehl	mail
mel biasa	mehl bee-ah-suh	surface mail
mel ekspres	mehl ehks-prehs	express mail
mel udara	mehl oo-dah-ruh	airmail
melakukan [laku]	me-lah-koo-kahn [lah-koo]	to do
melaporkan [lapor]	me-lah-por-kahn [lah-por]	to report
melawat [lawat]	me-lah-waht [lah-waht]	to visit
melayani [layan]	me-lah-yah-nee [lah-yahn]	to serve
meletakkan [letak]	me-le-tah(k)-kahn [le-tah(k)]	to put
melihat [lihat]	me-lee-haht [lee-haht]	to look
melihat-lihat saja [lihat]	me-lee-haht-lee-haht sah-juh [lee-haht]	to go window-shopping
melindungi [lindung]	me-lin-du-ngee [lin-dung]	to protect
melukis	me-loo-kis	painting (activity)
memaafkan [maaf]	me-mah-ahf-kahn [mah-ahf]	to forgive
memakai [pakai]	me-mah-kai [pah-kai]	to wear
memancing [pancing]	me-mahn-ching [pahn-ching]	to fish
memandu [pandu]	me-mahn-doo	to drive
memangga (col)	me-mahng-guh	padlock
membaca [baca]	mem-bah-chuh [bah-chuh]	to read
membantah [bantah]	mem-bahn-tah(h) [bahn-tah(h)]	to argue • to protest
membantu [bantu]	mem-bahn-too [bahn-too]	to help
membatalka [batal]	mem-bah-tahl-kah [bah-tahl]	to cancel
membawa [bawa]	mem-bah-wuh [bah-wuh]	to carry • to bring
membayangkan	mem-bah-yahng-kahn	imagine

membayar [bayar]	mem-*bah*-yahr [*bah*-yahr]	**to pay**
membeku [beku]	mem-*be*-koo [*be*-koo]	**to freeze**
membeli [beli]	mem-*be*-lee [*be*-lee]	**to buy**
membeli-belah [beli]	mem-*be*-le-be-*lah(h)* [be-*lee*]	**to go shopping**
membenarkan	mem-be-*nahr*-kahn	**to allow**
memberahikan [berahi]	mem-be-*rah*-hee-kahn [be-*rah*-hee]	**sexy**
memberi [beri]	mem-be-*ree* [be-*ree*]	**to give**
memberitahu [tahu]	mem-be-ree-*tah*-hoo [*tah*-hoo]	**to tell (inform)**
membersihkan [bersih]	mem-ber-*si(h)*-kahn [ber-*si(h)*]	**to clean**
membina [bina]	mem-*bee*-nuh [*bee*-nuh]	**to build**
membuat [buat]	mem-*boo*-aht [*boo*-aht]	**to make • to do**
membuat tempahan	mem-*boo*-aht *tem*-pah-hahn	**to make a booking**
membuka [buka]	mem-*boo*-kuh [*boo*-kuh]	**to open**
membunuh [bunuh]	mem-boo-*nuh(h)* [boo-*nuh(h)*]	**to kill**
memeriksa [periksa]	me-me-*rik*-sah [pe-*rik*-sah]	**to check**
memikirkan diri sendiri saja	me-mee-*kir*-kahn dee-*ree* sen-dee-*ree* sah-juh	**selfish**
memilih [pilih]	me-*mee*-li(h) [*pee*-li(h)]	**to choose**
meminjam [pinjam]	me-min-jahm [pin-jahm]	**to borrow**
meminta [minta]	me-*min*-tuh [*min*-tuh]	**to ask for something**
memisahkan [pisah]	me-mee-*sah(h)*-kahn [pee-*sah(h)*]	**to separate**
memotong [potong]	me-*mo*-tong [*po*-tong]	**to cut**
memperbaiki [baik]	mem-per-*bai*-kee	**to repair**
memulai [mula]	me-moo-*lah*-ee [moo-*luh*]	**to kick off**
memulakan [mula]	me-moo-*lah*-kahn [moo-*luh*]	**to start**
mempunyai [punya]	mem-*poo*-nyah-ee [*poo*-nyah]	**to have**
memutuskan [putus]	me-moo-*tus*-kahn [poo-*tus*]	**to decide**
menafikan [nafi]	me-nah-*fee*-kahn [nah-*fee*]	**to deny**
menaiki [naik]	me-*nai(k)*-kee [nai(k)]	**to ride (horse, bus, bike)**
menaip [taip]	me-*naip* (taip)	**to type**
menandatangani [tandatangan]	me-nahn-duh-*tah*-ngah-nee [tahn-duh-*tah*-ngahn]	**to sign**
menang	me-*nahng*	**to win**
menara	me-*nah*-ruh	**tower**
menarik	me-*nah*-ri(k)	**interesting**
menarik [tarik]	me-*nah*-ri(k) [*tah*-ri(k)]	**to pull**
mencampurkan [campur]	men-cham-*pur*-kahn [chahm-*pur*]	**to mix**

mencari [cari]	men-*chah*-ree [*chah*-ree]	to look for • to search
mencegah	men-che-*gah(h)*	prevent
mencium [cium]	men-*chee*-um [*chee*-um]	to kiss
mencuba [cuba]	men-*choo*-buh [*choo*-buh]	to try (attempt)
mencuci [cuci]	men-*choo*-chee [*choo*-chee]	to wash (something) • to develop (film)
mencuri [curi]	men-*choo*-ree [*choo*-ree]	to steal
mendaki gunung	men-*dah*-kee *goo*-nung	mountaineering
mendalam	men-*dah*-lahm	intense
mendapat [dapat]	men-*dah*-paht [*dah*-paht]	to earn
mendayung	men-*dah*-yung	to row
mendengar [dengar]	men-de-*ngahr* [de-*ngahr*]	to hear • to listen
menderita [derita]	men-de-*ree*-tuh [de-*ree*-tuh]	to suffer
mendesak	men-de-*sah(k)*	urgent
mendidik [didik]	men-dee-*di(k)* [dee-*di(k)*]	to educate
mendung	*men*-dung	cloudy
meneka [teka]	me-ne-*kuh* [te-*kuh*]	to guess
menelefon [telefon]	me-ne-*leh*-fon [teh-*leh*-fon]	to telephone
menemani	me-ne-*mah*-nee	to accompany
menembak [tembak]	me-*nehm*-bah(k) [*tehm*-bah(k)]	to shoot
menempah [tempah]	me-*nehm*-pah(h) [*tehm*-pah(h)]	to order
menentang	me-*nen*-tahng	against (opposed)
menerima [terima]	me-ne-*ree*-muh [te-*ree*-muh]	to accept • to receive
mengadu [adu]	me-*ngah*-doo [*ah*-doo]	to complain
mengajar	me-*ngah*-jahr	teaching
mengakhiri [akhir]	me-ngah-*khi*-ree [ah-*khir*]	to end
mengambil [ambil]	me-*ngahm*-bil [*ahm*-bil]	to pick up • to take away
mengambil foto/gambar	me-*ngahm*-bil *fo*-to/*gahm*-bahr	to take photographs
mengandung	me-*ngahn*-dung	to be pregnant
mengantuk	me-*ngah*-tu(k)	sleepy
mengapa	me-*ngah*-puh	why
mengatur [atur]	me-*ngah*-tur [*ah*-tur]	to organise
mengejek	me-*ngeh*-jeh(k)	to make fun of
mengeksport [eksport]	me-*ngehks*-port [*ehks*-port]	to export
mengakui [akui]	me-ngah-*koo*-ee [ah-*koo*-ee]	to recognise
mengembara	me-ngem-*bah*-ruh	to travel
mengerikan [ngeri]	me-nge-*ree*-kahn [nge-*ree*]	terrible • horrible
mengeringkan [kering]	me-nge-*ring*-kahn [ke-*ring*]	to dry

mengesahkan [sah]	me-nge-*sah(h)*-kahn [sah(h)]	to confirm (a booking)
mengesyorkan [syor]	me-nge-*shor*-kahn [shor]	to recommend
mengganggu [ganggu]	meng-*gahng*-goo [*gahng*-goo]	to annoy
menggigit [gigit]	meng-*gee*-git [*gee*-git]	to bite
menggunakan kembali	meng-goo-*nah*-kahn kem-*bah*-lee	to recycle
menghantar [hantar]	meng-*hahn*-tahr [*hahn*-tahr]	to send
menghasilkan [hasil]	meng-*hah*-sil-kahn [*hah*-sil]	to produce
menghiburkan [hibur]	meng-hee-*bur*-kahn [hee-*bur*]	entertaining
menghidu [hidu]	meng-hee-doo [hee-doo]	to smell
menghilangkan [hilang]	meng-hee-*lahng*-kahn [hee-*lahng*]	to lose (something)
menghiris [hiris]	meng-*hee*-ris [*hee*-ris]	to slice
menghukum [hukum]	meng-*hoo*-kum [*hoo*-kum]	to punish
mengikuti [ikut]	me-*ngee*-ku-tee [*ee*-kut]	to follow (join in)
mengira [kira]	me-*ngee*-ruh [*kee*-ruh]	to count
mengisi [isi]	me-*ngee*-see [*ee*-see]	to fill
mengizinkan	me-*ngee*-zin-kahn	to allow
mengkagumkan	meng-kah-*gum*-kahn	wonderful
mengulangi [ulang]	me-ngoo-*lah*-ngee [oo-*lahng*]	repeat
mengunci [kunci]	me-*ngun*-chee [*koon*-chee]	to lock
mengundi [undi]	me-*ngun*-dee [*un*-dee]	to vote
mengunjungi [kunjung]	me-*ngoon*-ju-ngee [*koon*-jung]	to visit
mengurat	me-*ngoo*-rut	to chat up
mengurut [urut]	me-*ngoo*-rut [*oo*-rut]	to massage
menikmati [nikmat]	me-*nik*-mah-tee [*nik*-maht]	to enjoy (oneself)
menimbang [timbang]	me-*nim*-bahng [*tim*-bahng]	to weigh
meninggal [tinggal]	me-*ning*-gahl [*ting*-gahl]	to die (person)
meninggal dunia	me-*ning*-gahl doo-ni-uh	dead (person)
menipu [tipu]	me-*nee*-poo [*tee*-poo]	to lie
menjaga [jaga]	men-*jah*-guh [*jah*-guh]	to look after
menjawab [jawab]	men-*jah*-wahb [*jah*-wahb]	to reply • to answer
menjerit [jerit]	men-je-*rit* [je-*rit*]	to shout
menjual [jual]	men-joo-*ahl* [joo-*ahl*]	to sell
menjumpai [jumpa]	men-*joom*-pah-ee [*joom*-pah]	to find
menolak [tolak]	me-no-*lah(k)* [to-*lah(k)*]	to refuse
menolong [tolong]	me-*no*-long [*to*-long]	to help
menonton [tonton]	me-*non*-ton [*ton*-ton]	to watch
mensyempu [syempu]	men-shehm-*poo* [shem-*poo*]	to shampoo

278

mentah	men-*tah(h)*	raw (food)
mentega	men-*teh*-guh	butter
menterjemahkan [terjemah]	men-ter-je-*mah(h)*-kahn [ter-je-*mah(h)*]	to translate
(rokok) mentol	(ro-ko(k)) *mehn*-tol	menthol (cigarettes)
mentul	*mehn*-tul	light bulb
menu	*meh*-noo	menu
menukar [tukar]	me-*noo*-kahr [*too*-kahr]	to change
menulis [tulis]	me-*noo*-lis [*too*-lis]	to write
menumpang	me-*noom*-pahng	to hitchhike
menunggang [tunggang]	me-*noong*-gahng [*toong*-gahng]	to ride (bus, car, plane, train)
menunjukkan [tunjuk]	me-*noon*-joo(k)-kahn [*toon*-joo(k)]	to show
menutup [tutup]	me-*noo*-tup [*too*-tup]	to close
menyakitkan	me-nyah-*kit*-kahn	painful
menyanyi [nyanyi]	me-*nyah*-nyee [*nyah*-nyee]	to sing
menyedari [sedar]	me-nye-*dah*-ree [se-*dahr*]	to realise
menyediakan [sedia]	me-nye-dee-*ah*-kahn [se-dee-*uh*]	to prepare
menyelam [selam]	me-nye-*lahm* [se-*lahm*]	to dive
menyelamatkan [selamat]	me-nye-*lah*-maht-kahn [se-*lah*-maht]	to save
menyentuh [sentuh]	me-nyen-*tu(h)* [sen-*tu(h)*]	to touch
menyesal [sesal]	me-nye-*sahl* [se-*sahl*]	to regret
menyewa [sewa]	me-*nyeh*-wuh [*seh*-wuh]	to hire (rent)
menyuntikkan [suntik]	me-nyun-*ti(k)*-kahn [sun-*ti(k)*]	to inject
merah	*meh*-rah(h)	red
merah jambu	*meh*-rah(h) *jahm*-boo	pink
merasuah	me-rah-soo-*ah(h)*	to bribe
merayakan [raya]	me-*rah*-yuh-kahn [*rah*-yuh]	to celebrate
mereka	me-*reh*-kuh	they
merindui [rindu]	me-*rin*-doo-ee [*rin*-doo]	to miss (feel absence)
merokok [rokok]	me-ro-ko(k) [*ro*-ko(k)]	to smoke
merompak [rompak]	me-rom-*pa(k)* [rom-*pa(k)*]	to rob
mesin	me-*sin*	machine
mesin basuh	me-*sin* bah-*su(h)*	washing machine
mesti	*mes*-tee	must
mesyuarat	me-*shoo*-ah-raht	meeting
meter	*mee*-ter	metre
migraine	*mai*-grehn	migraine
milimeter	*mi*-li-*mee*-ter	millimetre

minggu	*ming*-goo	week
minggu depan	*ming*-goo de-*pahn*	next week
minggu ini	*ming*-goo ee-nee	this week
minggu lepas	*ming*-goo le-*pahs*	last week
minit	*mi*-nit	minute
minum	*mee*-num	to drink
minuman	mee-nu-*mahn*	drink
minyak	*min*-yah(k)	petrol
minyak masak	*min*-yah(k) *mah*-sah(k)	oil (cooking)
misalan	mi-*sah*-lahn	example
miskin	*mis*-kin	poor
modem	mo-*dem*	modem
mogok	mo-*go(k)*	(on) strike
monyet	mo-*nyeht*	monkey
motosikal	mo-to-*see*-kahl	motorcycle
mual	*moo*-ahl	nausea
muda	*moo*-duh	young
mudah	moo-*dah(h)*	easy
muka	*moo*-kuh	face
mulakan	moo-*luh*-kahn	to begin
mulut	*moo*-lut	mouth
munasabah	moo-*nah*-sah-bah(h)	sensible
mungkin	*moong*-kin	maybe • perhaps
muntah	moon-*tah(h)*	vomit • to vomit
murah	*moo*-rah(h)	cheap
murah hati	moo-*rah(h)* hah-tee	generous
murid	moo-*rid*	student (school)
murni	*moor*-nee	pure
musim	*moo*-sim	season
musim bunga	*moo*-sim boo-nguh	spring (season)
musim luruh	*moo*-sim *loo*-ru(h)	autumn
musim panas	*moo*-sim *pah*-nahs	summer
musim sejuk	*moo*-sim se-*joo(k)*	winter
mutu	moo-*too*	quality
muzik	*moo*-zik	music
muzium	moo-*zee*-um	muse-
um		

N

naik	nai(k)	to board (ship, etc)
(jalan) naik bukit	(*jah*-lahn) nai(k) boo-*kit*	uphill (road)
nama	*nah*-muh	name
nama keluarga	*nah*-muh ke-loo-*ahr*-guh	surname
nama panggilan	*nah*-muh *pang*-gi-lahn	nickname

nama pertama	*nah*-muh per-*tah*-muh	first name
nanas	*nah*-nahs	pineapple
nanti	*nahn*-tee	later
naskhah	nahs-*kah(h)*	script
nasi	nah-*see*	rice (cooked)
nasib	nah-*sib*	luck
negara	ne-*gah*-ruh	country
nenas	*neh*-nahs	pineapple
nenek	neh-*neh(k)*	grandmother
nilai	nee-*lai*	value (price) • worth
nipis	*nee*-pis	thin
nombor	*nom*-bor	number
novel	no-*vel*	novel (book)
nyamuk (kelambu)	*nyah*-mu(k) (ke-*lahm*-boo)	mosquito (net)
nyaris-nyaris	*nyah*-ris-*nyah*-ris	almost

O

offside	of-*said*	offside
OK	*oh*-kay	OK
oksigen	ok-*see*-jen	oxygen
olahraga	o-*lah(h)*-rah-guh	track (sports)
ombak	om-*bah(k)*	waves
operasi	o-pe-*rah*-see	operation
operator (telefon)	o-pe-*reh*-tor (teh-*leh*-fon)	(telephone) operator
orang	o-rahng	person • people
orang asing	o-rahng *ah*-sing	foreigner
orang barat	o-rahng bah-*raht*	Westerner (col)
orang Eropah	o-rahng eh-ro-*pah(h)*	European
orang gaji	o-rahng gah-*jee*	servant
orang Islam	o-rahng *ees*-lahm	Muslim
orang suci	o-rahng soo-*chee*	saint
orang tua	o-rahng *too*-uh	parents
orang yang tidak dikenali	o-rahng yahng *tee*-dah(k) dee-ke-*nah*-lee	stranger
oren	o-*rehn*	orange (food, colour)
orgasma	or-*gahs*-mah	orgasm
orkestra	or-*kehs*-truh	orchestra
otak	o-*tah(k)*	brain
otot	o-*tot*	muscle

P

pada	pah-*duh*	at (time)
pada waktu tengahari	pah-*duh wahk*-too te-ngah-*hah*-ree	in the afternoon

padang pasir	*pah*-dahng *pah*-sir	desert
padang tenis	*pah*-dahng teh-*nis*	tennis court
paderi	pah-de-*ree*	priest (Catholic, Protestant)
(yang) paling	(yahng) pah-*ling*	most (the)
pagi	*pah*-gee	morning
pagi semalam	*pah*-gee se-*mah*-lahm	yesterday morning
paip	paip	pipe (plumbing)
pakar	pah-*kahr*	specialist
(kedai) pakaian	(ke-*dai*) pah-*kai*-ahn	clothing (store)
paku kayu	pah-*koo* kah-*yoo*	tent pegs
paling penting	*pah*-ling *pen*-ting	essential
pam	pahm	pump
pameran	pah-*meh*-rahn	exhibition
panas	*pah*-nahs	hot (temperature) • heat
pancang khemah	pahn-*chahng* kheh-*mah(h)*	tent pegs
panggang	*pahng*-gahng	roasted
panggung sandiwara	*pahng*-gung sahn-dee-*wah*-rah	theatre (play)
panggung wayang	*pahng*-gung *wai*-yahng	cinema
panjang	*pahn*-jahng	long (measurement) length
pantai	*pahn*-tai	beach
pantas	pahn-*tahs*	quick • quickly
papan kekunci	pah-*pahn* ke-*koon*-chee	keyboard
papan markah	pah-*pahn* mahr-*kah(h)*	scoreboard
papan mata	pah-*pahn* *mah*-tuh	scoreboard
papan selancar	pah-*pahn* se-*lahn*-chahr	surfboard
parlimen	*pahr*-lee-men	parliament
parti	*pahr*-tee	party (political)
pas naik	pahs nai(k)	boarding pass
pasar (malam)	*pah*-sahr *(mah*-lahm)	(night) market
pasaraya	pah-sah-*rah*-yuh	supermarket
pasir	*pah*-sir	sand
(nombor) pasport	(*nom*-bor) pahs-port	passport (number)
pasukan	pah-*su(k)*-kahn	team (sport)
patah	pah-*tah(h)*	broken
patung	*pah*-tung	statue
payung	*pah*-yung	umbrella
pecah	pe-*chah*	break (fracture)
pedang	pe-*dahng*	sword
pedas	pe-*dahs*	hot (spicy)
pegas	pe-*gahs*	spring (coil)

Malay	Pronunciation	English
pegawai pengawas stesen keretapi	pe-gah-wai pe-ngah-wahs steh-sehn ke-reh-tah-ah-pee	stationmaster
peguam	pe-gwahm	lawyer
pejabat maklumat pelancong	pe-jah-baht mah(k)-loo-maht pe-lahn-chong	tourist information office
pejabat pos	pe-jah-baht pos	post office
pejabat tiket	pe-jah-baht tee-keht	ticket office
pejalan kaki	pe-jah-lahn kah-kee	pedestrian
pekak	pe-kah(k)	deaf
pekerja	pe-ker-juh	employee
pekerja pejabat	pe-ker-juh pe-jah-baht	office worker
pekerjaan	pe-ker-jah-ahn	job • occupation
pelabuhan	pe-lah-bu-hahn	port • harbour
pelacur	pe-lah-chur	prostitute
pelajar	pe-lah-jahr	student (school)
pelan	pe-lahn	plan
pelancong [lancong]	pe-lahn-chong [lahn-chong]	tourist
pelarian	pe-lah-ree-ahn	refugee
pelayan	pe-lah-yahn	waiter
pelepasan	pe-le-pah-sahn	departure
pelik	pe-li(k)	strange
peluang	pe-loo-ahng	chance
peluk	pe-lu(k)	hug
pelukis	pe-loo-kis	painter (artist)
pelukis potret	pe-loo-kis po-treht	portrait sketcher
pemain	pe-main	player
pemain muzik	pe-main moo-zik	musician
pemain sukan	pe-main soo-kahn	sportsplayer
pemakaman	pe-me-mah-kah-mahn	funeral
pemenang	pe-me-nahng	winner
pemandangan [pandang]	pe-mahn-dah-ngahn [pahn-dahng]	scenery • view
pemandu	pe-mahn-doo	guide (person, audio)
pembasmi kuman	pem-bahs-mee koo-mahn	antiseptic
pemberian [beri]	pem-be-ree-ahn [be-ree]	present (gift)
pembuka botol	pem-boo-kuh bo-tol	bottle opener
pembuka tin	pem-boo-kuh tin	can opener
pemeriksaan kembali	pe-me-rik-sah-ahn kem-bah-lee	review
pemetik api	pe-me-ti(k) ah-pee	lighter
pemilik	pe-mee-li(k)	owner
pemimpin [pimpin]	pe-meem-pin [peem-pin]	leader

283

pemungut tiket	pe-moo-*ngut* tee-*keht*	ticket collector
pen	pehn	pen
(penagih) heroin	(pe-*nah*-gi(h)) heh-ro-in	heroin (addict)
penanaman hutan semula	pe-nah-*nah*-mahn hoo-*tahn* se-*moo*-luh	reforestation
penangguhan	pe-*nahng*-gu-hahn	delay
penat	pe-*naht*	tired
pencacaran	pen-chah-*chah*-rahn	vaccination
pencemaran	pen-che-*mah*-rahn	pollution
pencuri	pen-choo-*ree*	thief
(kaunter) pendaftaran	(*kown*-ter) pen-*dahf*-tah-rahn	check-in (desk)
pendakian tebing batu	pen-dah-*kee*-ahn te-*bing* bah-*too*	rock climbing
pendapat	pen-*dah*-paht	opinion
pendek	*pehn*-deh(k)	short (length, height)
pendidikan	pen-dee-*di(k)*-kahn	education
pendingin udara	pen-*dee*-ngin oo-*dah*-ruh	air-conditioner
penebangan hutan	pe-ne-*bah*-ngahn hoo-*tahn*	deforestation
penerbangan	pe-ner-*bah*-ngahn	flight
penerbit [terbit] (filem)	pe-*ner*-bit [*ter*-bit] (*fee*-lem)	producer (of film)
pengadil	pe-*ngah*-dil	referee
penganggur	pe-*ngahng*-gur	homeless • unemployed
penganut Buda	pe-*ngah*-nut boo-*duh*	Buddhist
pengarah (filem)	pe-*ngah*-rah(h) (*fee*-lem)	director (of film)
pengembalian wang	pe-ngem-*bah*-lee-ahn wahng	to refund
pengembaraan [kembara]	pe-ngem-*bah*-ruh-ahn [kem-*bah*-ruh]	to trek
pengemis	pe-*nge*-mis	beggar
pengenalan	pe-*nge*-nah-lahn	identification
pengguguran	peng-goo-*goo*-rahn	abortion
penggunting rambut	peng-*gun*-ting *rahm*-but	barber
penghibur jalanan	*peng*-hi-bur *jah*-lah-nahn	busker
penginapan	pe-*ngee*-nah-pahn	accommodation
pengsan	*pehng*-sahn	to faint
pengurus	pe-*ngoo*-rus	manager
pening	pe-*ning*	dizzy

Penipu!	pe-nee-*poo*!	Cheat!

Malay	Pronunciation	English
penjaga anak	pen-*jah*-guh *ah*-nah(k)	babysitter
penjaga gol	pen-*jah*-guh gol	goalkeeper
penjagaan anak	pen-*jah*-*gah*-ahn *ah*-nah(k)	childminding
penjara	pen-*jah*-ruh	prison
penjual dadah	pen-joo-*ahl* dah-*dah*(h)	drug dealer
penjuru	*pen*-joo-roo	corner
pensyarah	pen-shah-*rah*(h)	lecturer
pentas	pen-*tahs*	stage
penting	*pen*-ting	important • urgent
penuh	pe-*nuh*(h)	full
penuh sesak	pe-*nuh*(h) se-*sa*(k)	crowded
penulis	pe-*noo*-lis	writer
penumpang	pe-*noom*-pahng	passenger
penyakit	pe-*nyah*-kit	disease
penyakit berak darah	pe-*nyah*-kit beh-*ra*(k) dah-rah(h)	dysentery
penyakit kelamin	pe-*nyah*-kit ke-*lah*-min	venereal disease
penyakit sengal-sengal tulang	pe-*nyah*-kit se-*ngahl*-se-*ngahl* too-*lahng*	rheumatism
penyampai	pe-*nyahm*-pai	presenter (TV, etc)
penyampaian [sampai]	pe-*nyahm*-pai-ahn [*sahm*-pai]	presentation
penyanyi	pe-*nyah*-nyee	singer
penyeluk saku	pe-nye-*lu*(k) sah-*koo*	pickpocket
penyembahan	pe-nyem-*bah*(h)-hahn	worship
penyokong [sokong]	pe-*nyo*-kong [*so*-kong]	fan (of a team)
penyunting	pe-*nyun*-ting	editor
perak	peh-*ra*(k)	silver
perahu	pe-*rah*-hoo	boat
perang	pe-*rahng*	war
perasaan [rasa]	pe-*rah*-sah-ahn [*rah*-suh]	feelings
peraturan	pe-*rah*-tu-rahn	rules
perayaan	pe-*rah*-*yah*-ahn	festival
percaya	per-*chah*-yuh	to trust
percintaan	per-*chin*-tah-ahn	romance
percuma	per-*choo*-muh	free (of charge)
perdana menteri	per-dah-*nuh* men-te-ree	prime minister
perempuan	pe-*rem*-pwahn	female (human) • woman
pergaduhan	per-gah-*du*(h)-hahn	fight
pergi	*per*-gee	to go
(tiket) pergi balik	(tee-*keht*) *per*-gee bah-li(k)	return (ticket)

Pergilah!		
per-*gee*-la(h)!		**Get lost!**

pergunungan	per-goo-*nu*-ngahn	mountain range
perhentian bas	per-*hen*-tee-ahn bahs	bus stop
perhimpunan	per-*him*-pu-nahn	rally (demonstration)
peribadi	pe-ree-*bah*-dee	personality • private
periuk	pe-*ree*-u(k)	pot (cooking)
perjalanan	per-jah-*lah*-nahn	trip • journey
perjalanan [jalan]	per-jah-*lah*-nahn [*jah*-lahn]	to trek
perkahwinan	per-*kah(h)*-wi-nahn	marriage
pernikahan	per-nee-*kah(h)*-hahn	wedding
perkataan	per-kah-*tah*-ahn	word
perlahan	per-*lah*-hahn	slow
perlu	per-*loo*	need
perlumbaan	per-*loom*-bah-ahn	race (sport)
permaidani	per-*mai*-dah-nee	rug
permainan	per-*mai*-nahn	game (board game, sport)
permainan komputer	per-*mai*-nahn kom-*piu*-ter	computer game
permit	per-*mit*	permit
permit kerja	per-*mit ker*-juh	work permit
pernah	per-*nah(h)*	already
perniagaan	per-nee-ah-*gah*-ahn	business
pernikahan	per-nee-*kah(h)*-hahn	wedding
perogolan [rogol]	pe-ro-*go*-lahn [ro-*gohl*]	rape
perpustakaan	per-poos-*tah*-kah-ahn	library
persatuan	per-sah-*too*-ahn se-*ker*-juh	unions
persendirian	per-sen-dee-*ree*-ahn	private
persimpangan	per-*sim*-pah-ngahn	intersection
pertama	per-*tah*-muh	first
pertanyaan	per-*tah*-nyuh-ahn	question
pertemuan	per-te-*moo*-ahn	meeting
pertolongan	per-*to*-lo-ngan	assistance
(kadar) pertukaran	(kah-*dahr*) per-too-*kah*-rahn	exchange (rate)
pertunjukan [tunjuk]	per-toon-*joo(k)*-kahn [toon-*joo(k)*]	performance • show
perut	pe-*rut*	stomach
pesanan	pe-*sah*-nahn	message
pesara	pe-*sah*-ruh	pensioner
pesta	*pehs*-tuh	party (fiesta)
peta	pe-*tah*	map
peta jalan	pe-tah *jah*-lahn	road map
petang	pe-*tahng*	afternoon
petang esok	pe-*tahng* eh-so(k)	tomorrow afternoon
petang ini	pe-*tahng* ee-nee	this afternoon
petang semalam	pe-*tahng* se-*mah*-lahm	yesterday afternoon

Malay	Pronunciation	English
petani	pe-*tah*-nee	farmer
peti besi	pe-*tee* be-*see*	safe (vault)
peti sejuk	pe-*tee* se-*ju(k)*	refrigerator
petrol	peh-trol	petrol
Piala Dunia	pee-*ah*-luh doo-ni-*uh*	World Cup
pidato politik	pee-*dah*-to po-*lee*-tik	political speech
pil	pil	pill
pilihanraya	pee-lee-*hahn*-rah-yuh	elections
pinggan	*ping*-gahn	plate
pinggang	*ping*-gahng	back (of body)
pinggir bandar	*ping*-gir *bahn*-dahr	suburb
pinggir laut	*ping*-gir lowt	coast
ping-pong	ping-*pong*	table tennis
pintu	*peen*-too	door
pintu masuk	*peen*-too mah-*su(k)*	entrance
pisang	*pee*-sahng	banana
pisau	*pee*-sow	knife
pisau cukur	*pee*-sow *choo*-kur	razor
pisau lipat	*pee*-sow *lee*-paht	penknife
planet	plah-*neht*	planet
plastik	*plahs*-tik	plastic
plug	pluhg	plug (electricity)
PMS	pee em es	premenstrual tension
pohon	po-hon	tree
poker	po-ker	poker (the game)
poket	po-*keht*	pocket
pokok	po-ko(k)	tree
polis	po-lis	police
pondok	pon-*do(k)*	mountain hut
popular	po-*piu*-luhr	popular
poskad	pos-*kahd*	postcard
poskod	pos-*kod*	postcode
poster	*pos*-ter	poster
potong	*po*-tong	piece
presiden	preh-*see*-den	president
projektor	pro-*jehk*-tor	projector
Puan	pwahn	Mrs
puisi	poo-*ee*-see	poetry
pulang	poo-*lahng*	to go home
pulau	poo-*low*	island
pun	pun	also • too
puncak	*poon*-chah(k)	peak (of mountain)
purba	*pur*-buh	ancient
purse	puhrs	purse

pusat membeli-belah	poo-*saht* mem-be-*lee*-be-*lah(h)*	department stores
pusing	poo-*sing*	turn
pusingan	poo-*si*-ngahn	leg (of a race)
putih	poo-ti(h)	white

R

radiator	rah-*dee*-ah-tor	radiator
rakaman	rah-*kah*-mahn	recording
raket	rah-*keht*	racquet
ramah-tamah	rah-*mah(h)*-tah-*mah(h)*	outgoing
ramai	rah-*mai*	busy (place, party)
rambut	*rahm*-but	hair
rancangan	rahn-*chah*-ngahn	program (TV)
rantai	*rahn*-tai	necklace
rasa	*rah*-suh	taste
rasisme	rah-*sis*-muh	racism
rehat	reh-*haht*	rest (relaxation)
rendah	ren-*dah(h)*	low
rentak	ren-*tah(k)*	rhythm
republik	ree-*puhb*-lik	republic
resit	re-*sit*	receipt
restoran	rehs-*to*-rahn	restaurant
resume	reh-siu-*meh*	resumé
ribut	ree-*but*	storm
ringan	ri-*ngahn*	light (not heavy)
risau	ree-*sow*	worried
risiko	ree-*see*-ko	risk
roda	ro-*duh*	wheel
(kertas) rokok	(ker-*tahs*) ro-ko(k)	cigarette (papers)
rosak	ro-*sah(k)*	rotten
roti	ro-tee	bread
roti bakar	ro-tee bah-kahr	toast (bread)
ruam	roo-*ahm*	rash
ruam bayi	roo-*ahm* bah-yee	nappy rash
ruang	roo-*ahng*	space (area)
ruang tamu	roo-*ahng* tah-moo	lounge (room)
rumah	roo-mah(h)	house
rumput	*room*-put	grass
runtuhan	run-*tu*-hahn	ruins
runtuhan bersejarah	run-*tu*-hahn ber-se-*jah*-rah(h)	historical ruins
rusa	*roo*-suh	deer

S

saat	sah-*aht*	second (unit of time)
sabar	sah-*bahr*	patient (adj)
sabun	sah-*bun*	soap
sains	sains	science
saintis	*sain*-tis	scientist
saiz	saiz	size
sajak	sah-*jah(k)*	poetry
sakit	*sah*-kit	sick • pain
sakit gigi	*sah*-kit *gee*-gee	toothache
sakit haid	*sah*-kit haid	period pain
sakit kepala	*sah*-kit ke-*pah*-luh	headache
sakit lelah	*sah*-kit le-*lah(h)*	asthma
sakit perut	*sah*-kit pe-*rut*	indigestion • stomachache
saku	sah-*koo*	pocket
salah	sah-*lah(h)*	wrong
salah faham	sah-*lah(h)* fah-*hahm*	misunderstanding
sama	*sah*-muh	same
sambil	*sahm*-bil	while (currently)
sampah	*sahm*-pah(h)	rubbish
sampai	*sahm*-pai	to arrive
sampan	*sahm*-pahn	boat
sampul surat	*sahm*-pul *soo*-raht	envelope
sangat	sah-*ngaht*	very • intense
sangat baik	sah-*ngaht* bai(k)	excellent
sangat lemak	sah-*ngaht* le-*mah(k)*	rich (food)
sangat ulung	sah-*ngaht* oo-lung	excellent
sarapan pagi	sah-rah-*pahn pah*-gee	breakfast
sarung bantal	sah-*rung bahn*-tahl	pillowcase
satu saja	*sah*-too *sah*-juh	just one
sawan babi	sah-*wahn bah*-bee	epilepsy
saya	*sai*-yuh	I
sayang	*sah*-yahng	love
sayap	sah-*yahp*	wings
sayap kanan	sah-*yahp kah*-nahn	right-wing
sayap kiri	sah-*yahp* ki-ree	left-wing
sayuran saja	*sai*-yu-rahn *sah*-juh	vegetarian (food)
sayur-sayuran	*sai*-yur-*sai*-yu-rahn	vegetables
sebab	se-*bahb*	because
sebarang	se-*bah*-rahng	any
sebelum	se-be-*lum*	before
seberang	se-be-*rahng*	across

sedap	se-*dahp*	**delicious**
sederhana	se-der-*hah*-nuh	**simple**
sedia	se-dee-*uh*	**ready**
sedih	se-*di(h)*	**sad**
sedikit	se-*dee*-kit	**little (amount)**
segan	se-*gahn*	**shy**
segar	se-*gahr*	**fresh**
segiempat	se-gee-*em*-paht	**square (shape)**
(tiket) sehala	(tee-*keht*) se-*hah*-luh	**one-way (ticket)**
sehingga (Jun)	se-*hing*-guh (joon)	**until (June)**
sejak	se-*jah(k)*	**since**
sejarah	se-*jah*-rah(h)	**history**
sejuk	se-*ju(k)*	**cold**
sekali	se-*kah*-lee	**once**
sekali lagi	se-*kah*-lee *lah*-gee	**once again**
sekarang	se-*kah*-rahng	**now • present**
sekarang juga	se-*kah*-rahng *joo*-guh	**right now**
sekejap lagi	se-ke-*jahp lah*-gee	**soon**
sekolah	se-ko-*lah(h)*	**school**
sekolah menengah (SM)	se-ko-*lah(h)* me-ne-*ngah(h)*	**high school**
seks	sehks	**sex**
seks selamat	sehks se-*lah*-maht	**safe sex**
seksisme	sehk-*sis*-muh	**sexism**
selalu	se-*lah*-loo	**always**
selama	se-*lah*-muh	**for (length of time)**
selama-lamanya	se-*lah*-muh-*lah*-muh-nyuh	**forever**
selamat	se-*lah*-maht	**safe (secure)**

Selamat datang. se-*lah*-maht dah-*tahng*	**Welcome.**
Selamat hari jadi! se-*lah*-maht *hah*-ree *jah*-dee!	**Happy Birthday!**
Selamat jalan. se-*lah*-maht *jah*-lahn	**Goodbye. (speaker staying)**
Selamat malam. se-*lah*-maht *mah*-lahm	**Good night.**
Selamat pagi. se-*lah*-maht *pah*-gee	**Good morning.**
Selamat petang. se-*lah*-maht pe-*tahng*	**Good afternoon.**
Selamat tengahari. se-*lah*-maht te-ngah-*hah*-ree	**Good day.**

selatan	se-lah-*tahn*	**south**
selepas	se-le-*pahs*	**after**
selesa	se-*leh*-suh	**comfortable**
selimut	se-*lee*-mut	**blanket**
selipar	se-*lee*-pahr	**sandals**
seluar dalam	se-loo-*ahr* dah-*lahm*	**underwear**
seluar panjang	se-loo-*ahr* pahn-*jahng*	**trousers**
seluar pendek	se-loo-*ahr* pehn-*de(k)*	**shorts (clothes)**
seluruh	se-loo-*ru(h)*	**whole (all)**
semacam	se-*mah*-chahm	**similar**
semalam	se-*mah*-lahm	**yesterday**
sembahyang	sem-*bah*-yahng	**prayer**
sembelit	*sem*-be-lit	**constipation**
sempadan	*sem*-pah-dahn	**border**
sempit	*sem*-pit	**tight**
sempurna	sem-*pur*-nuh	**perfect**
semua	se-*moo*-uh	**all**
semua orang	se-*moo*-uh o-rahng	**everyone**
semuanya	se-moo-*uh*-nyuh	**everything**
semula	se-*moo*-luh	**again**
semut	se-*mut*	**ant**
senang	se-*nahng*	**easy**
seni	se-*nee*	**art**
seni prasejarah	se-*nee* prah-se-*jah*-rah(h)	**prehistoric art**
seni tembikar	se-*nee* tem-*bee*-kahr	**pottery**
seni ukir	se-*nee* oo-kir	**sculpture**
senibina	se-nee-*bee*-nuh	**architecture**
seni foto	se-*nee* fo-to	**photography**
seniman/seniwati	se-*nee*-mahn/ se-*nee*-wah-tee **(m/f)**	**artist**
sentiasa	*sen*-tee-ah-sah	**always**
senyap	se-*nyahp*	**quiet**
senyum	se-*nyum*	**to smile**
sepasang	se-*pah*-sahng	**pair (a couple)**
sepi	se-*pee*	**quiet**
serangan	se-*rah*-ngahn	**assault**
serangga	se-*rahng*-guh	**bug · insect**
seratus	se-*rah*-tus	**a hundred**
sering	se-*ring*	**often**
serius	see-*ree*-uhs	**serious**
seronok	se-*ro*-no(k)	**fun**

serupa	se-*roo*-puh	similar
seseorang	se-se-*o*-rahng	someone
sesuai	se-soo-ai	appropriate
sesuatu	se-soo-*ah*-too	something
sesudah	se-soo-*dah(h)*	after
setelah	se-te-*lah(h)*	after
setem	se-*tehm*	stamp
setengah	se-te-*ngah(h)*	half
setengah liter	se-te-*ngah(h) lee*-ter	half a litre
setia	se-*tee*-uh	loyal
setiap	se-*tee*-ahp	each • every
setiap hari	se-*tee*-ahp *hah*-ree	every day
setiausaha	se-*tee*-uh-oo-suh-huh	secretary

Setuju.	
se-*too*-joo	Agreed.

siap	see-*ahp*	ready
siapa	see-*ah*-puh	who
siar-siar	see-*ahr*-see-*ahr*	stroll
sibuk	si-*bu(k)*	busy (time)
sihat	si-*haht*	healthy
sikap	see-*kahp*	bad (attitude)
silakan	see-*lah*-kahn	please
simpang jalan	sim-*pahng jah*-lahn	crossroad
sinseh	sin-seh(h)	herbalist (person)
sintetik	sin-*teh*-tik	synthetic
sisa	see-suh	rest (what's left)
sisa buangan toksik	see-suh boo-ah-*ngahn tok*-sik	toxic waste
smir	smir	pap smear
soalan	so-*ah*-lahn	question
sosialis	so-see-*ah*-lis	socialist
stadium	stah-*dee*-um	stadium
standard	stahn-*dahrd*	standard (usual)
stesen	steh-sehn	station
stesen bas	steh-sehn bahs	bus station
stesen keretapi	steh-sehn ke-reh-tuh-*ah*-pee	railway/train station
stoking	sto-king	socks
studio	stoo-*dee*-o	studio
suam	soo-*ahm*	warm
suami	soo-*ah*-mee	husband
suara	soo-*ah*-ruh	voice • volume (sound)

suasana	soo-*ah*-sah-nuh	environment • atmosphere
subang	soo-*bahng*	earrings
suci	soo-*chee*	pure
sudah	soo-dah(h)	already
sudu	soo-*doo*	spoon
sudut	soo-*dut*	corner
suhu badan	soo-*hoo* bah-*dahn*	temperature (fever)
suhu udara	soo-*hoo* oo-*dah*-ruh	temperature (weather)
suka	soo-kuh	to like
suka menerima rasuah	soo-kuh me-ne-*ree*-muh rah-soo-ah(h)	corrupt (adj)
sukan	soo-*kahn*	sport
sukar	soo-*kahr*	difficult
suku	soo-*koo*	quarter
sundal	soon-*dahl*	prostitute
sungai	soo-*ngai*	river
suntikan [suntik]	sun-*ti(k)*-kahn [sun-*ti(k)*]	injection
sunyi	soo-*nyee*	quiet
surat	soo-*raht*	letter
surat beranak	soo-*raht* be-rah-*nah(k)*	birth certificate
surat berdaftar	soo-*raht* ber-*dahf*-tahr	registered mail
surat khabar	soo-*raht kah*-bahr	newspaper
susah	soo-*sah(h)*	difficult
susu	soo-*soo*	milk
sutera	soo-te-ruh	silk
syarahan	shah-rah-hahn	lecture
syarikat	shah-ree-kaht	company (business)
syiling	shee-ling	coins

T

tadika	tah-*dee*-kah	kindergarten
tafakur	tah-*fah*-kur	meditation
tahi	tai(k)	shit
tambah	tahm-bah(h)	plus

Tahniah!
tah(h)-nee-ah(h)!   **Congratulations!**

tahu	tah-hoo	to know (something)
tahun ini	tah-hoon *ee*-nee	this year
tahun depan	tah-hoon de-*pahn*	next year

tahun lepas	*tah*-hoon le-*pahs*	last year
tak apa	ta(k) *ah*-puh	never mind
takut	tah-*kut*	afraid
tali	tah-*lee*	rope • string
tali kasut	tah-*lee* kah-sut	shoelaces
tali pinggang keledar	tah-*lee* peeng-gahng ke-leh-*dahr*	seat belt
taman negara	tah-*mahn* ne-*gah*-ruh	national park
tampon	*tahm*-pon	tampon
tanah	tah-*nah(h)*	land (ground)
tanaman	tah-*nah*-mahn	plant
tanda	*tahn*-duh	sign
tanda lebam	*tahn*-duh le-*bahm*	bruise
tandas	*tahn*-duhs	toilet
tandas awam	*tahn*-duhs ah-*wahm*	public toilet
tandatangan	*tahn*-duh-*tah*-ngahn	signature
tangan	tah-*ngahn*	hand
tangga	*tahng*-guh	stairs
tanggungjawab	tang-gung-*jah*-wahb	responsibility
tanpa	*tahn*-puh	without
tanpa filter	*tahn*-puh *fil*-ter	without filter
taraf	tah-*rahf*	standard (adj)
taraf kehidupan	tah-*rahf* ke-hee-*du*-pahn	standard of living
tarikh	tah-*rikh*	date (time)
tarikh lahir	tah-*rikh* lah-*hir*	date of birth
taruhan	tah-*ru*-hahn	bet
tasik	tah-*si(k)*	lake
tatabahasa	tah-tah-bah-*hah*-suh	grammar
tawaran	tah-*wah*-rahn	offer
tawar-menawar [tawar]	*tah*-wahr-me-*nah*-wahr [*tah*-wahr]	to bargain
tayar	*tai*-yahr	tyre
tebing tinggi	te-*bing ting*-gee	cliff
teduh	te-*du(h)*	shade
teh	teh(h)	tea
telah	te-*lah(h)*	already
tekak	te-*kah(k)*	throat
tekanan	te-*kah*-nahn	pressure
tekanan darah	te-*kah*-nahn *dah*-rah(h)	blood pressure
teks	tehks	subtitles
telanjang	te-*lahn*-jahng	nude
telefon	teh-*leh*-fon	telephone
telefon awam	teh-*leh*-fon *ah*-wahm	phone box
telefon bimbit	teh-*leh*-fon *bim*-bit	mobile phone

telegram	teh-leh-*grahm*	telegram
teler (col)	teh-ler	teller
televisyen	teh-leh-*vee*-shen	television • TV
telinga	te-*lee*-nguh	ear
telur	te-*lur*	egg
teman	te-*mahn*	friend
teman lelaki	te-*mahn* le-*lah*-kee	boyfriend
teman wanita	te-*mahn* wah-*nee*-tah	girlfriend
tembakau	tem-*bah*-kow	tobacco
tembikai	tem-*bee*-kai	watermelon
tembok	tehm-*bo(k)*	wall (outside)
tempahan	tem-*pah(h)*-hahn	reservation
tempat	tem-*paht*	location • place
tempat duduk	tem-*paht doo*-du(k)	seat
tempat letak kereta	tem-*paht* le-*tah(k)* ke-*reh*-tuh	car park
tempat kelahiran	tem-*paht* ke-lah-*hi*-rahn	place of birth
tempat suci	tem-*paht* soo-*chee*	shrine
tempatan	tem-*pah*-tahn	local
temujanji	te-*moo*-jahn-jee	date (appointment)
tenaga nuklear	te-*nah*-guh noo-*klee*-er	nuclear energy
tenang	te-*nahng*	calm
tendangan [tendang]	ten-dah-ngahn [*ten*-dahng]	kick
tengah malam	te-*ngah(h) mah*-lahm	midnight
tengahari	te-ngah-*hah*-ree	noon
(padang) tenis	(pah-*dahng*) teh-*nis*	tennis (court)
tepat pada masanya	te-*paht pah*-duh mah-*sah*-nyuh	on time
tepi (jalan)	te-*pee* (*jah*-lahn)	side (of street)
tepi laut	te-*pee* lowt	seaside
terakhir	te-rah-*khir*	last (final)
terang	te-*rahng*	light (not dark)
terbaik	ter-bai(k)	best
terburu-buru	ter-boo-*roo*-boo-roo	in a hurry

Terima kasih.
te-*ree*-muh *kah*-si(h)   **Thank you.**

terkenal	ter-ke-*nahl*	famous
terlalu	ter-*lah*-loo	too (excessive)
terlalu banyak makan ubat	ter-*lah*-loo *bah*-nya(k) *mah*-kahn oo-baht	overdose
terlalu mahal	ter-*lah*-loo mah-*hahl*	rip-off
termasuk	ter-*mah*-su(k)	included
teropong	te-*ro*-pong	binoculars

terpencil	ter-pen-*chil*	remote
terseliuh	ter-se-*lee*-uh(h)	sprain
tersesat [sesat]	ter-*se*-saht [*se*-saht]	lost
terus ke hadapan	te-*rus* ke hah-dah-*pahn*	straight ahead
tetamu	te-*tah*-moo	guest
tetapi	te-*tah*-pee	but
tiada	tee-*ah*-duh	none
tiap-tiap	tee-ahp-*tee*-ahp	each • every
tiba	*tee*-buh	to come (arrive)
tidak	*tee*-dah(k)	no
tidak apa-apa	*tee*-dah(k) *ah*-puh-*ah*-puh	nothing
tidak kemas	*tee*-dah(k) ke-*mahs*	sleazy (person)
tidak pernah	*tee*-dah(k) per-*nah(h)*	never
tidak selamat	*tee*-dah(k) se-lah-*maht*	unsafe
tidur	*tee*-dur	to sleep • asleep
tifoid	tai-*foid*	typhoid
tikar	*tee*-kahr	mat
tiket	tee-*keht*	ticket
tikus	*tee*-kus	rat
tilam	tee-*lahm*	mattress
timun	*tee*-mun	cucumber
timur	*tee*-mur	east
tinggal	*ting*-gahl	to live (somewhere)
tinggi	*ting*-gee	tall • high
tingkap	*ting*-kahp	window
tingkat	*ting*-kaht	floor (storey)
tipis	*ti*-pis	thin
tisu	*tee*-soo	toilet paper • tissues
tokong Buda	*to*-kong boo-*dah*	temple (Buddhist)
tokong Cina	*to*-kong *chee*-nuh	temple (Chinese)
tolong	*to*-long	help • please
topeng	*to*-*pehng*	mask (face)
topi	*to*-pee	hat
topi keledar	*to*-pee ke-leh-*dahr*	helmet
trek perbandu	trehk ber-*pahn*-doo	guided trek
tua	*too*-uh	old (person)
tuala	too-*ah*-luh	towel
tuala wanita	too-*ah*-luh wah-*nee*-tah	sanitary napkins
Tuan	*too*-ahn	Mr
Tuhan	too-*hahn*	God (Muslim)
tukang jahit	too-*kahng* jah-*hit*	tailor
tukang tenung	too-*kahng* te-*nung*	fortune teller
tukang tilik	too-*kahng* tee-*li(k)*	fortune teller
tulang	*too*-lahng	bone

tulen	too-*lehn*	**pure**
tuli	too-lee	**deaf**
tumbuh-tumbuhan	toom-*bu(h)*-toom-*bu(h)*-hahn	**vegetation**
tunangan	too-*nah*-ngahn	**fiance(e)**
tunggu	*toong*-goo	**wait**
tunjuk perasaan	toon-*ju(k)* pe-rah-*sah*-ahn	**demonstration**
tuntutan bagasi	*toon*-tu-tahn bah-*gah*-see	**baggage claim**
tutup	*too*-tup	**shut**

U

ubat	oo-*baht*	**medicine**
(kedai) ubat Cina	(ke-*dai*) oo-*baht chee*-nuh	**herbalist shop**
ubat gigi	oo-*baht gee*-gee	**toothpaste**
ubat pencegah hamil	oo-*baht* pen-che-*gah(h)* hah-mil	**the Pill**
ubat pencuci perut	oo-*baht* pen-*choo*-chee pe-*rut*	**laxatives**
ubat tahan sakit	oo-*baht* tah-*hahn sah*-kit	**painkillers**
ubat tidur	oo-*baht tee*-dur	**sleeping pills**
ucapan politik	oo-*chah*-pahn po-*lee*-tik	**political speech**
udang	oo-*dahng*	**shrimp**
udara	oo-*dah*-ruh	**air**
ujian (peperiksaan)	oo-*jee*-ahn (pe-pe-*rik*-sah-ahn)	**test (exam)**
ujian darah	oo-*jee*-ahn *dah*-rah(h)	**blood test**
ujian nuklear	oo-*jee*-ahn noo-*klee*-er	**nuclear testing**
ukiran kayu	oo-ki-*rahn* kah-yoo	**woodcarving**
ular	oo-*lahr*	**snake**
umum	*oo*-mum	**general**
umur	*oo*-mur	**age**
undang-undang	oon-*dahng*-oon-*dahng*	**law**
ungu	oo-*ngoo*	**purple**
universiti	yu-ni-*ver*-si-tee	**university**
untuk	oon-*tu(k)*	**for (purpose)**
untuk berseronok	oon-*tu(k)* ber-se-*ro*-no(k)	**to have fun**
urat darah	oo-*raht dah*-rah(h)	**vein**
urutan	*oo*-ru-tahn	**massage**
utama	oo-*tah*-muh	**main**
utara	oo-*tah*-ruh	
north		

V

van	vahn	**van**
virus	vi-*rus*	**virus**
visa	*vee*-sah	**visa**
vitamin	vi-*tah*-min	**vitamin**

W

wain	wain	wine
waktu makan tengahari	wak-too mah-kahn te-ngah-hah-ree	lunchtime
wang	wahng	money
wang tunai	wahng too-nai	cash
wanita/perempuan	wah-nee-tah/ pe-rem-pwahn	woman
wap	wahp	steam
warung	wah-rung	food stall
warna	wahr-nuh	colour
wartawan	wahr-tah-wahn	journalist
wawancara	wah-wahn-chah-ruh	interview
wayar	wah-yahr	wire

Y

ya	yah	yes
yang	yahng	which
yang berikutnya	yahng be-ree-kut-nyah	next
yang lalu	yahng lah-loo	past (before)

Z

zakar	zah-kahr	penis
zebra	zeh-brah	zebra
zoo	zoo	zoo

SIGNS

AWAS	**CAUTION**
TUTUP	**CLOSED**
BUKA	**OPEN**
MASUK	**ENTRY**
KELUAR	**EXIT**
INFORMASI	**INFORMATION**
DILARANG MASUK	**NO ENTRY**
DILARANG MEROKOK	**NO SMOKING**
DI TEMPAH	**RESERVED**
POLIS	**POLICE**
TARIK	**PULL**
TOLAK	**PUSH**
TELEFON	**TELEPHONE**
TANDAS	**TOILETS**